How Barack Obama Won

Chuck Todd—Political Director, NBC News—also serves as on-air political analyst for *NBC Nightly News with Brian Williams*, *Meet the Press*, *Today*, and MSNBC shows, including *Hardball with Chris Matthews* and *Morning Joe*.

Sheldon Gawiser—Elections Director, NBC News—is the senior executive in charge of election information for all of NBC News productions, including exit poll analysis. He is responsible for projections as the head of the NBC News Decision Desk.

Book One: A Question of War

HOW BARACK OBAMA WON

A State-by-State Guide to the

Historic 2008 Presidential Election

CHUCK TODD
Political Director, NBC News

and

SHELDON GAWISER
Elections Director, NBC News

with Ana Maria Arumi and G. Evans Witt

VINTAGE BOOKS
A Division of Random House, Inc.
New York

A VINTAGE BOOKS ORIGINAL, JANUARY 2009

Cataloging-in-Publication Data for *How Barack Obama Won*
has been filed at the Library of Congress.

ISBN: 978-0-307-47366-0

Book design by Cathryn S. Aison and Claudia Martinez

www.vintagebooks.com

Printed in the United States of America
10 9 8 7 6 5 4 3 2 1

This book is dedicated to Tim Russert,
student, colleague, friend, and mentor.
We really miss you, Tim.
Go Bills!!

CONTENTS

A personal note from Sheldon Gawiser

I knew Tim Russert longer than anyone else at NBC News; he was a student of mine at John Carroll University. At that time, while there was a lot of unrest on campuses across the country, at John Carroll the problem was getting the students to challenge professors in class, getting them to ask pointed questions. That was never a problem with Tim. We always assumed he would become a litigator.

A week or two before the 2000 election, Tim came to me and wanted to know what the chances were that one candidate would get a majority of the electoral votes and another candidate would win the popular vote. We discussed that possibility, and Tim promised to buy me a new Mercedes if I managed to get that result. A week after the election, I went to my local dealer and got an invoice for a new car and sent it to Tim. He immediately responded that the car was in the works and that a John Carroll man always keeps his word.

In mid-December, a package arrived at my house from Tim. Inside was a toy Mercedes sedan, with the Gore and Bush electoral votes painted on the doors and the Gore margin in the popular vote on the trunk. His note read, "Here it is. A brand-new Mercedes with all the relevant data. A John Carroll man always keeps his word. Happy New Year, Tim."

I last saw Tim the night of the June 3 primaries. He was having the time of his life with this never-ending primary season. While all of us were exhausted, the extended coverage pleased him no end. What a time he would have had at the conventions and during this campaign.

But while most people knew the public Tim, for those of us who worked with him, he was more than a colleague. He never missed asking about my boys and telling me the latest story about his son, Luke. And when my grandson arrived, he added Zac to the conversation. When my wife was ill, he made sure that she was in his prayers. I like to think the reason the Bills are doing much better this year is that Tim is looking out for them.

A personal note from Chuck Todd

I may be the polar opposite of Sheldon in that I may have known Tim for less time than anyone else at NBC News, the short 15 months I spent working with him. And yet, the fact that I got to work so closely with him during this campaign, spent time on the campaign trail with him, had him let me in on the joke that is this business sometimes, is 15 months I'd never trade for the world.

There was nothing more challenging than trying to tell Tim something that he didn't know already. Yet he always wanted to know more, and there was no more rewarding feeling than giving him a tidbit that he hadn't known. I sure hope there are a few tidbits in here he'll want to use. He was a heckuva role model in many ways. I kinda feel like Clete Boyer, the not so well-known third baseman for the New York Yankees in the early 1960s. Because the one thing you can't take away from Boyer is this: he got to bat in the same lineup as Mickey Mantle. Well, I got to work with Tim Russert for a brief period of time; you can't take that away from me. So, Tim, because Shelly couldn't get you those exit polls in November, we figured why not a full-fledged book; so you can devour the data as you configure that whiteboard for 2012 and beyond.

ACKNOWLEDGMENTS

We want to express our gratitude to Ana Maria Arumi and Evans Witt. Without their thoughtful analysis and persistence, this book would not have been possible.

The authors would like to thank all our colleagues at NBC News for their hard work and support during this intense political campaign, from the front office to the specials unit to the fine folks at the key NBC News programs covering politics, as well as the "place for politics" itself, MSNBC. We would have lost the little sanity we have left without their assistance. We would also like to thank our families for putting up with us all year long and particularly during the writing of this book that took place after we had promised that the election insanity would end.

Chuck would like to thank, in particular, the NBC News political unit, specifically Mark Murray, Domenico Montanaro, Carrie Dann, and Abby Livingston. The four of them had the thankless job of reading Chuck's mind when he would make semirandom requests about lists of "this voting group" or "that bunch of states." Not only did Mark, Dom, Carrie, and Abby read Chuck's mind with ease, they will notice how much of their research inspired many parts of this tome. Chuck would also like to single out Sheldon for being an incredible writing partner in this project. We were brought together in some trying circumstances and grew to more than tolerate each other. It's been an honor to learn from and work with Sheldon, and the rest of the NBC elections teams.

Sheldon would especially like to thank Phil Alongi, Cliff Kappler, and particularly Katie Primm for their help and guidance throughout this crazy year at NBC News. In addition, our decision and poll analysis team made election nights tolerable. Chuck had a very tough task in a tough year, and he had to step into some very large shoes this summer. I would also like to thank Naomi Gawiser for taking on the completely thankless job of editing this material. It is a wonder she can still read after many hours looking for our all too many mistakes.

And thanks to the great staff at Vintage Books, led by our editor Erroll McDonald. He came to us late in the election season and somehow talked us into a crazy writing and publishing schedule. And then there's our agent, Matthew Carnicelli, who probably thought he'd never get Chuck to meet these audacious deadlines. Then again, he never realized how Sheldon doesn't like to miss deadlines.

Finally, we would like to thank our Founding Fathers, who, when writing the Constitution, designed the most interesting and complex political system possible. Of course, they had no idea that was what they were doing. The law of unintended consequences proven once again.

How Barack Obama Won

INTRODUCTION

Once in a Generation?

So how does one sum up the 2008 presidential campaign in just 12,000 words? Who is arrogant enough to think he or she can capture precisely the historical nature of this campaign and election, at a time when the nation seems vulnerable on so many fronts?

It's possible a historian 50 years from now might be able truly to understand what happened and why the country was ready to break through the color barrier, particularly if said historian looks at the 2008 election through the prism of post–Cold War America.

Since 1992, the country has witnessed nearly two decades of political tumult of a kind it has experienced only once or twice a century. Right now, the country is so enamored with the fact that we've broken the political color barrier of the American presidency that we haven't stepped back and appreciated just what a wild political ride our country has been on.

Since the Cold War ended and America lost its most significant enemy, the Soviet Union, the country has been looking for its political center. Consider the upheaval we've experienced as a nation since 1992. First, we had a three-way presidential election in which the third-party candidate was the front-runner for a good part of the campaign. Then, in 1994, we saw the House of Representatives switch control for the first time in 40 years. Next, in 1996, the winning presidential candidate failed to secure 50% of the vote for the second straight election, something that hadn't happened before in two straight presidential elections in 80 years. Then, in 1998, the nation watched as a tabloid presidential soap opera became a

Constitutional crisis, and Congress impeached a president for only the second time in this nation's history. In 2000, the nation's civics lesson on the Constitution continued, thanks to the first presidential election in over 100 years in which the winner of the Electoral College failed to win the popular vote, followed by the Supreme Court ruling, which eventually ended the protracted vote count controversy in Florida. In 2001, this nation was the victim of the worst terrorist attack in our history. Then, in 2004, a president won reelection by the smallest margin of any successfully reelected president in modern times. Finally, in 2006, control of Congress flipped after what, historically, was a fairly short stint for the Republicans. All of which brings us to 2008 and what for many Americans is the campaign commonly referred to as "the election of our lifetimes."

Is this the election that ends a 20-year period of political chaos? The serious problems this country is facing may be the reason that 2008 puts the exclamation point on the country's post–Cold War search for its political center.

Nine Years in the Making

The 2008 election got started early, before the first candidate, Tom Vilsack, officially announced in November 2006. The campaign began in 1999, when word first leaked that then first lady Hillary Clinton was seriously contemplating a run for U.S. senator from New York. Her election in 2000 set off the anticipation for what would be a historic first: the potential election of this country's first woman president.

There was some scuttlebutt that Clinton would run for president in 2004, but ultimately she decided to keep her eye on the 2008 ball. That was when she'd be into her second term as senator and when the field would be cleared of an incumbent president. This country rarely fires presidents after one term. It's happened just three times in the last 100 years.

The long march of the Hillary Clinton candidacy shaped much of the presidential fields for both parties. The Republicans who announced in 2008 all made their cases within the framework of challenging Hillary. In fact, it was Hillary's presence on the Democratic side that gave Rudy Giuliani the opportunity to be taken seriously by Republicans as a 2008 presidential candidate. As for the Democrats, consider that many an analyst and media critic like to talk about how wrong so-called conventional wisdom was during the 2008 campaign. But much of it was right. One early piece of such wisdom was that the Democratic primary campaign would be a primary within the primary between all the Democrats not named Clinton to establish an alternative to Hillary.

This sub-Democratic primary, which started in earnest after the 2004 presidential election, looked as if it was going to be a campaign between a lot of white guys and Washington insiders looking for their last chance at the brass ring. Familiar faces like Joe Biden, Chris Dodd, John Edwards, and Bill Richardson must have thought to themselves, *If I could only get into a one-on-one with Hillary, I could beat her.* Some new names were also seriously considering a run, like Virginia Governor Mark Warner and Iowa Governor Tom Vilsack. None of these potential candidates scared the Clinton camp, because they all were just conventional enough that Hillary's ability to put together a base of women and African-Americans would be sufficient to achieve the Democratic nomination.

But there was one potential candidate whose name was being talked about by activists and the blogosphere who did have the Clinton crowd nervous: the freshman senator from Illinois, Barack Obama. The factor that kept the Clintons confident about their 2008 chances was the notion that there was just no way, despite his popularity with the Democratic activist base, that a guy who, until 2004, was in the Illinois state senate would somehow have the audacity to run for president so soon. The Clintons were very familiar with the strategy of figuring out the timing of when best to run. They knew 1988 was too soon for Bill, and they took the advice of many and waited until 1992, and they knew that 2004 was too soon for Hillary, and she took the advice of many and waited. Surely, the Clintons must have thought, Obama would follow the same advice.

The Most Remarkable Primary Campaign
No One Seemed to Care About

While the Democrats were positioning themselves, the Republicans were in the midst of their own turmoil. This turned out to be a hard-fought primary that few cared about, as the country became obsessed with the most amazing Democratic primary campaign in a generation.

The Republican nomination was seen as completely wide open, mostly because the outgoing incumbent Republican president had not identified an heir apparent. President Bush's vice president, Dick Cheney, had lost his presidential ambition long ago, and the only other potential Bush heir, his brother Jeb, decided that trying to immediately succeed his brother was probably not the wisest move.

But Republicans love order, or so their presidential nomination contests in the past have indicated. What does order mean for the GOP? If there's no incumbent president or sitting vice president in the field, then the runner-up from the last contested nominating fight would be deemed the de facto front-runner. In this case it was John McCain since he was the runner-up to George W. Bush in the 2000 primary. Of course, McCain ended up with the nomination, but to this day, it's a miracle that he was able to win it.

McCain initially portrayed himself as the inevitable nominee, creating a behemoth campaign organization, participating in endorsement buy-offs with his deep-pocketed competitor, Mitt Romney, and trying to enhance his image as a maverick while making nice with various conservatives, including the late Jerry Falwell and evangelist Pat Robertson.

Still, many activists were searching for an alternative to McCain. As a result, McCain struggled mightily to raise money in the first six months of his campaign. His fund-raising was further hampered when he became the highest profile Republican other than George W. Bush to push for comprehensive immigration reform. This legislation, cosponsored by conservative bogeyman Massachusetts Senator Ted Kennedy, fired up the conservative talk radio base and McCain got scorched, drying up his fund-raising and putting him on the brink of having to end his campaign before Labor Day 2007.

But instead of dropping out, McCain essentially filed for Chapter 11 and did a massive reorganization. He drastically reduced his staff to a small band of campaign operatives determined to win the nomination one early primary state at a time. There was one great illustrative moment in the summer of 2007 of this new campaign, postreorganization, when McCain carried his own bags in an airport while traveling alone to a campaign event in New Hampshire.

During McCain's apparent demise, there was a massive effort by the other Republicans to fill the vacuum. Mitt Romney was vying to be the conservative alternative to McCain early on, which meant he had to tack back on a number of positions he took when he ran for office in liberal Massachusetts. But even with McCain apparently out of the mix, Romney decided not to fill the center but still aimed to become the front-runner by appeasing conservatives. Former New York City Mayor Rudy Giuliani was also in the race but was running on a different plane. He was certainly taken seriously by his opponents because he raised decent money, and his name identification as the mayor of New York on 9/11 meant he led in just about every national poll during the run-up to the Iowa caucuses. But there was always something about his candidacy that seemed like a house of cards. It really wasn't a matter of *if* his candidacy would collapse, but *when*. The collapse began in December 2007, when the New York tabloid press just unloaded, well, everything from Giuliani's past, from his secretive courtship of his third wife to his relationship with his now disgraced former police chief, Bernard Kerik. Giuliani's personal problems turned out to be as debilitating as many analysts had predicted. Adding to this politics of self-destruction, Giuliani's team had crafted a nonsensical campaign strategy that banked on Giuliani skipping Iowa, New Hampshire, South Carolina, and Michigan, while focusing solely on the Florida primary to launch his candidacy. Giuliani joins a long list of presidential wannabes who have attempted and failed to get the nomination by bypassing *both* Iowa and New Hampshire. While every campaign rule of presidential politics is bound to be broken, this one has yet to be, at least since 1976 when Jimmy Carter used a win in Iowa to catapult himself to the Democratic nomination.

There were two other major players in the Republican contest: on-again, off-again actor and former Senator Fred Thompson and former Baptist preacher and former Arkansas Governor Mike Huckabee.

Thompson's rise ended on the day he actually announced his candidacy. The idea of a Thompson candidacy began to develop in the conservative blogosphere and Washington salons in the spring of 2007, and when McCain's campaign nearly collapsed, the idea quickly gathered speed. Essentially, he was one of the best noncandidates in the history of presidential politics. But then he got in the race and his prospects began to deteriorate. The minute he announced, he became ordinary and quickly earned a reputation as being lazy and unenergetic. He just seemed to wing it, hoping the lack of interest in the rest of the GOP field would consolidate support for his candidacy.

If Thompson had a polar opposite when it came to hunger for the nomination, it was Huckabee. Never meeting a TV camera he didn't like, Huckabee quickly became a media darling of the primary campaign. With each passing Republican debate, it was Huckabee who seemed to be creating immeasurable buzz. While he had little campaign cash, he had a devoted support network, comprised of many social conservatives, including homeschooling advocates, who tirelessly put together a very impressive Iowa field organization.

As Thompson was fizzling and Giuliani was campaigning in his own world down in Florida, McCain was hunkering down in New Hampshire, trying to recapture the 2000 magic. The buzz for McCain was not nearly as intense in the fall of 2007 as it was in the fall of 1999, when he came from behind, nearly toppling George W. Bush in the 2000 presidential primaries. But there was something about McCain's 2008 candidacy that seemed salvageable.

McCain, of course, was helped by the basic fact that none of his other opponents seemed to catch fire. Romney was mired in a fight with Huckabee for the hearts and minds of Iowa conservatives. And Thompson and Giuliani were in free fall. This meant McCain had his opening. The formula was simple: if Huckabee could upset Romney in Iowa, McCain had a good shot to beat Romney in New Hampshire. This would provide McCain a shot of momentum that could carry him through Michigan, South Carolina, and Florida and bring the nomination fight to a close before Super Tuesday.

As it turns out, the nomination fight would end before Super Tuesday, which in 2008 was on February 5. Super Tuesday appeared to be an obvious end date for both primary contests because so many states, more than 20, had decided to move their primary or caucus up to that day.

McCain got what he needed in Iowa as Huckabee upset Romney by a considerable margin, leaving the Massachusetts Republican in poor shape. With New Hampshire coming just five days after Iowa, it was nearly impossible for Romney to turn things around in time. Sure enough, McCain prevailed and got the media spark he was hoping for. In fact, nothing benefited McCain more than his still strong relationship with the national press corps, who seemed eager to write the McCain comeback story out of New Hampshire. When McCain won, the press fell in love with him again for a brief period, just long enough for him to sweep the nomination.

After Iowa and New Hampshire, the only significant speed bump on McCain's road to victory came in Romney's onetime home state of Michigan. Romney made a last-ditch effort in the state, eked out a win over McCain, and lived to see another day. But Michigan turned out to be a blessing for McCain. Why? McCain could not have won South Carolina if it were a two-man race against the more socially conservative Huckabee. But with Romney back in the game, Thompson decided to stick around and turned South Carolina into a quasi-four-person race. This was exactly what McCain needed; he won the South Carolina primary without garnering even a third of the vote. Now he had the all-important momentum going into Florida, the last big contest before Super Tuesday.

Romney refused to give up, but he knew it would all come down to Florida. He might have succeeded had it not been for Huckabee. Both McCain and Romney were battling for first, as the third and fourth place contenders—Giuliani and Huckabee—each took support from the top. Giuliani was a drag on McCain, and Huckabee was a drag on Romney. What eventually put McCain over the top was a last minute endorsement by Florida's popular governor, Charlie Crist. The endorsement was not just in name only. It also meant the governor unofficially mobilized his get-out-the-vote machine within the state party. This effort changed what was supposed to be a conservative primary electorate into something more moderate, and proved to be just what McCain needed.

McCain's was a remarkable comeback story in which he had to make bank shot after bank shot to win the nomination. Florida was the final one on January 29. Romney would continue on through Super Tuesday along with Huckabee. When the votes from the Super Tuesday states were tallied, McCain ended up winning more delegates than either of the two more conservative candidates, leaving Romney defeated and Huckabee ecstatic that he actually mattered. Huckabee had made no secret of his distaste for Romney and spent much of his latter days on the campaign praising McCain, even as he forced the Arizona Republican to run a semicompetitive series of primaries through March officially to get a majority of the delegates. Only then did Huckabee drop out. And that's when McCain's general election troubles began.

The Rise of Obama

While the Republican nomination was fascinating, it didn't hold a candle to what was going on inside the Democratic party. The decision by Obama to run transformed the Democratic primary instantly from a subprimary campaign to determine the anti-Hillary alternative to a two-person clash of the titans. From the moment Obama formalized his candidacy, Clinton's campaign was transformed into a rapid response operation focused solely on Obama.

When word leaked that Obama was going to form an exploratory committee and would do so on YouTube, Clinton quickly crafted her "I'm in it to win it" announcement, which was also done via the Web.

Interestingly, though, while Obama used new media to announce the formation of his exploratory committee, he went the old school route when formally announcing his actual candidacy—he gave a "Why I'm running for president" announcement speech in front of thousands of supporters in his home state. Clinton never gave a formal "Why I'm running" speech akin to what Obama delivered on February 10, 2007, in front of the Old State Capitol in Springfield, Illinois. This fundamental fact sums up the primary contest about as well as any primary result or delegate count.

Obama outlined the organizing principle for that candidacy via his announcement speech. In fact, the basic themes Obama introduced in that first speech in Springfield would be repeated on the stump throughout the campaign—all the way until his victory speech on Election Night in November 2008.

That initial announcement speech included plenty of phrases which would become familiar to his supporters, such as: "What's stopped us is the failure of our leadership, the smallness of our politics—the ease with which we're distracted by the petty and trivial, our chronic avoidance of tough decisions, our preference for scoring cheap political points instead of rolling up our sleeves and building a working consensus to tackle big problems." In that first speech, Obama also constantly used the refrain, "Let's be the generation," as a way to talk directly to new voters; he hinted that his speeches would be a big part of his campaign strategy when he uttered the phrase, "There is power in words."

While much of Obama's campaign rationale was evident in his announcement speech, the same cannot be said for either Clinton or McCain. Stunningly, neither gave a "Why I'm running for president" speech. Neither made a formal announcement in his or her home state or any other. Neither outlined in the traditional way a philosophy or program as Obama had done. Clinton made her Web video speech and that was it, nothing else other than "I'm in it to win it." McCain announced on *The Tonight Show with Jay Leno*. Just on the basis of announcement strategies, is it any wonder why Obama appeared to be the candidate who constantly was able to stay on message while his two opponents, Clinton in the primary and McCain in the general, were grasping for anything that would stick?

There are several reasons why Obama ultimately won the presidency, but one of the central factors was he always made the case for why he was the candidate of change, the candidate who was change from Bush. Clinton and McCain, when running against Obama, were always caught up in trying to contrast themselves with Obama and highlight his inexperience. Neither offered consistent "change from Bush" arguments. And in a time when President Bush had approval ratings ranging from 25% to 30%, change mattered the most to voters over any other issue.

Of course, Obama didn't win his nomination by simply holding an impressive kickoff, but he did quickly cement his place as the chief challenger to the then front-runner Clinton. In one fell swoop, Obama was able to displace all of the other anti-Hillary challengers and relegate them to second-tier candidates. John Edwards was the strongest of these second-tier challengers because of his near victory in the 2004 Iowa caucuses. In fact, it was Edwards who started out as the Iowa front-runner simply because of the strength of his organization. But when he didn't win Iowa, he was toast.

Edwards and the rest of the second-tier Democratic candidates did play important roles in the primary. It was Chris Dodd who may have delivered the knockout blow to Clinton in an October primary debate. He called foul on an answer Clinton gave on whether she supported a New York state proposal to give drivers' licenses to illegal immigrants. Dodd's attack on her answer (or nonanswer) started a firestorm and managed to get political reporters worked up over whether Clinton was capable of answering a question directly or whether she was prone to do what her husband was famous for doing and equivocate. Dodd helped the media play up the narrative that a Clinton doesn't give direct answers.

It was a near-fatal moment for Clinton. While her campaign believes the media pounced unfairly, from that point on, the die was cast, and her lead in the polls began to shrink.

The 2007 preprimary campaign was one of the oddest reality shows in presidential campaign history. It seemed a week didn't go by without one of the two major parties participating in a debate. These debates turned into must-see TV for many, as the ratings kept going up as Iowa got closer. And as the field of candidates shrank, particularly on the Democratic side, these debates became more important.

But for Obama, 2007 was about getting his sea legs. While his kickoff was near perfect, he struggled in the first five to six months of his candidacy as he tried to build a campaign that was more than just an idea. Resources weren't a problem as his campaign kept up with Clinton dollar for dollar and, as it turns out, was spending those dollars much more wisely. Obama's problem in the summer and early fall of 2007 was that he wasn't breaking through, particularly in the debates.

But debates were never Obama's strong suit. The key to his campaign were his speeches. At every moment in the primary when he was in need of a lift, it was a formal speech that jump-started his campaign. When questions were building among the chattering class about Obama's presidential campaign and his inability to catch Clinton in the polls, Obama delivered a stem-winder of a speech at the Iowa Jefferson-Jackson dinner in November 2007, drowning out the other speeches. In hindsight, if there was a moment that Obama truly caught fire in Iowa, it was that night in Des Moines in front of 10,000 Democratic activists.

Of course, the other big speech that bailed Obama out of a

tough spot came after the Reverend Jeremiah Wright episode. Wright was Obama's pastor in Chicago and became a familiar face to many Americans; in March 2008, excerpts of some of Wright's more controversial sermons were aired almost nonstop on cable news channels. There was hateful, and to some, un-American rhetoric being spewed by Wright, who was described as the man who helped Obama find God and the man who married him and baptized his children. This was not some made-up close relationship pushed by Obama's opponents, as with 1960s radical Bill Ayers.

Obama had treaded carefully on the race issue for much of the campaign, doing what he could to be "postracial." It's not as if he ran away from his ethnicity; it's that he didn't dwell on it. But he didn't have to; everyone else did in every profile of him written early in his political career. Of course, his unique background, being an African-American with no U.S. black roots, meant many white voters viewed him through a different prism than they had other black presidential candidates, most notably, Jesse Jackson.

But the Wright episode had the potential to upend Obama's candidacy and the candidate knew it, hence the decision to give a major speech about race. His March 2008 race speech in Philadelphia was very well received, as he did his best to send the message that he viewed the race issue through the eyes of both black and white America. It seemed to put a period on the Wright affair, and most important got the cable news channels to stop running the Wright sermons on a continuous loop. Wright would resurface just before the May primaries in Indiana and North Carolina. His bizarre appearance before the National Press Club was so antagonistic that Obama decided to quit Wright's church and publicly rebuke him. It appears that whatever close relationship the two did have at one time no longer existed. Wright wouldn't pop up again during the campaign, and he really wasn't used in any negative TV ads against Obama. John McCain pledged early on that he wouldn't do it and he kept his promise, to the chagrin of some Republican strategists.

The Empire Strikes Back?

Of course, after Obama won Iowa, thanks to the launching pad of his November Jefferson-Jackson speech, it seemed as if he was going to do what John Kerry did in 2004, roll up primary and caucus victories quickly, and win the Democratic nominating fight before it even got to Super Tuesday.

But something happened in the five days between Obama's

stunning Iowa victory and the New Hampshire primary. Hillary Clinton became more human, at least for a day. As pundit after pundit and poll after poll were in the midst of declaring Clinton's candidacy DOA (even the Clinton campaign thought it was over; a bunch of staffers were preparing to be fired), Clinton got a tad emotional at one famous event less than 24 hours before the polls opened in the Granite State. It was the tears felt round the world; whether she actually cried or just got choked up, the important thing was Hillary showed a pulse and New Hampshire voters, particularly women, were smitten. She came back to win New Hampshire and eke out a victory in the Nevada caucuses, putting the pressure back on Obama to do well in South Carolina at the end of January.

It was at this point in the campaign that the Democratic electorate started to break into two very formidable coalitions. The Obama coalition was made up of African-Americans, college-educated whites, and young voters. Clinton's coalition was Latinos, women, and non-college-educated whites. Depending on the state, these coalitions were fairly matched and the national polls showed it. But Obama's coalition proved to be the winning one for a few reasons, mostly a matter of timing. The primaries in February featured states that were dominated by Obama's coalition, while Clinton's coalition really didn't dominate any state primaries until much later when the campaign was all but over. Had the Kentucky, West Virginia, and Pennsylvania contests been held in February, and Virginia, Wisconsin, and Mississippi in May, there may have been another nominee.

After Clinton's win in Nevada, her campaign was cocky enough to believe it could be competitive in South Carolina. Why? Bill Clinton's supposed popularity with African-Americans was thought to be strong enough to secure Hillary at least a quarter of the black vote. Winning 25% of blacks in the Palmetto State wouldn't be enough to stop Obama from winning in South Carolina, but it would be enough to keep him from blowing the doors off the Clinton campaign. But the more Bill campaigned, the more he kept tripping up on the racial front. He seemed publicly to be too dismissive of Obama for many black voters. In effect, Bubba was seen as dissing Obama, and this caused the black vote to solidify for Obama in a way that even the Obama campaign didn't expect.

During the summer of 2007, Clinton would regularly outpoll Obama among black voters, particularly older black voters. But the more Bill Clinton ramped up in his critiques of Obama, the more black voters started moving toward Obama. It also helped that black voters viewed Obama as electable. Besides Bill Clinton, the other important moment for Obama in his capability to solidify the black vote was winning Iowa. When African-Americans saw Obama win that very white state of Iowa, it sent the message that maybe their vote wouldn't be wasted on the young rising star of the Democratic Party.

Obama won South Carolina by a landslide, setting the stage for Super Tuesday, though with one hiccup. A few days after South Carolina, Florida was holding what the Democratic National Committee (DNC) called an unsanctioned primary; Michigan held a similar one in mid-January of 2008, but Obama successfully pulled his name off the ballot there. Clinton won Florida big since Obama never campaigned there. But the key to Obama's success in states where he campaigned was TV advertising. So in both Florida and Michigan where Obama didn't buy TV ads, he was a distant second choice behind Clinton. These primary victories would later serve as a rallying point for Clinton supporters—particularly when they made the argument about which candidate was winning the national primary vote—during their desperate attempt to catch up to Obama in the delegate count. The party would eventually resolve this dispute by halving the delegation in Florida and splitting up Michigan nearly evenly, making Clinton's victories as hollow in the delegate count as they were when the primaries were actually held.

Subtracting Florida and Michigan, Clinton and Obama were even in the number of contests won going into Super Tuesday at two apiece. But while the two candidates looked even on paper, it was a misnomer, as this was the point where the Clinton campaign would lose the nomination. The Clinton campaign had a money problem, a big one, so they had to pick and choose their spots on Super Tuesday, a day when more than 20 states were holding primaries and caucuses. This was not an issue for Obama. Low on resources, Clinton decided not to spend a lot of money organizing in the caucus states on Super Tuesday. Instead the campaign concentrated on the big delegate prizes of New York, California, New Jersey, and Arizona, among others. In many ways, Clinton's strategy was successful. In just about every state in which she spent serious time organizing and campaigning, she won. But Obama organized and campaigned in every state, even ones he lost. He dominated the primaries in the South, but he also won in the Midwest and Northeast, but more important, he swept all of the caucus states, including Colorado and Minnesota, and also smaller states like Idaho. So, while Clinton won the more glamorous big states, Obama was racking up Democratic delegates everywhere, including in those so-called big states he lost.

As close followers of the Democratic nominating fight will remember, the Democratic Party awards delegates to any candidate earning at least 15% of the vote in any congressional district of any state. So even if Clinton won California by some 20 points, Obama was still picking up sizable chunks of delegates. But Clinton was getting trounced in the caucus states, so badly that she came close to getting shut out in a few states. The most glaring example of this Clinton miscalculation was the delegates earned by Obama in Idaho versus the number earned by Clinton in New Jersey. Obama won Idaho and netted 15 more delegates than Clinton. She won New Jersey, not by an insignificant margin, but netted fewer delegates than Obama's gain in Idaho. It was miscalculations like this one that cost the Clinton campaign dearly.

The Obama delegate operation ran circles around the Clinton campaign and by the time all of the delegates were counted after Super Tuesday, it was Obama, not Clinton, who won more delegates that day. (He also won more states and was about even in total votes so there really wasn't a barometer for the Clintons to prove they were ahead.) Clinton may have won the bigger states, but Obama was garnering the votes that mattered. When Super Tuesday came and went, the Clinton campaign was broke and behind. The Obama campaign was just getting started. A week later, Obama would sweep the Potomac primaries, Maryland, Virginia, and D.C., and go on to win 11 straight contests, forcing Clinton to make a final stand on Junior Tuesday, the March 4 primaries in Ohio and Texas.

But while the news media was soaking up the Clinton theatrics about the Ohio-Texas do-or-die, a very important event had already occurred: Obama had built a delegate lead that was close to insurmountable, thanks to the proportional system of delegates. His 100-plus delegate lead from his February sweep through post-Super Tuesday states may have looked close in the raw total, but it wasn't.

While Clinton did well on Junior Tuesday by winning Ohio and Texas, she netted less than a dozen delegates for her efforts. The die was cast and all Obama had to do was run out the clock. But all was not smooth going: there was the aforementioned Reverend Wright episode in the run-up to the Pennsylvania primary. And Obama's loss in the Pennsylvania primary raised concerns among some Democrats that he couldn't win the working-class white vote in the general election and gave Clinton even more life, or so it seemed. Then Obama won North Carolina by double digits and nearly upset Clinton in white working-class-heavy Indiana on May 6, leading smart observers to publicly acknowledge that the race was over. In fact, on that famous May night, the late Tim Russert said first what every smart politico knew, "We now know who the Democratic nominee is going to be." And that nominee was Barack Obama.

It was a primary campaign for the ages; one that probably lasted longer than it should have because of the media's fascination with the Clintons. But it was still something else. Every Tuesday night, more and more folks kept tuning in to see what would happen next in America's favorite reality show. Could Obama win working-class white voters? Would college-educated white women start breaking more for Clinton? Would Hillary finally drop out? What would Bill Clinton say next?

To think that we're writing a book on how Obama won and mostly talking about the general election is to dismiss a very important, if not more important, part of Obama's rise and maturation as a presidential candidate. The long, drawn-out primary campaign with Clinton did more to help Obama than hurt him. He became a better debater, not a great debater, but a better one. He became a candidate who could speak a bit more from the heart than the head on economic issues. And of course, without Clinton, he never would have had to run campaigns in all 50 states (and Guam and the Virgin Islands and Puerto Rico . . .). If Obama never had to run a 50 state campaign in the primaries, would he have been able to put Indiana in play in the general election? What about North Carolina? And would Virginia have turned blue so easily without Obama's early primary efforts?

Many an Obama operative seethed at the selfishness of the Clinton campaign during those draining primary moments in March, April, and May, because they knew she couldn't win and she had to know that as well. But Clinton staying in this race as long as she did only helped Obama. And Obama, the candidate-turned-president, knows it. It's why the highest-ranking cabinet slot went to her.

McCain's Wasted Opportunities

The most interested spectator for the greatest reality show on earth in the spring of 2008 was John McCain. While Obama had to trudge through 48 states (not including Florida and Michigan) and Puerto Rico to fend off Clinton, McCain was able to wrap up his nomination by campaigning in all of four states. Being the nominee on the sidelines should have been an enormous advantage. This should have been the time for McCain to ratchet up his national organization, hone his general election message, begin the VP vetting process, and raise the boatload of money he would need to keep up with the financial juggernaut that was and still is Barack Obama.

As it turns out, McCain apparently did very little of those things. Many a McCain apologist argues that his candidacy was doomed by outside events, like the economic meltdown in the fall of 2008 or the fact that President George W. Bush had the lowest ratings of any two-term president since the archiving of polling numbers began. But while Bush and the economy were enormously heavy anchors on McCain, it does not excuse the wasted three month head start he had on Obama.

Summer Slumber

Sensing the country needed a breather from the primary, both McCain and Obama sparred at a low level for much of the summer. There was the McCain challenge to Obama to keep his word on taking public financing, rather than paying for his general election with private donations. Also, McCain attempted to push Obama into holding a series of 10 joint town hall meetings, an idea that many in Obama's orbit liked but the top leadership did not. The thinking by some Obama aides was that the more Obama debated or appeared with McCain, the more presidential he would look because he'd be soaking up the gravitas McCain exuded. But the chief deciders in Obamaland believed the McCain town hall gambit was designed to keep Obama tied down, and they didn't want to be spending days prepping for town halls, instead of putting new states in play by visiting Montana, Indiana, or North Carolina. If the Obama campaign was going to play in 20 or more states, they needed as much summer travel flexibility as they could find. Ultimately, the Obama camp agreed to do a few town halls but the McCain stand was "10 or nothing" and nothing happened.

As for the campaign finance challenge, McCain made it because 1) he was the father of campaign finance reform via the McCain-Feingold legislation and 2) he couldn't raise the money Obama could raise privately so the only way he could level the financial playing field was to make an issue of Obama's keeping the public financing pledge he had made during the primary campaign. But the Obama folks backed out of the deal because they knew how much money they'd be leaving on the table. They also knew the public didn't care about campaign financing as long as money was being raised legally. It may be hard for campaign finance reform advocates to read this, but the evidence is clear.

Obama and the Democratic Party raised approximately $1 billion for this campaign; McCain's haul wasn't shabby as the combined total of his campaign and the Republican Party stash was over half a billion dollars, but that nearly two to one advantage in spending is why Obama could afford to experiment with putting new states in play like Indiana, North Carolina, and Georgia, while McCain had to take risks like holding off on buying Florida TV time and calling Obama's bluff in Indiana, Georgia, and Montana.

European Vacation

The general election really didn't take off until Obama set out on his weeklong international tour of world hotspots and European capitals. The culmination of the trip was a speech in Berlin in front of some 200,000 spectators, a scene that seemed to leave much of this country awestruck by Obama's worldwide popularity.

With their backs against the wall, the McCain campaign was desperate to bring Obama back down to earth. They launched perhaps the most famous TV ad of the 2008 campaign, calling Obama the "biggest celebrity in the world" and comparing him to Paris Hilton and Britney Spears. Needless to say, this ad served as cable news catnip and got tons of attention. The McCain strategy was clear; they intended to make Obama's popularity a liability. The McCain campaign was attempting to win the experience argument against Obama by invoking celebrity lightweights like Paris Hilton.

The tactic worked. Obama didn't get the big bump from his very well orchestrated international trip. If anything, Obama's narrow three to six point lead throughout the summer started to shrink a bit, as the race fell within the margin of error in the polls. The more important aspect about this moment in the campaign is that it really did signal the start of the general election. And everything from this point on in the race was a blur.

The McCain folks were proud of their ability to deflate the bounce they expected Obama to receive from his overseas adventure. But the campaign leadership may have learned the wrong lesson from this moment: that tactics were the secret to keeping McCain viable. The campaign would never have as effective a hit on Obama after the Paris Hilton ad but would spend a lot of energy trying. Whether it was the pick of Sarah Palin as running mate, the decision to suspend the campaign, or the introduction of "Joe the Plumber," the McCain campaign used a series of tactics with no overall strategy.

As we've mentioned before, it is telling that McCain never gave a formal announcement speech for president. If he had no organizing principle from the beginning, how was he expected to find it as the campaign wore on? Our NBC colleague, Tom Brokaw, liked to compare the McCain campaign team to guerilla war fighters. They could do quick strikes and shock their foes for a day or two, but like many unsuccessful guerilla armies, the McCain campaign could never advance on the general election battlefield. They never took new ground, never forced the Obama campaign into retreat. The best the McCain campaign could ever do was slow the Obama campaign from advancing; they never stopped them.

VPMatch.com Selects Biden

If there was one month the Obama campaign would like to forget, it's August. Obama's chief strategist, David Axelrod, said as much in many of the campaign postmortems. It all started with Paris Hilton. The Obama campaign was caught flat-footed; they really thought this overseas trip would help Obama on the question of "Is he ready?" but the Paris Hilton attack blunted any benefit. The campaign muddled through the month, focused on their vice presidential selection process and orchestrating their convention. There were two potential pitfalls at the convention: figuring out a role for the Clintons and living up to the hype on Obama's own acceptance speech, since the decision was made to move the convention's final night to an 80,000 seat football stadium. The Clintons' convention speeches were very well received and seemed truly to bury the primary hatchet. As for Obama's convention speech, it's hard to evaluate it since a certain Republican vice presidential candidate completely sucked the air out of it a mere 12 hours later.

Obama's vice presidential selection process was fairly predictable. This is another case in which the campaign and the conventional wisdom crowd were in sync. Despite all of the cable chatter by uninformed hype-analysts about putting Hillary Clinton on the ticket, the campaign believed Obama needed someone safe, and safe meant an older white guy with impeccable foreign policy credentials. Obama, himself, wanted to be a bit more daring. He was personally impressed with two of his early primary supporters, Kansas Governor Kathleen Sebelius and Virginia Governor Tim Kaine. But the political reality was that he couldn't pick a woman running mate not named Clinton, and he couldn't pick a running mate who had been in his current position for less time than Obama's own tenure as senator. So the campaign quickly zeroed in on Delaware Senator Joe Biden, one of Obama's primary opponents.

The Biden pick checked all of the conventional wisdom boxes, including experience, working-class roots (the Scranton, Pennsylvania–raised Democrat was one of the poorest members of the Senate, one of just a handful who were not millionaires), and he'd been publicly vetted a more than 30 year Senate career. This is not to say that Biden didn't have a little excess baggage from his unsuccessful bids for the presidency, but nothing disqualifying. Much of the baggage that knocked Biden out of the presidential race in 1988 seemed to have faded away, particularly since he comported himself well during the 2008 primary campaign. More often than not, Biden was judged as one of the better debate performers during the never-ending primary debate series.

But because the Biden rollout was conventional, it did little on the polling front, as Obama got virtually no bounce. But he wasn't hurt either. Much of Obama's goal for the final months of the general election campaign was making voters who didn't like Bush and wanted change feel comfortable with him. Biden did that. As the candidate himself would say, Obama is the change, and voters knew that visually. It meant, though, that he needed to surround himself with folks who were reassuring. The Biden pick would foreshadow many of Obama's initial cabinet appointments as the folks he picked were the conventional, experienced choices, not risky change agents.

The Greatest Sideshow on Earth: Sarah Palin

McCain's search for a running mate was much less chronicled in the media because the campaign seemed to do a pretty good job keeping their short list close to the vest. One thing they were counting on though, was Obama not picking Biden. It was the one pick the leadership of the McCain campaign thought would be the safest and smartest choice for Obama, the pick that would create the least amount of drama. As one McCain senior adviser put it, "Obama doesn't have the guts to pick Biden." What did he mean by that? Biden's too logical of a choice and too qualified for the job; Obama doesn't believe he needs that, so pontificated this senior McCain strategist.

But that's just the thing: the McCain folks constantly misjudged Obama. They believed the stereotype they were trying to create, that he was this out-of-control, egomaniacal, power-hungry politician. It's one thing to attempt to create that image; it's another to believe it when you are in charge of setting the campaign's strategy.

McCain's presumed short list was Joe Lieberman, the sometime Democratic senator who was supporting McCain; Tim Pawlenty, the blue-collar-rooted conservative governor of Minnesota; and Mitt Romney, McCain's chief primary rival, who was thought to be helpful in the swing states of Michigan and New Hampshire. The only pick among those three who got McCain's juices flowing was Lieberman. He loved the idea of sending the maverick message again while also trying to steal a bit of Obama's postpartisan thunder. What better way to show off anti-Bush credentials than picking a running mate who essentially ran against Bush, not once, but twice? (Lieberman ran once against Bush as the Democratic VP in 2000 and again as a failed Democratic presidential candidate in 2004.) However, the senior leadership of the campaign talked McCain out of this pick because they believed it would cause a floor fight at the Republican convention, due mostly to Lieberman's pro-choice position on abortion. The campaign believed it could not control its delegates on the floor and prevent them from nominating an alternative running mate, say, Mike Huckabee. Did McCain really want to cause intraparty turmoil this late in the campaign? (Actually, in hindsight, yes.)

But just because McCain couldn't pick Lieberman didn't mean he didn't want to make a splash. So he went back to the drawing board and asked about a candidate whom two of McCain's close aides, Steve Schmidt and Rick Davis, had been pushing for for some time: Alaska Governor Sarah Palin. After a fairly brief meeting, McCain gave the nod.

The Palin pick was announced approximately 12 hours after Obama finished giving what the Democratic campaign believed was a historically significant acceptance speech, in front of 80,000 Democrats. The speech was so effective that 13 hours later, barely a word was being replayed. Why? The entire political world was focused on one person, Sarah Palin.

That she took the country by storm is an understatement. The irony, of course, is that she instantly became a celebrity of the level the McCain campaign hadn't seen since, well, Obama in Europe. There were so many things to learn about her: her husband was half-Eskimo; she had five children, one of whom was less than a year old; her oldest daughter was pregnant; she was a dead-ringer for *Saturday Night Live* veteran Tina Fey; and she was a self-described "hockey mom."

Notice what wasn't on that list: she was a successful governor who had done X, Y, and Z. Or, she was an expert in subject matter X. The pop culture story of Sarah Palin and the image of a working mother was a great narrative. But after that, a perception quickly developed that there wasn't a lot of "there" there. Of course, she became fodder for the media, was even ridiculed, and that only got the Republican base fired up. To the GOP base, she was a breath of fresh air; the *Republican* the Republican Party had been waiting to rally around for two years. While the base had never been enamored with McCain, they were taken with Palin. Here was a woman who was practicing what many in the social conservative movement were preaching, whether it was choosing to have a Down syndrome child or pushing her unmarried daughter to keep her baby and get married.

But it would be Palin's lack of experience that would eventually prove her undoing. Was she the reason McCain lost? No. Did she, in fact, help McCain in certain states like North Carolina and Georgia? Absolutely. But the campaign did her no favors when she was rolled out more as a pop icon and less as someone ready to be president, particularly when voters consistently told pollsters that McCain's age was a bigger factor than Obama's race. One of the issues McCain said she was an expert on was energy. But did the campaign ever allow Palin to hold an event in front of an oil rig or a nuclear power plant or a wind farm? The campaign did nothing to reinforce the energy issue in Palin's background other than to insinuate that any elected official from Alaska is by definition an energy expert because of energy's importance to the state's economy.

Palin proved to be an excellent political performer in controlled settings but stumbled in some TV interviews, most famously with Katie Couric of CBS. The experience seemed to scar Palin a bit as she became harder to deal with for rest of the campaign. This was always going to be a tougher political marriage than the McCain campaign team understood. Palin's political experiences were limited. Sure, she had run for quite a few offices and mostly won, but her staff was limited and her chief strategist was her husband. When she parachuted onto the national stage, she suddenly found herself with political handlers. And when those handlers, in her mind, failed her during the early rollout, she rebelled and refused to take any advice from anyone, relying instead on her gut instincts and her husband.

What the future holds for Palin is unclear. At the start of 2009, she was the most popular Republican in the country with a certain segment of the party. And for candidates running for office in 2009 and 2010, she'll be the biggest draw for fund-raisers and events. But in order truly to have a national impact on her party and be a player in 2012, she's going to need to improve her issue credentials. Cult of personality can only get a candidate so far; a proven ability to get things done or pushing a set of substantial issues is necessary to be taken seriously.

As for the verdict of voters, it's clear, according to the 2008 National Exit Poll, Palin was polarizing. Four out of ten voters said Palin's selection was an important factor in their vote, but those voters split their votes about evenly between the Republican and Democratic tickets. Fully two-thirds of voters believed Joe Biden was ready to serve as president if required, but 60% of voters nationwide held the opposite view of Palin, saying she was not qualified.

	TOTAL	OBAMA	McCAIN
IMPORTANCE OF PALIN SELECTION			
IMPORTANT	41	48	51
NOT IMPORTANT	53	53	45
PALIN QUALIFIED TO BE PRESIDENT			
YES	38	8	91
NO	60	82	16
BIDEN QUALIFIED TO BE PRESIDENT			
YES	66	71	28
NO	32	17	80

Palin energized social conservatives behind McCain. There was greater consensus on the qualifications of the two vice presidential candidates. For example, 74% of Republicans, 66% of conservatives, and 62% of white Evangelicals thought Palin was qualified to be president. She may have helped shore up the Republican base, but she made it far more difficult for McCain to broaden his appeal. Outside of core Republican groups, Palin's standing was weak. Sixty-four percent of Independents believed her to be unqualified, as did college graduates. Even voters who say they favored Hillary Clinton over Obama as the Democratic nominee, a group some Republicans expected to defect to McCain because of his inclusion of a woman on the ticket, were not enthusiastic about Palin's qualifications. Only 12% of Clinton supporters thought Palin had the necessary background to become president.

Election Day Comes Early: The September 15 Economic Crash

The Palin pick did prove to be a short-term spark in early September 2008, as McCain took the lead in many of the national polls for the first time all year. But that lead wouldn't last for long, as the Palin bounce was nothing more than a bubble just waiting to be popped. And it was. On September 15, Lehman Brothers, one of the financial world's biggest institutions, failed, leading to a panicky feeling in the country that the worst was yet to come for the economy. It was just after the Lehman announcement that McCain voiced a phrase on the campaign trail, which he will regret for the rest of his life. As the country was watching its economy collapse, McCain claimed that the "fundamentals of our economy are strong." Within an hour of uttering the phrase at a rally in Florida, a claim McCain had made nearly two dozen times before this dark day, Obama was on the trail mocking McCain's statement and implying the Republican, like Bush, was deeply out of touch on the economy.

McCain, to his credit, tried to fix the error, but the seeds were sewn; he had lost the economic issue and with it, any remote chance he may have had at the presidency. From this point on, Obama's numbers would only go up, slowly building a five to ten point lead in the national polls and substantial leads in states like Pennsylvania and Michigan, two blue states McCain was hoping to pick off. In addition, the economic turn for the worse hit four red states particularly hard and created an electoral map that was unnavigable for McCain. Florida, North Carolina, Indiana, and Ohio were all red states that were especially hit hard by the economic downturn.

McCain would try various gambits to attempt to get back in control of his fortunes, from suspending his campaign to work out the deal to get a financial bailout package passed in Congress to introducing the country to a working-class hero named "Joe the Plumber." None worked, and if anything the public saw through the efforts as nothing but political stunts.

After the Lehman collapse, much of the presidential campaign, believe it or not, seemed to play second fiddle to the events of the moment. Bush's treasury secretary, Hank Paulson, was as familiar a face on the tube as either McCain or Obama in the final weeks of the campaign.

The debates, not surprisingly, were dominated by the economic crisis, even those debates that were supposed to be about national security. But the debates provided McCain no breakthrough moments, as it seemed every debate was held on a day when the nation was gripped with economic anxiety. On the day of two of the three presidential debates, the stock market dropped 500 points, making a bigger impact on the average voter than anything the candidates said in their 90 minute exchanges.

Obama won the debate season, according to the polls, and from then on, things were smooth sailing. The only unknown, at least as far as many observers were concerned, was the role of race. Would there be a "Bradley effect"? Would McCain overtly play the race card at the end in order to test the notion?

Well, neither occurred. The Bradley effect was never proven to be real. The theory is that white voters lie to pollsters about their support for a black candidate, only to enter the voting booth and pull the lever for a white candidate. What seemed true in the past for some major black candidates is that some white voters would say they were undecided if they feared seeming racist to a pollster, but they wouldn't lie about supporting the candidate. The correct term for this is the "Wilder effect." Doug Wilder was the first black governor elected by a Southern state (Virginia) since Reconstruction. He had a big lead in the polls going into Election Day 1989; one trusted poll had Wilder up 50% to 41% with the rest undecided. Well, just about all of the undecided went to Wilder's opponent and Wilder squeaked out a victory, barely garnering over 50%.

It was *this* Wilder effect the McCain camp was hanging its hat on. And, in fact, there was some evidence that there was a mini-Wilder effect in the Democratic primaries. Clinton regularly was judged as the better "closer" and would always do better among the "late deciders" than she did overall. Obama would never lose support from the preelection primary polling; his levels just wouldn't grow at the rate Clinton's support levels would grow.

But as we learned on Election Day itself, there was no Wilder effect; late deciders split evenly and Obama's seven to nine point lead and his lead in most of the battleground states held up. If race was a major factor for some voters, it was for a very limited set of voters.

To McCain's credit, he never played the race card. Did some of his supporters? Yes, but McCain's campaign never did it; it was not the way McCain wanted to win as he knew it would mean he'd have a compromised presidency. McCain's senior leadership, in fact, feared that they might somehow win a narrow Electoral College majority while losing the popular vote and race would be the reason why.

The Election Is as It Was Supposed to Be

In many ways, the actual results of the presidential race were as expected; they were quite unremarkable if one understood how the fundamentals of the political landscape so favored the Democrats throughout all of 2008. Obama's victory margin was what it should have been for a generic Democrat against a generic Republican. Yes, it was a long, strange trip to this eventual normalcy that the electorate delivered, but it was what it should have been.

Republicans were trying to win a third term in a year in which the economy was extremely weak and the Republican Party brand was as poor as it had been since the Great Depression. As many a McCain apologist would utter postelection, it's remarkable they were in the race as long as they were.

Before we delve into the numbers of how Obama won and debate whether 2008 is another year like 1980, in which the country experiences a long-term political realignment, it's worth discussing a few lessons from the 2008 campaign for candidates in 2012 and beyond.

1. Campaigns matter: Obama proved that the old Woody Allen adage is still true, "Eighty percent of success is showing up." Obama showed up in more battleground states than any presidential candidate in 20 years, spending resources in places Democrats hadn't seriously contested in decades. And the gamble paid off. Sure, Obama was assisted by an awful economy that made voters in places like Indiana and North Carolina more susceptible to his change message than they would normally be, but he never would have known whether he could compete if he hadn't shown up.

2. TV ads are overrated: had it not been for the sheer saturation of the television airwaves Obama's financial advantage allowed him, 2008 might have been known as the year the 30 second TV ad died. It's becoming more and more difficult for political TV ads to be "sticky," so good as to be remembered by voters for a period of time. When a campaign comes up with one, it's gold, but it's harder and harder now. Campaigns need to diversify their attempts at branding beyond the 30 second spot unless they truly have unlimited resources, like Obama. For all of his money, it's still very difficult to single out one Obama ad as memorable.

3. Don't forget radio and the Internet: while TV ads may be overrated in their importance in 2008; radio and the Internet are underrated. Obama didn't let a medium go without advertising in it, whether it was a social networking site like Facebook or old-fashioned radio or even video games. McCain barely contested Obama on the radio and didn't do nearly as much on the Internet.

4. Everything old is new again: the key to Obama's impenetrable community of supporters is just that, they are a community. As much as the new technology allows these folks to connect in ways they have not connected before, it was only the first step in organizing them. The tools were used to make sure it was Iowans canvassing Iowans for their support or young people meeting up with young people or African-American men pushing other African-American men to campaign. All in all, the Obama cam-

paign was no different than a campaign for a local office; it was peer to peer and person to person.

5. Early bird gets the worm: one of the more underrated decisions by Obama was the timing of his announcement. Before he got in the race, he was advised by many to hold off getting in formally. The thinking was that the later he got in, the longer he could play the initial "phenomenon card" in order to ride a wave of momentum to victory. But presidential politics is now trench warfare, particularly for candidates who, like Obama, lack the conventional résumé. Obama's decision to get in early meant that by the time the general election started, of the Iowa caucuses, he'd already been on the presidential scene for nearly a year. By the start of the general election, he'd been running for 18 months—the equivalent of about three political lifetimes. And time on the campaign trail is perceived as experience by many voters.

6. Speaking of "early," the early voting phenomenon is here to stay. In 10 states, a majority of the vote was cast *before* Election Day. Among those states are the battlegrounds of Colorado, Florida, Nevada, New Mexico, North Carolina and the emerging battlegrounds of Georgia and Texas. Democrats dominated the early vote like never before and if the Republicans don't catch up quickly, they'll lose an election or two that they shouldn't simply because of the Democrats out-organizing them.

7. Don't forget the lesson of Roger Mudd. During the 1980 presidential campaign, Ted Kennedy infamously could never spell out in a TV interview with journalist Roger Mudd why he wanted to be president. There's no harder lesson for Clinton and McCain than this one, as neither one of them ever laid out a vision for why they were running. Both believed it was simply their turn. Obama was the only one of the three who actually made the case for why he wanted to be president. You've heard the adage, "You can't win if you don't play." Well, in presidential politics, "You can't win if you don't know why you're running."

8. Money still matters: John McCain will be the last candidate who ever takes public financing unless there is a massive overhaul in how campaigns are funded in this country. To date, Congress has never been able to legislate money for the future; it only responds to problems of the past. McCain-Feingold may have wanted to keep big-money special interests out of campaigns, but it didn't account for the fact that millions of small donors could, over time, become their own big-moneyed special interest group. Obama created a massive fund-raising machine. The

billion dollar figure is staggering; does this mean Obama will raise twice this when or if he runs for reelection? Is there a point at which the average American responds negatively to Obama's ability to raise money? Can a sitting president get away with raising $1.5 billion for an election? This is a daunting figure for the Republicans to face. In a span of four years, the party of money, the GOP, has suddenly become political paupers.

9. Primary calendar chaos: one of the most warped aspects of this campaign was that the voters spent more time, 17 months, deciding who the two major nominees were than they did deciding who would be the better president, McCain or Obama, five months. We're not advocating for a longer campaign, just a reversed ratio. Give the country more time to decide on the eventual president. This can happen with a more disciplined primary calendar, one that has the conventions held earlier in the process, say mid-July and early August, and one that allows the first primaries to be held in February or March, rather than two days after New Year's. But whether these recommendations are followed or not, one thing is for sure: future candidates need to take the primary calendar seriously and only assume that the most important contest is the one that's coming up next, not one you are wishing matters. (This means you, Rudy Giuliani, who tried skipping four states.)

Debating Realignment: We Don't Yet Know but . . .

There are plenty of ways to slice this election and proclaim that X is what won Obama the election. X could equal Bush or the economy or African-Americans or new voters or money or the suburbs or, well, you get the picture.

But let's start with the simple question on the minds of many political observers; was the 2008 election the start of a political realignment in favor of the Democrats?

The answer is: we don't yet know. Political realignments aren't known until a few years after they happen. Frankly, it wasn't crystal clear that 1980 was a political realignment until as early as 1988 and maybe as late as 1994.

But here's what we do know: there is an opportunity for Democrats to make 2008 a realignment election; they simply have to govern smartly and popularly. If they do that, they could see themselves in power with a 52% to 55% coalition of supporters for a decade or more.

Inside the American Election 2008

Demographically Speaking, Times Are Tough for GOP

Obama's victorious coalition in 2008 was impressive but not radical. The portrait of the electorate in 2008 was roughly the same as it was in 2004, with a couple slight, but important differences.

While the coalition of voters that supported Obama reflected the increasing diversity of America, and while Obama made gains across almost all demographic subgroups, the majority of his support came from white voters. Sixty-one percent of his supporters were white, 23% were African-Americans, and 11% were Hispanic. In contrast, 90% of John McCain's supporters were white.

There were fewer white voters to win or lose. This is a *huge* potential problem for the GOP especially if you consider that in 1976, only one in ten voters was not white, 10%. In 2008, one in four voters was not white, 26%, and guess what, the white vote isn't enough to power the GOP.

Obama did as well among white voters as any previous Democratic presidential candidate since Jimmy Carter in 1976, when 47% of whites cast their votes for the Democrat. In 2008, 43% of white voters nationwide voted for Obama, while McCain won 55% of the white vote.

Apart from whites under 30, McCain won a majority of every other age group of white voters. This appeared to limit Obama in many traditionally Republican states. Southern whites seemed resistant to Obama's appeal, voting 68% to 32% for McCain. Even so, Obama managed to peel off North Carolina and Virginia the fastest-growing states in the South outside of Texas.

	2008			2004		
	TOTAL	OBAMA	McCAIN	TOTAL	KERRY	BUSH
RACE						
WHITE	74	43	55	77	41	58
BLACK	13	95	4	11	88	11
HISPANIC	9	67	31	8	60	40

African-Americans

African-American voters increased their percentage of the electorate to 13%. In 2004, they accounted for 11% of voters. Although they were already strongly Democratic, Obama outperformed John

Kerry among blacks by five points to the highest level of Democratic support. He won 95% of the black vote, compared to just 4% for McCain.

Significant Trend in Latinos

Obama also built up a big advantage among Hispanic voters. Over the last two elections, the Bush campaign was able to make inroads among Latinos. However, in 2008, Latinos came back to the Democratic Party. Hispanics were 9% of the electorate and Obama beat McCain by more than two to one. Obama led 67% to 31% among these voters, the best ever showing for a Democratic presidential candidate.

What's more, Hispanic turnout was up in 19 states, including some that will have the average political observer scratching their head. The obvious places where Hispanic turnout was up were Arizona, Colorado, Nevada, and New Mexico. The not so obvious states were Indiana, Iowa, Michigan, Minnesota, Missouri, Montana, New Hampshire, North Carolina, North Dakota, Ohio, Pennsylvania, South Dakota, Virginia, West Virginia, and Wisconsin.

The Hispanic population is increasing all over the country; no longer are Hispanics only a significant voting bloc in Border States or states with big cities. This migration is shaking up the political map. For example, Hispanics can be credited as the voting group that swung Indiana. If no Hispanics had voted McCain, not Obama, would have carried Indiana.

Youth Vote Overrated?

At the age of 47, Obama will become one of the nation's youngest presidents. He won partly because of an unprecedented level of support among young people and new voters. Obama was supported by those voters under 30 by an impressive 66% to 31% margin, much higher than in any previous election, as well as 68% of first-time voters.

This is an especially important statistic for one reason, also familiar to marketing professionals: picking a party for the first time is akin to picking between Diet Coke and Diet Pepsi. Once you become loyal to one, you usually stay loyal for some time.

| | **2008** | | | **2004** | | |
	TOTAL	OBAMA	McCAIN	TOTAL	KERRY	BUSH
AGE						
18–29	18	66	32	17	54	45
30–44	29	52	46	29	46	53
45–64	37	50	49	38	47	52
65+	16	45	53	16	47	52

This year the gap between young and old increased a lot. Obama outperformed Kerry with all age groups except seniors. McCain retained the Republican advantage among seniors but lost among the middle-aged, who had supported Bush in 2004. Obama got just over half of the vote among those 30 to 64 years old.

The consistent growth in the margins among the youth vote over the last eight years is one of the best signs for the Democratic Party in terms of their push for realignment. In 2000, Gore beat Bush by a couple of points among voters aged 18 to 29. In 2004, Kerry beat Bush by nine points in this group. And in 2008, Obama beat McCain by 34 points, 66% to 32%.

Young voters are more diverse racially and ethnically than older voters and are growing more so over time. Just 62% of voters under 30 are white, while 18% are black and 14% Hispanic. Four years ago, this age group was 68% white; in 2000, nearly three-quarters, 74%, were white. They are also more secular in their religious orientation and fewer report regular attendance at worship services, and secular voters tend to vote Democratic.

At the same time, it's important not to overstate the significance of the youth vote in Obama's victory. In spite of the expectation of a significant increase in voting among young people, the youth share of the vote was 18% of the electorate this year, just one percentage point more than in 2004. And while almost a quarter of Obama's vote was under 30, 77% was over 30.

To hammer this point home, consider this stunning fact: if no one under the age of 30 had voted, Obama would have won every state he carried with the exception of two: Indiana and North Carolina.

New Voters Mattered to a Point

The Obama campaign did really well in their effort to increase their support among new voters. One in ten of those voting in 2008 did so for the first time, the same proportion of the electorate as in 2004. But they were quite different in their vote preference. A huge majority of new voters supported Obama by 69% to 30%. This compares to just a seven point advantage that the Democrats had in 2004 when Kerry won by 53% to 46%.

| | **2008** | | | **2004** | | |
	TOTAL	OBAMA	McCAIN	TOTAL	KERRY	BUSH
NEW VOTER						
YES	11	69	30	11	53	46
NO	89	50	48	89	48	51

Two-thirds of new voters were under 30, and one in five was black, almost twice the proportion of blacks among voters overall. And nearly as many new voters are Hispanic, about 18%. Almost half were Democrats, and a third called themselves Independents.

Gender Gap Lives

Obama made a strong showing among women, winning them by 13 points, 56% to 43%, even more than the usual Democratic margin. This was partly because of the increased proportion of minority women voting for Obama. While Obama won women overall, and nonwhite women overwhelmingly, he performed slightly worse with white women in 2008 than Gore did in 2000. In that year, white women split their vote 48% for Gore to 49% for Bush. In 2008, McCain won the votes of white women, 53% to 46%.

| | **2008** | | | **2004** | | |
	TOTAL	OBAMA	McCAIN	TOTAL	KERRY	BUSH
GENDER						
MEN	47	49	48	46	44	55
WOMEN	53	56	43	54	51	48
GENDER BY RACE						
WHITE MEN	36	41	57	36	37	62
WHITE WOMEN	39	46	53	41	44	55
BLACK MEN	5	95	5	5	86	13
BLACK WOMEN	7	96	3	7	90	10
LATINO MEN	4	64	33	4	55	42
LATINO WOMEN	5	68	30	4	61	37
ALL OTHER RACES	5	64	32	2	53	43

When people discuss the gender gap they often concentrate on how much more Democratic women are than men. In a dramatic shift, Obama flipped men in this election in part because Obama narrowed the white male gap to 16 points, 41% to 57%. Not since

Carter had any Democratic nominee earned more than 38% of the white male vote. This narrowing among a group of voters who account for 36% of the electorate allowed Obama to split the male vote overall, eking out a one point advantage, 49% to 48%, over McCain. This erased the advantage that President Bush enjoyed among men in 2004, 55% to 44%.

Obama Did Well Among the Better-Educated

Obama ran stronger this year than Kerry did in 2004 among several voter groups that typically vote Republican.

	2008			2004		
	TOTAL	OBAMA	McCAIN	TOTAL	KERRY	BUSH
EDUCATION BY RACE						
WHITE, COLLEGE DEGREE	35	47	51	43	44	55
WHITE, NO COLLEGE DEGREE	39	40	58	34	38	61
NONWHITE, COLLEGE DEGREE	9	75	22	14	68	28
NONWHITE, NO COLLEGE DEGREE	16	83	16	9	70	29

Obama nearly tied with McCain among the 35% who are college-educated white voters. They broke for McCain 51% to 47%, marking roughly a three point gain for Obama compared to Kerry's 44% showing. There has been a trend for at least a decade, as more and more college-educated white suburban professionals have been moving toward the Democrats. The improved showing by Obama was particularly relevant in Virginia and Colorado, where white college graduates helped Obama win. Both states are in the top 10 states in terms of the highest rates of college education. They are the only two of those 10 states that Kerry lost in 2004.

Obama outperformed Kerry among all income groups by at least five to eight points. Four years ago, George W. Bush carried voters nationwide with incomes over $100,000 by 17 points, 58% to 41%. In 2008, affluent voters split their votes evenly, 49% for Obama and 49% for McCain.

The biggest gains were among households with incomes over $200,000 where Obama improved the 2004 performance by 17 points. This was true even though McCain regularly harped on the fact that Obama was going to raise taxes on folks making over $200,000.

	2008			**2004**		
	TOTAL	OBAMA	McCAIN	TOTAL	KERRY	BUSH
INCOME						
LESS THAN $50,000	38	60	38	45	55	44
$50–100,000	36	49	49	37	43	55
MORE THAN $100,000	26	49	49	18	41	58

Middle-of-the-Road Voters

Obama's persistent attention to the middle also paid off. When McCain sealed the nomination, his path to the White House seemed to be based on winning moderates and Independents. In the end, those who describe themselves as moderates, 44% of the electorate, voted for Obama by a huge margin, 60% to 39%. Obama also beat McCain among Independents by eight points, 52% to 44%, three points better than Kerry did in 2004.

Catholics, about 26% of the electorate, and a vital swing group, were among the Republican-leaning groups that moved into the Democratic column for Obama, 54% to 45%. Obama also improved slightly among non-Hispanic, white Catholic voters, although McCain held a narrow majority, 52% to 47%.

There are several other interesting groups in Obama's coalition: he won 83% of Hillary Clinton Democrats, 17% of 2004 Bush voters, and 62% of every voter who did not identify themselves as white Evangelicals. Despite worries among Democrats about Obama's chances with Jewish voters, he won more than three-quarters of them nationally, a slight improvement over Kerry.

	2008			**2004**		
	TOTAL	OBAMA	McCAIN	TOTAL	KERRY	BUSH
IDEOLOGY						
LIBERAL	22	89	10	21	85	13
MODERATE	44	60	39	45	54	45
CONSERVATIVE	34	20	78	34	15	84
RELIGION						
PROTESTANT	54	45	54	54	40	59
WHITE PROTESTANT	42	34	65	41	32	67
WHITE EVANGELICAL PROTESTANT	23	26	73	21	20	79
WHITE PROTESTANT, NOT EVANGELICAL	19	44	55	20	44	55
BLACK PROTESTANT	9	94	4	8	86	13
BLACK EVANGELICAL PROTESTANT	2	95	3	5	81	18

	2008			2004		
	TOTAL	OBAMA	McCAIN	TOTAL	KERRY	BUSH
BLACK PROTESTANT, NOT EVANGELICAL	7	95	5	3	92	8
HISPANIC PROTESTANT	2	67	32	3	40	58
CATHOLIC	27	54	45	27	47	52
WHITE CATHOLIC	19	47	52	20	43	56
HISPANIC CATHOLIC	6	72	26	5	58	39
JEWISH	2	78	21	3	74	25
OTHER	6	73	22	7	74	23
NONE	12	75	23	10	67	31

Republican Base

One group McCain held on to were white Protestant Evangelicals, who made up 23% of the entire electorate. This group voted three to one for the Republican despite attempts by Obama to reach out to faith groups. However, McCain received about five percentage points less support than Bush received four years ago.

McCain, 72, was the choice of just over half, 53%, of those in his peer group, senior citizens, coveted because of their turnout rate. Those 65 years and older were 16% of all voters, similar in number to those under 30.

Obama fared relatively poorly among white voters without a college education. He lost this group by 18 points, a small improvement over Kerry's performance. John McCain courted working-class whites, calling out repeatedly to "Joe the Plumber," a symbol of these voters, and drew some of his strongest support from them, winning 58%. In fact, he even flipped a few counties in southwest Pennsylvania where the "Joe the Plumber" message may have resonated best. But the group's share of the electorate dropped by four points and McCain's margins were shy of the 23 points by which Bush won this group in 2004.

The Suburbs

The lynchpin of any realignment in American politics is the suburbs. The nation's suburbs have sometimes been portrayed as lily-white enclaves of the middle and upper classes, detached from the problems and diversity of the cities. The suburbs have also long been characterized as Republican strongholds, at least in presidential races, areas where the GOP overcomes usual Democratic margins in the nation's big cities.

But none of those stereotypes about the nation's suburbs are accurate anymore, if they ever were. In particular, the political geography of the suburbs is a battleground, not a partisan bastion.

The battle for the White House in 2008 was decided, in large part, in the suburbs. Obama won the suburbs over McCain, if narrowly, the first Democrat to achieve that since Bill Clinton in 1996. Obama won 50% of the vote in the suburbs, while McCain took 48%.

That performance in the suburbs, matched with Obama's good showing in the big cities (although not as good as some expected), was enough for victory. But Obama's win in the suburbs was not a huge surprise. First, the suburbs have been fought over in the twenty-first-century presidential campaigns, with neither party holding a decisive edge for what is about one-half of all the votes in the country. Bush won the suburbs by only two percentage points in 2000 and only five percentage points in 2004.

Presidential Vote in the Suburbs

	2008	2004	2000
OBAMA/KERRY/GORE	50%	47%	47%
MCCAIN/BUSH	48%	52%	49%

The preelection polls in 2008 depicted a seesaw battle for the suburbs, with Obama holding a lead in the spring, but McCain taking the lead in mid-summer and holding that into September. But close to the election, several polls, including the National Suburban Poll for Hofstra University, showed Obama moving into the lead in the suburbs.

Obama won the big cities by a 63% to 35% margin, an overwhelming victory. That 28 point win was a substantial improvement over Kerry's 54% to 46% victory in the urban areas in 2004, but it was only slightly better than Gore's 61% to 35% win in the cities in 2000.

McCain did well in the rural areas, although again, not as well as past GOP candidates. He won 53% to 45%, certainly the poorest showing there for a Republican since 1996. McCain's eight point margin trailed Bush's 22 point edge in 2000 and his 15 point win in 2004.

Presidential Vote in Urban, Suburban, and Rural Areas

2008	TOTAL	OBAMA	McCAIN
URBAN	30%	63%	35%
SUBURBS	49%	50%	48%
RURAL	21%	45%	53%

2004	TOTAL	KERRY	BUSH
URBAN	30%	54%	45%
SUBURBS	46%	47%	52%
RURAL	25%	42%	57%

2000	TOTAL	GORE	BUSH
URBAN	29%	61%	35%
SUBURBS	43%	47%	49%
RURAL	28%	37%	59%

Comparing results in the suburbs over time is a tricky business, because the suburbs have been a constantly shifting and expanding area over the past several decades.

In just about every red state Obama flipped or every blue state he won substantially, it was a flip in the suburban counties that led the way, whether one looks at the northern Virginia suburbs, which powered Obama's victory in the Old Dominion to the Research Triangle in North Carolina to county flips in the I-4 corridor in Florida and the surrounding suburban counties in Denver, Colorado.

The building blocks for Obama's victory in the suburbs were the same as those he used in the cities: he won big majorities among the young, those with college degrees, minority group members, and those who are not married. Obama won the votes of those age 18 to 29 by 20 points and those in their 30s by a 51% to 47% margin, compared to an eight point GOP margin among these suburbanites in 2004.

Obama improved his showing among both suburban men and suburban women by seven percentage points over 2004, but it was suburban women who moved firmly into the Democratic camp, 52% to 46%.

Two groups led this change: working women and women with children, particularly married women with children. Suburban working women were evenly divided in 2004, 49% to 49%, but Obama won them by 21 points, 60% to 39%. Married suburban women with children also pivoted in a major way: Obama won their votes by 52% to 48%, compared with Bush's 17 point victory in 2004.

Religion played an interesting role in the suburbs in the 2008 election. Evangelicals did turn out in the suburbs, rising from 28% of the suburban voters to 36%. And they did back McCain, by a hefty 58% to 39% margin. But that was far short of the 66% to 33% edge Bush won among these suburbanites in 2004.

Obama improved the Democratic showing among many income groups, although the gain among those suburbanites making less than $50,000 a year was only four percentage points. Again, among white suburbanites making less than $50,000, Obama actually did worse: he lost the group by six points while it split almost evenly four years before when Kerry lost by two points.

The inner and outer suburbs have also helped power the Democrats back into impressive majorities in both houses of Congress. Take a look at the map of Democratic House victories in both 2006 and 2008. Many of the seats they've won are in suburban areas of the country, from Florida's 8th Congressional District in and around Orlando to Virginia's 11th District that includes Fairfax County. The GOP slippage in the suburbs has been evident for some time.

Firing the Republicans

Identity politics is just one way to determine how Obama won. But forget gender, age, and ethnicity a minute and remember this election may have been decided by one, simple, four letter word: *B-U-S-H*. This election took place during one of the longest sustained periods of voter dissatisfaction in modern history. The vote was a verdict on the past eight years of Republican rule. Three-quarters of Americans thought America was on the "wrong track" and two-thirds disapproved of Bush's performance as president.

	2008			**2004**		
	TOTAL	OBAMA	McCAIN	TOTAL	KERRY	BUSH
COUNTRY MOVING						
RIGHT DIRECTION	20	27	71	49	10	89
WRONG TRACK	75	62	36	46	86	12

In 2000, voters who felt the country was headed in the right direction outnumbered those with negative assessments by two to one: just 31% said the country was on the wrong track that year. In 2004, 46% held that view. In this election, 75% of voters said the country was "seriously off on the wrong track." This included majorities of key swing groups such as Independents and moderates. Among those who thought the country was off on the wrong track, Obama beat McCain 62% to 36%.

Only 27% approved of Bush's job performance, while 71% disapproved. The last time a sitting president had an approval rating this low in an election year was 1952, long before the exit poll was invented. A Gallup Poll in February 1952 reported a 22% approval rating for Democrat Harry S. Truman. Truman did not run for reelection that year, but Dwight D. Eisenhower soundly defeated Adlai Stevenson, the Democratic Party's candidate. Even in Utah, one of the nation's most Republican state, a majority, 51%, disapproved of the job Bush was doing. This compares to 53% approval among Utah voters in 2004.

	2008			**2004**		
	TOTAL	OBAMA	McCAIN	TOTAL	KERRY	BUSH
BUSH JOB						
APPROVE	27	10	89	53	9	90
DISAPPROVE	71	67	31	46	93	6
WILL JOHN McCAIN						
CONTINUE BUSH'S POLICIES	48	90	8	–	–	–
MOVE IN A DIFFERENT DIRECTION	48	13	85	–	–	–

Bush's job rating was an important factor in determining which states would turn red or blue. With the single exception of Missouri, which barely went for McCain, Obama won every state where Bush's approval rating was below 35% in the exit polls, and he lost every state where Bush's approval rating was over 35%.

McCain spent much of the campaign trying to disassociate himself from Bush. But Obama never let him forget his mostly loyal Republican record. McCain proclaimed in his final debate with Obama, "I am not President Bush. If you wanted to run against President Bush, you should have run four years ago." While McCain may have said he would bring change, he failed to convince. When voters were asked whether they thought McCain would continue Bush's policies or take the country in a new direction, half of them said McCain would continue on Bush's path. And of those voters, nine in ten voted for Obama.

War in Iraq

It could be said that the issue of the Iraq war is what propelled both McCain and Obama to their respective nominations. Obama's stance against the Iraq war is what gave him his initial presidential credibility. For McCain, his stubbornness in sticking with the Iraq surge was enough to convince conservatives in the party, never McCain fans, to hold their nose and tolerate his nomination.

By the time of the election, though, Iraq crumbled as an important issue, with only 10% of voters considering it most important. The Iraq war had become most salient to opponents of the war; those who chose Iraq as their top issue favored Obama. While McCain won handily among those who approved of the war in Iraq, 86% to 13%, they represented only about one in three voters, 36%. Among the 63% of the electorate who disapproved of the war, Obama won 76% to 22%.

	2008			2004		
	TOTAL	OBAMA	McCAIN	TOTAL	KERRY	BUSH
WAR IN IRAQ						
APPROVE	36	13	86	51	14	85
DISAPPROVE	63	76	22	45	87	12
WORRIED ABOUT TERRORISM						
VERY	25	43	54	22	56	44
SOMEWHAT	45	51	48	53	43	56
NOT TOO	23	67	31	19	47	51
NOT AT ALL	5	69	27	5	48	50

The Magic of *Change*

Obama had a singular, consistent theme from day one and he ran on it for two years: *change*. Obama was about change, both the man and his message, and what that meant was never ambiguous. It was the opposite of Bush and the Republicans. It was clear and simple. And it was very difficult for McCain, McCain the reformer, McCain the maverick, McCain the anti-earmark guy, to be the change candidate. The ability to bring change edged out all other candidate qualities with 34% reporting that "change" was the most important candidate quality to them. Only 20% said experience was the most important candidate quality. Those who were focused on change supported Obama by a stunning ratio of nine to one.

	TOTAL	OBAMA	McCAIN
CANDIDATE QUALITIES			
CHANGE	34	89	9
VALUES	30	32	65
EXPERIENCE	20	7	93
CARES	12	74	24
HAS THE RIGHT EXPERIENCE			
McCAIN DOES	59	29	59
McCAIN DOES NOT	40	89	8
OBAMA DOES	51	93	5
OBAMA DOES NOT	48	12	85

	TOTAL	OBAMA	McCAIN
McCAIN HAS RIGHT JUDGMENT TO BE PRESIDENT			
YES	49	19	80
NO	49	89	8
OBAMA HAS RIGHT JUDGMENT TO BE PRESIDENT			
YES	57	90	9
NO	42	5	92

While Obama ran largely on a message of change, he was still able to meet the threshold when it comes to having experience. A majority, 51%, said Obama has the right experience to be president, while 59% said the same about McCain.

Over the course of the campaign, during the debates and the economic crisis, the public also began to assess the candidates' judgment. Almost six in ten, 57%, of voters said that Obama had the right judgment to make a good president, while 49% said the same for McCain.

Obama's Race vs. McCain's Age

Race is a difficult subject for a lot of people, but given the historic nature of the election with the first African-American nominee of a major party, Americans were talking about it a lot during the campaign. Plenty of voters said race was at least one of several important factors in deciding how to cast their vote.

Most white voters, 92%, said race was not important. But for 7% race *was* at least a somewhat important factor, 27%. Race did have a negative impact on Obama's vote as white voters who *acknowledged* that race was important voted for McCain by a two to one margin. But, remarkably, one-third of white voters who said Obama's race was important voted *for* Obama.

Twice as many African-American voters than white voters said the race of the candidate was important in their vote, just a little over one in five. However, the level of support for Obama among all black voters was so high that there is no significant difference between those who said race was important and those who said it wasn't.

The issues of McCain's age and Obama's race may have canceled each other out. At 72 years old, McCain would have been the oldest first-term president and in the end, McCain's age may have been a bigger issue than Obama's race. Twice as many voters overall said the age of the candidates was a factor in their vote than said race was. And those concerned about age favored Obama by a two to one margin, 77% to 22%.

	TOTAL	OBAMA	McCAIN
FUTURE OF NATIONAL RACE RELATIONS			
BETTER	47	70	28
STAY THE SAME	34	44	54
WORSE	15	27	70
IMPORTANCE OF CANDIDATE'S RACE, AMONG WHITES			
IMPORTANT	7	33	66
NOT IMPORTANT	92	44	54
IMPORTANCE OF CANDIDATE'S RACE, AMONG BLACKS			
IMPORTANT	16	98	2
NOT IMPORTANT	83	96	4
IMPORTANCE OF CANDIDATE'S AGE			
IMPORTANT	15	77	22
NOT IMPORTANT	84	47	51

The Enthusiasm Gap

Another major factor in deciding the election was the enthusiasm gap, the difference between the intensity of feeling of McCain and Obama supporters. One-third of the Obama voters were "excited" by the prospect of his victory, as opposed to just 14% of McCain voters. Even among his supporters, enthusiasm for McCain was tepid, as it had been all through the campaign. Just 28% of McCain voters were "excited" about the prospect of his becoming president. By contrast, twice as many Obama supporters, 56%, were excited about the prospect of an Obama presidency.

	TOTAL	OBAMA	McCAIN
FEELINGS IF McCAIN ELECTED			
EXCITED	14	7	92
OPTIMISTIC	32	13	86
CONCERNED	25	79	18
SCARED	28	95	2

	2008		
	TOTAL	OBAMA	McCAIN
FEELINGS IF OBAMA ELECTED			
EXCITED	30	98	2
OPTIMISTIC	24	77	20
CONCERNED	20	18	80
SCARED	24	4	95

The "It's Always the Economy, Stupid" Portion of the Book

The economy was by far the dominant concern in the election, with 63% citing it as the most important issue facing the United States. Nothing else was even close. Among these voters, Obama won by a solid 53% to 44% margin.

An unprecedented number of voters held negative views about the state of the economy. In 2004, 47% said the nation's economy was good and 52% said it was not so good. In 2008, only 7% rated the current condition of the national economy good while 93% rated it as not so good or poor. Those who said it was in the direst straits were also the strongest backers of Obama. Among those who rate the nation's economy as not so good or poor, Obama beat McCain 54% to 44%. On Election Day, McCain won the whopping 7% of Americans who said the economy was good.

For many families, their financial situation has worsened over the last four years. Forty-two percent of voters said their family's financial situation was worse than it was four years ago, the most since the question first was asked in exit polls in 1992. Two-thirds expressed concern about affording health care. But looking ahead, voters are more optimistic. Forty-seven percent think the economy will get better in the coming year. Just 23%, primarily McCain backers, say the economy will get worse next year.

The centerpiece of McCain's closing argument charged that a Democrat in the White House, especially in combination with a Democratic-controlled Congress, would mean an approach to governing based on "tax and spend" and redistribution of wealth. He said a Republican in the White House could change that. But that story didn't sell. A majority of voters thought taxes would go up if Obama were elected, 71%, but nearly as many, 61%, thought taxes would go up if McCain were elected.

	2008			**2004**		
	TOTAL	OBAMA	McCAIN	TOTAL	KERRY	BUSH
MOST IMPORTANT ISSUE						
ECONOMY	63	53	44	–	–	–
IRAQ	10	59	39	–	–	–
TERRORISM	9	13	86	–	–	–
HEALTH CARE	9	73	26	–	–	–
ENERGY	7	50	46	–	–	–
BEING ABLE TO AFFORD HEALTH CARE						
WORRIED	66	60	38	–	–	–
NOT WORRIED	33	42	56	–	–	–
STATE OF THE ECONOMY						
EXCELLENT OR GOOD	7	26	72	47	13	87
NOT GOOD OR POOR	93	54	44	52	79	20
WORRIED ABOUT THE NATIONAL ECONOMY						
WORRIED	85	54	44	–	–	–
NOT WORRIED	14	33	65	–	–	–
PERSONAL FINANCIAL SITUATION COMPARED TO FOUR YEARS AGO						
BETTER	24	37	60	32	19	80
SAME	34	45	53	39	50	49
WORSE	42	71	28	28	79	20
FUTURE OF THE NATIONAL ECONOMY NEXT YEAR						
BETTER	47	61	38	–	–	–
SAME	25	52	46	–	–	–
WORSE	23	43	54	–	–	–
McCAIN WOULD RAISE TAXES						
YES	61	62	36	–	–	–
NO	36	40	59	–	–	–
OBAMA WOULD RAISE TAXES						
YES	71	43	55	–	–	–
NO	27	82	16	–	–	–

Partisan Shifts

Any political realignment starts with a surge of voters identifying with one party over the other. In 1976, Democrats had a 16 point advantage in their share of the electorate. In 1984, the first four years of Reagan's presidency shrank the Democratic advantage to just two points. And this move to a narrow Democratic advantage helped propel the Republicans for 20 years, culminating in 2004 when there was partisan parity.

This year, in a dramatic turnaround, Democrats outnumbered Republicans by seven points, 39% to 32%, the fewest Republicans in 28 years. Much of the electorate may not have looked all that different from 2004, but the likelihood that members of that electorate would call themselves Republicans was dramatically different. The question is: how many formerly Republican voters stayed home versus those who voted but did not identify as Republican?

Given the massive registration efforts waged by the Obama campaign, that Republicans fell as a proportion of the electorate might not be surprising. But the big shift in the makeup of the electorate did not come from an increase in Democrats, but rather from an increase in Independents and a decreased percentage identifying themselves as Republican. The share of voters describing themselves as "liberal," "moderate," and "conservative" stayed roughly the same compared to four years ago. This speaks more to moderates and Independents fleeing the GOP than to a lack of turnout on the part of the base.

Moreover, it was men and women alike—indeed slightly more men—who were responsible for the sharp shift in partisanship.

The polls also show party identification shifting away from the Republicans even more strongly in some states that voted for Obama this time, after supporting George W. Bush in the last two elections. The pattern can be seen at the regional level. The Midwest, West, and South showed a steep decline in Republican identification losing six points over the last four years. The Northeast, which has had a steady Democratic advantage for decades, had a three point decline in Republican identification.

Party Identification by Year

	DEMOCRAT	INDEPENDENT	REPUBLICAN	DEMOCRATIC ADVANTAGE
1972	46%	19%	35%	11%
1976	41%	34%	25%	16%
1980	45%	26%	30%	15%
1984	38%	26%	36%	2%
1988	38%	26%	35%	3%
1992	38%	27%	35%	3%
1996	39%	26%	35%	4%
2000	39%	27%	35%	4%
2004	37%	26%	37%	0%
2008	39%	29%	32%	7%

Party Identification by Gender by Year

| | MALE | | | FEMALE | | |
	DEMOCRAT	INDEPENDENT	REPUBLICAN	DEMOCRAT	INDEPENDENT	REPUBLICAN
1972	44%	22%	34%	47%	17%	36%
1976	39%	38%	23%	43%	30%	27%
1980	42%	27%	31%	48%	24%	28%
1984	35%	29%	36%	41%	23%	35%
1988	33%	28%	39%	42%	25%	33%
1992	34%	30%	36%	41%	26%	34%
1996	34%	29%	37%	44%	23%	33%
2000	33%	29%	38%	44%	25%	32%
2004	31%	29%	39%	41%	24%	35%
2008	35%	32%	33%	43%	26%	31%

	1972	1984	1992	2000	2004	2008
NORTHEAST						
DEM.	42%	40%	39%	40%	41%	44%
IND.	20%	29%	30%	30%	30%	29%
REP.	38%	31%	31%	30%	30%	27%
MIDWEST						
DEM.	41%	36%	36%	36%	37%	39%
IND.	21%	27%	29%	31%	25%	29%
REP.	38%	37%	35%	34%	38%	32%
SOUTH						
DEM.	55%	39%	40%	40%	35%	37%
IND.	18%	26%	25%	22%	22%	27%
REP.	27%	35%	35%	38%	42%	36%
WEST						
DEM.	48%	39%	36%	39%	34%	38%
IND.	18%	21%	26%	25%	30%	32%
REP.	34%	41%	38%	36%	36%	30%

And it isn't just party identification; there are some slight attitudinal shifts that have taken place, which might be enough for a realignment to stick.

The number of voters who said they thought the government should be more active was slightly higher than in 2004; in 2008, 51% said they wanted the government to do more, and only 43% thought the government was doing too much. Those wanting more of an activist government swung 20 points more Democratic this time. And while it's not clear that racism is a thing of the past, the country just elected the first African-American president, which certainly marks a long-term liberalization in racial attitudes. While the center might not have moved ideologically, the new voters and those under the age of 30 have come of age politically in a climate that inclines them toward greater support of activist government, greater opposition to the war in Iraq, less social conservatism, and a greater willingness to describe themselves as liberal politically.

Building Blocks Are in Place

The building blocks for a political realignment are clearly in place. The Democratic Party's advantages in fast-growing states and fast-growing demographics indicate the possibility the party could go on a run that mirrors the Republican success story from 1980 to 2004.

The rest of this book takes a detailed look at each state, how it voted, and where it's headed on the political spectrum. It's a scary book to some Republican strategists because the numbers in 2008 were so dire. It's possible Obama was a unique candidate, running in a unique year that will never be mirrored again. After all, maybe a soft-spoken Midwestern African-American Democratic politician is a more powerful political weapon to defeat Republicans than moderate Southern Democrats, the previous recipe for Democrats. Obama's dominance in the region of Illinois (Iowa, Wisconsin, and Indiana), combined with his ability to mobilize minority and new voters in New South states like Virginia, North Carolina, and Florida, allowed him to put together an unparalleled electoral coalition, which even Bill Clinton couldn't do and Clinton had the help of Ross Perot peeling away Republican voters.

But maybe the floor of the Democratic Party has risen to a point where the party's ability to forge a majority is a lot easier right now than it is for the Republican Party. Consider this amazing statistic, courtesy of longtime Democratic strategist Mike Berman. Democrats have carried 18 states plus D.C. in five straight presidential elections, totaling 248 electoral votes, just 22 short of the 270 to win. In contrast, Republicans have carried just 13 states in five straight elections, totaling a mere 95 electoral votes. If you include states where Democrats have won in four of the last five presidentials, the electoral vote floor for the Democrats rises to 264. And these numbers do not count Colorado, Virginia, Florida, or Nevada, four states, which sure look like they've forever taken a turn toward the battleground with a couple looking like blue bets in 2012.

The Republican Party has a lot of work to do. They haven't won a Democratic-held Senate seat since 2004; they don't hold a single U.S. House seat in all of New England; the party is at an all-time low in number of House seats they hold in New York state (just 3 of 29). According to the Cook Political Report, Democrats hold regional advantages in the U.S. House in the Midwest by 10 seats, in the West by 28 seats, and in the Northeast by a whopping 59 seats. The only region where the GOP holds an advantage in U.S. House seats is in the South, where their lead is 16 seats. There may not be a better stat to underscore the GOP's geographic problem than this one.

As the exit poll and the election results suggest, the Republican Party is in danger of becoming a Southern and rural party and nothing more. The party's slow drain of support in the suburbs and its ideological shift away from its pre-Reagan moderate Midwestern and New England roots have cost the party big-time.

It's unclear where the GOP will head next. More than likely, there will be an ideological debate about whether the party was conservative enough. The argument will be that Bush campaigned as a conservative but didn't govern as one and McCain never governed as a conservative and only masked himself as one during the campaign. But if conservatives win this debate, will that help them win back the northern Virginia suburbs? Will that help the party compete more effectively in Pennsylvania? What about New Hampshire, Colorado, and Arizona?

And then there is the GOP's Hispanic problem. After two straight elections making gains among Hispanics, the party's support levels slipped badly to numbers the party hadn't seen since 1996. The GOP already loses African-Americans by large margins. Can the party afford to see a faster growing minority group voting in larger and larger majorities for the Democrats?

Finally, there's the GOP's education deficit. For yet another cycle, college-educated white voters have moved toward the Democrats. Some in the GOP are warning that all of this anti-intellectual rhetoric is chasing away onetime suburban Republicans.

Republicans can always hope the Democrats overreach with their political power; it's something all political parties eventually do when they achieve the status that the Democrats now have, which is control of both houses of Congress and the presidency. But Obama's campaign team turned governing team doesn't look like a gang that will shoot itself in the foot often. And for the GOP, rebuilding its party can't start with hoping the other guys self-destruct; it starts with getting its act together state by state, county by county, demographic group by demographic group.

Battleground States

(8 States)

These are the eight states that were the most contentious in this election. Some have been battlegrounds for the last several elections, such as Florida, Missouri, and Ohio. Others were battleground states for the first time this year, such as Indiana, Colorado, North Carolina, and Virginia. In 2008, the candidates focused a great deal on these states. Some were very close, Missouri and North Carolina in particular, while others such as Iowa had a wider margin than in the past. But each and every one of these states was a contest and probably should be keyed on as folks put together their battleground state lists for 2012.

COLORADO
Can Democrats Continue Their Recent Sweeps?

9 ELECTORAL VOTES

Colorado has voted Republican in all but three elections since World War II. But today Colorado is considered a battleground state due in large measure to changes in population. And in 2008 Obama won the battle by a significant margin. The polls showed a consistent Obama lead after the conventions that widened in October. The polls slightly underestimated the final Obama margin.

	2008		2004	
Obama	1,288,568	53.7%	Kerry	47.0%
McCain	1,073,584	44.7%	Bush	51.7%
Other candidates	39,197			
	2,401,349			

Note: 100% 3,215 of 3,215 precincts; 100% 64 of 64 counties. Chart based on final, official vote totals.

Turnout was up 2.7 percentage points, to 69.4%, from 2004. Obama won 28 of the 64 counties, flipping six from the GOP slate in 2004. McCain won 38 counties.

The biggest Obama wins were in Arapahoe and Jefferson counties, Denver suburbs that the campaign targeted and where they did well. The two counties are mostly part of the state's 6th Congressional District, the one once held by former conservative Republican Congressman Tom Tancredo. And Coors Brewing Company and the conservative Coors family have long been associated with Golden in Jefferson County.

McCain needed big majorities out of Douglas, El Paso (Colorado Springs), and Mesa. He got them, but the majorities shrank substantially from 2004.

One minor item of note: the nation's newest county, Broomfield, carved out of Boulder County in 2001, flipped from Republican in its first ever presidential election in 2004 to Democratic in 2008. In the caucus of February 5, 2008, Obama received 66.6% of the vote and Clinton received 32.3%.

	2008			2004		
	TOTAL	OBAMA	McCAIN	TOTAL	KERRY	BUSH
GENDER						
MALE	50	49	50	44	45	53
FEMALE	50	56	41	56	48	51
AGE						
♦ *18–29*	14	–	–	15	51	47
30–44	33	53	46	31	48	51
45–64	39	56	42	38	47	52
65+	13	44	53	16	40	60
RACE						
WHITE	81	50	48	86	42	57
BLACK	4	–	–	4	87	13
♦ *HISPANIC*	13	61	38	8	68	30
PARTY						
DEMOCRAT	30	92	7	29	93	7
REPUBLICAN	31	13	87	38	6	93
♦ *INDEPENDENT*	39	54	44	33	52	45
IDEOLOGY						
LIBERAL	17	93	6	22	88	11
MODERATE	46	63	35	43	54	45
♦ *CONSERVATIVE*	36	18	79	35	12	88
EDUCATION BY RACE						
♦ *WHITE, COLLEGE DEGREE*	49	56	42	41	35	64
WHITE, NO COLLEGE DEGREE	32	42	57	45	48	50
NONWHITE, COLLEGE DEGREE	9	–	–	8	72	27
NONWHITE, NO COLLEGE DEGREE	10	–	–	6	63	35
WHITE EVANGELICAL OR BORN-AGAIN						
♦ *YES*	21	23	76	26	13	86
NO	79	61	37	74	58	41
NEW VOTER						
YES	7	–	–	10	53	47
NO	93	54	45	90	45	54
INCOME						
LESS THAN $50,000	25	57	41	42	49	50
$50–100,000	42	51	48	38	47	52
♦ *MORE THAN $100,000*	33	56	43	20	44	55
WORRIED ABOUT THE NATIONAL ECONOMY						
WORRIED	84	56	42	–	–	–
NOT WORRIED	15	41	57	–	–	–
WAR IN IRAQ						
APPROVE	39	10	89	54	9	90
DISAPPROVE	60	82	16	44	90	9

	2008			**2004**		
	TOTAL	OBAMA	McCAIN	TOTAL	KERRY	BUSH
BUSH JOB						
APPROVE	30	9	90	53	4	95
DISAPPROVE	69	73	25	46	94	4
WILL JOHN McCAIN						
CONTINUE BUSH'S						
POLICIES	46	94	5	–	–	–
MOVE IN A DIFFERENT						
DIRECTION	51	17	81	–	–	–
CANDIDATE QUALITIES						
VALUES	32	42	56	–	–	–
CHANGE	29	93	5	–	–	–
EXPERIENCE	23	8	91	–	–	–
CARES	12	72	26	–	–	–
CONTACTED BY						
McCAIN'S CAMPAIGN						
YES	34	48	51	–	–	–
NO	64	57	41	–	–	–
CONTACTED BY						
OBAMA'S CAMPAIGN						
♦ *YES*	**51**	**64**	**34**	–	–	–
NO	47	42	56	–	–	–
ATTACKED OTHER						
CANDIDATE UNFAIRLY						
McCAIN DID	73	61	38	–	–	–
McCAIN DID NOT	24	31	68	–	–	–
OBAMA DID	61	44	55	–	–	–
OBAMA DID NOT	37	69	29	–	–	–
HAS THE RIGHT						
EXPERIENCE						
McCAIN DOES	66	33	66	–	–	–
McCAIN DOES NOT	33	92	5	–	–	–
OBAMA DOES	55	91	9	–	–	–
OBAMA DOES NOT	44	6	92	–	–	–
OBAMA'S POSITIONS						
ON THE ISSUES ARE						
TOO LIBERAL	44	7	92	–	–	–
TOO CONSERVATIVE	2	–	–	–	–	–
ABOUT RIGHT	51	93	5	–	–	–

Obama's performance with white college graduates put him over the top in Colorado. More than half, 58%, of voters in Colorado were college graduates and 49% were white college graduates. Obama did even better with them in Colorado than he did nationally. Obama won college-educated white voters, beating McCain 56% to 42%. Four years ago, white voters with a college education just barely favored Kerry over Bush, 51% to 47%, while whites with no college education went for Bush 62% to 36%.

Obama also had significant support among the one-third of voters whose families earn more than $100,000. Fifty-six percent of those voters were for Obama compared to 43% for McCain. In 2004 these upper-income individuals only represented one in five voters, and they went for Bush over Kerry 55% to 44%.

Colorado is home to dozens of conservative megaministries (including James Dobson's Focus on the Family) that employ tens of thousands of people. Evangelical voters made up a quarter of the vote in 2004 and voted overwhelmingly for Bush. In addition to the 2008 presidential race, Evangelicals also rallied to vote on a ballot measure that would define "the term 'person' to include any human being from the moment of fertilization." McCain continued to receive support among these conservative voters. White Evangelicals were 24% of the electorate and went 75% for McCain. However, Obama improved his standing over Kerry among white Evangelicals in Colorado by 10 points.

In most of the swing states where Obama campaigned heavily, such as Colorado, Florida, Indiana, Michigan, Pennsylvania, and Virginia, he posted substantial gains among white Evangelicals.

In the last four presidential elections, about one-third of Colorado voters were unaffiliated with either party. Independents backed Bush in 2000, but swung to Kerry in 2004. In 2008, the share of Independents increased six points; they went with Obama at about the same rate as they had for Kerry in 2004, 54% for Obama to 44% for McCain. The increased Independent share of the electorate was yet another reason for the uptick in the overall Democratic vote.

White voters in Colorado, who made up 81% of the electorate, evenly split their votes between Obama and McCain.

If there was a minor surprise in Colorado, it was the weaker than expected performance by Obama among Hispanics. The Hispanic share of the electorate has shifted within the exit polls' margin of error: in 2000 Hispanics were 14% of the vote; in 2004, they were 8%. In 2008, they were 13% of the electorate and they went for Obama, 61% to 38%. Latinos were one of the few groups in Colorado to become less Democratic this election. While they have been heavily Democratic in the presidential voting in Colorado, Republicans have been making steady inroads. In 1996, 12% of Hispanics voted Republican. In 2000, 25% did and in 2004, 30% did. In 2008, the number grew to 38% of Hispanics voting Republican.

Also surprising in Colorado, the proportion of the vote that was

18 to 29 was the lowest share of the vote since 1992 and was down five points from 2000. In 2008, they basically split their vote about evenly between Obama and McCain. Voters under 30 have been behind the Democratic candidate in each election since 1992. The largest Democratic advantage was in 1996 when Clinton won 49% to Dole's 39%.

Part of the reason for the change from red to blue was the impressive get-out-the-vote efforts by the Obama campaign. In Colorado, 51% of voters said they were reached by the Obama campaign, while only 34% of voters were reached by the McCain campaign.

THE FOUR YEAR SPRING FROM RED TO BLUE

The first hints of a Democratic resurgence in Colorado were in 2004 when, in the face of a strong Republican tide nationally, Democrats won a U.S. Senate seat, netted a new U.S. House seat, took control of both houses of the state legislature, and the Kerry-Edwards ticket (without truly targeting the state) cut the Bush-Cheney 2000 eight point victory nearly in half. The Democratic ticket lost Colorado by less than five points in 2004, signaling, frankly, that the Democratic ticket erred in pulling out of the state that year.

At the time, Republicans chalked up Ken Salazar's 2004 U.S. Senate win as nothing to be too concerned with. He was a pro-gun Democrat who did his best to distance himself from the national party. But as it turns out, Salazar's win (and that of his brother in a swing congressional seat in 2004) was a sign of things to come.

Democrats continued their successful push for political power in the state in 2006 when Democrat Bill Ritter won the governor's race. In addition, the party netted yet another U.S. House seat.

As if to telegraph their intent to make Colorado a seriously con-tested battleground state, the Democrats decided to hold their 2008 national convention in Denver.

From the trend that started in 2004 to the very sophisticated campaign the Obama team put together to win Colorado to yet another strong performance down the ballot, Democrats have not only turned Colorado into a serious battleground but, right now, an argument can be made that it is more blue than purple.

Consider this: the three top elected officials in the state are all Democrats, the state legislature is still controlled by the Democrats, and the party owns five of the state's seven U.S. House seats with only one that will be in serious jeopardy in 2010. And let's not forget

Obama's nine point victory is a 14 point swing from 2004, one of the larger swings for the Democrats of any state, battleground or not.

The Obama organizational juggernaut started in Colorado with the state party's decision to move up its presidential nominating caucuses to Super Tuesday, February 5, 2008. As the Clinton campaign is painfully aware, the Obama team was very proficient at organizing these caucus states. It's not a coincidence that in some of the general election battleground states that featured the caucus process during the primary season, Obama not only won the states but put the states away fairly early in the fall. Besides Colorado, other battleground states that held caucuses during the primaries include: Iowa, Minnesota, and Nevada. In all four states, Obama won by a relatively comfortable margin.

The key to Obama's success in the general election is that his campaign rarely shut down a state campaign during the primary season. If anything, the primary campaigns were used as building blocks for the fall. Such was the case with Colorado. In addition, the Obama folks took full advantage of the fact the state was the host of the Democratic convention. The penultimate organizing moment for the campaign in the state came on the final night of the convention when the Obama folks moved from Denver's basketball and hockey arena to the Broncos' home stadium. Obama's acceptance speech, in front of 80,000 attendees (mostly Coloradoans) at the football stadium also served as a massive in-state organizing tool. Based on the Election Day results, it's hard to argue that this focus on organizing didn't give Obama a distinct advantage.

As for 2010, it's difficult to imagine the Republican comeback will be under way. The Republican bench in the state is a mess. The Republicans have tried a few methods to bail them out of their mess this century, including recruiting well-knowns (such as Pete Coors) running moderates (Bob Beauprez for governor in 2006), or running conservatives (Bob Schaffer for Senate in 2008). Nothing has worked. The party needs one of two things to happen: some sort of Democratic overreach in the state or a slow rebuilding of the party from the ground up, in which the party doesn't get caught up in nasty ideological fights. The pressure to move right for Republicans is high because of the social conservative powerhouses that reside in Colorado Springs. But as the state holds on to its very moderate and independent roots, that pressure hasn't been a help to the GOP.

FLORIDA
The Country's Biggest Battleground
27 ELECTORAL VOTES

Florida, like the rest of the South, almost always voted Democratic from the Civil War until tilting Republican in 1952. Ever since the disputed vote count in 2000, Florida has been the ultimate battleground state. At the same time, Florida's population has changed with migration of Cubans, Central and South Americans, Caribbean Islanders, retirees, and other workers that have made the state much less Southern and more heterogeneous. Obama's victory here makes it virtually certain that Florida will continue as a battleground state. The polls showed a narrow McCain lead until October when Obama became the leader by a narrow margin. Obama kept the lead in the polls until the end, and the polls accurately predicted the final margin.

	2008			2004	
Obama	4,282,074	51.0%	Kerry	47.0%
McCain	4,045,624	48.4%	Bush	51.7%
Other candidates	63,064			
	8,390,744			

Note: 100% 7,005 of 7,005 precincts; 100% 67 of 67 counties. Chart based on final, official vote totals.

Turnout in Florida was up 2.7 percentage points to 69.1% from 2004, one of 13 states where turnout rose that much. Early voting was a big item on both campaigns' agendas in Florida and it showed as more than half of the votes were cast early or via absentee ballot. The total number of votes cast rose from 2004 in 65 of the state's 67 counties. This quick adoption of the early vote in Florida will forever change political strategies for winning in this state. During the contentious 2000 campaign, early voting wasn't much of a factor as absentee balloting was the early vote of choice.

In this classic battleground state, five counties turned Democratic after voting for Bush in 2004. The two largest make up the bulk of the Tampa-St. Petersburg area: Hillsborough and Pinellas counties. The GOP won Hillsborough by 31,444 votes four years ago; the Democrats won it by 58,831 votes in 2008. In Pinellas, a 226 vote Republican victory turned into a 38,233 vote Democratic win in 2008.

In Orange County, home to Disney World, Democrats eked out an 815 vote victory in the 2004 presidential race. That was not much of a surprise in a county that has been decided by less than 6,000 votes every year since 1996. But not in 2008, turnout was up by nearly 75,000 votes . . . and Obama won by 86,177 votes. In the primary of January 29, 2008, Clinton received 49.8% of the vote and Obama received 32.9%.

	2008			**2004**		
	TOTAL	OBAMA	McCAIN	TOTAL	KERRY	BUSH
GENDER						
MALE	47	51	47	46	46	53
FEMALE	53	52	47	54	49	50
AGE						
♦ *18–29*	15	61	37	17	58	41
30–44	25	49	49	27	46	53
♦ *45–64*	37	52	47	28	42	57
65+	22	45	53	27	47	52
RACE						
WHITE	71	42	56	70	42	57
♦ *BLACK*	13	96	4	12	86	13
♦ *HISPANIC*	14	57	42	15	44	56
PARTY						
DEMOCRAT	37	87	12	37	85	14
REPUBLICAN	34	12	87	41 ·	7	93
INDEPENDENT	29	52	45	23	57	41
IDEOLOGY						
♦ *LIBERAL*	19	91	8	20	81	18
MODERATE	47	57	41	47	56	43
CONSERVATIVE	35	21	77	34	13	86
EDUCATION BY RACE						
WHITE, COLLEGE DEGREE	34	43	55	31	41	57
WHITE, NO COLLEGE DEGREE	38	41	58	39	42	58
NONWHITE, COLLEGE DEGREE	11	65	34	19	52	47
NONWHITE, NO COLLEGE DEGREE	18	79	20	12	65	34
BUSH JOB						
APPROVE	28	9	90	54	8	92
DISAPPROVE	70	69	29	45	94	4
WORRIED ABOUT THE NATIONAL ECONOMY						
♦ *WORRIED*	83	53	45	–	–	–
NOT WORRIED	16	44	54	–	–	–
RELIGION						
PROTESTANT	52	43	55	–	–	–
WHITE PROTESTANT	38	30	68	–	–	–

	2008			**2004**		
	TOTAL	OBAMA	McCAIN	TOTAL	KERRY	BUSH
WHITE EVANGELICAL PROTESTANT	22	18	81	–	–	–
WHITE PROTESTANT, NOT EVANGELICAL	17	45	53	–	–	–
BLACK PROTESTANT	9	94	5	–	–	–
CATHOLIC	28	50	49	–	–	–
WHITE CATHOLIC	19	46	53	–	–	–
HISPANIC CATHOLIC	8	56	43	–	–	–
JEWISH	4	–	–	–	–	–
OTHER	6	80	18	–	–	–
NONE	10	71	26	–	–	–
NEW VOTER						
YES	12	59	40	–	–	–
NO	88	50	48	–	–	–
INCOME						
LESS THAN $50,000	39	61	37	–	–	–
$50–100,000	38	44	54	–	–	–
MORE THAN $100,000	24	44	55	–	–	–
CANDIDATE QUALITIES						
VALUES	26	30	69	–	–	–
CHANGE	34	92	7	–	–	–
EXPERIENCE	23	6	93	–	–	–
CARES	14	69	28	–	–	–
CONTACTED BY McCAIN'S CAMPAIGN						
YES	20	39	58	–	–	–
NO	77	55	44	–	–	–
CONTACTED BY OBAMA'S CAMPAIGN						
YES	29	60	37	–	–	–
NO	69	48	51	–	–	–
ATTACKED OTHER CANDIDATE UNFAIRLY						
McCAIN DID	64	62	36	–	–	–
McCAIN DID NOT	33	30	69	–	–	–
OBAMA DID	48	33	65	–	–	–
OBAMA DID NOT	48	69	30	–	–	–
HAS THE RIGHT EXPERIENCE						
McCAIN DOES	59	25	75	–	–	–
McCAIN DOES NOT	40	92	6	–	–	–
OBAMA DOES	50	93	6	–	–	–
OBAMA DOES NOT	49	9	89	–	–	–

(continued)

	2008			**2004**		
	TOTAL	OBAMA	McCAIN	TOTAL	KERRY	BUSH
WILL JOHN McCAIN						
CONTINUE BUSH'S POLICIES	47	92	7	–	–	–
MOVE IN A DIFFERENT DIRECTION	48	12	87	–	–	–
OBAMA'S POSITIONS ON THE ISSUES ARE						
TOO LIBERAL	43	6	92	–	–	–
TOO CONSERVATIVE	3	–	–	–	–	–
ABOUT RIGHT	50	93	6	–	–	–

Boom! That's about the best way to describe the surge for Obama in Florida. The baby boom generation gave Obama the edge in the Sunshine State. Not only did Obama swing the 45- to 64-year-old age group 20 points from John Kerry in 2004—one of the single biggest swings in 2008—the baby boomers also accounted for the largest uptick in turnout. In 2004, approximately one in four Florida voters were aged 45 to 64, 28%; in 2008, more than one in three Florida voters were baby boomers, 37%. Forget young voters or minority voters, it was baby boomers that delivered Florida for Obama.

Groups who supported Obama at exceptionally strong levels included 95% of blacks, 91% of liberals, and 64% of voters under the age of 30.

Hispanics, another highly courted group in Florida politics, made up 12% of the registered voters statewide. In the densely populated region of South Florida, Hispanics represent about 55% of registered voters. A key objective for John McCain was to retain the Hispanic vote gains that George W. Bush achieved in 2004. Not only did he not retain these votes, the loss of votes for the Republicans in the Hispanic community was significant.

In the highly contested 2000 vote, George W. Bush split the Hispanic vote with Al Gore and then went on in 2004 to beat John Kerry with 56% among Hispanics. But McCain lost the ground gained by Bush, getting only 45% of the Hispanic vote.

With home foreclosure and unemployment rates exceeding the national average, Florida voters entered the polls with strong concerns about the direction of the nation's economy. More than eight out of ten voters said they were personally worried about the nation's economy.

Florida voters held the key in the first election of George W.

Bush, but they concluded his term with a vastly more negative assessment of his administration. Just four years ago, a 54% majority of Florida voters approved of the way George W. Bush handled his job as president, while on Election Day 2008, 70% disapproved.

ECONOMY DEALS REPUBLICANS HUGE BLOW

For much of the general election the conventional wisdom was that Obama was going to have an uphill battle putting Florida in play. There were two reasons this perception took hold in the political community: 1) Obama did not have to campaign here during the Democratic primary season. Florida was one of two states where the state party had a dispute with the national party about when they could hold their presidential primary. (The other state was Michigan.) The dispute never did get worked out in time for voters to have a say about who should get the Florida delegates. Eventually, a compromise was worked out. But the lack of a primary campaign was thought to put Obama behind the proverbial eight ball in the state. 2) There was a lot of ink wasted by members of the media convinced that older Jewish voters would never vote for a black candidate whose middle name was Hussein. Of course, like much of the media's conventional wisdom about how voters would react to Obama, this turned out to be an overhyped piece of analysis. Jewish voters were 4% of the 2008 Florida vote. They went more than three to one for the Democrat, just as they did in 2004.

But it wasn't just Obama's perceived primary problems in the state that were supposed to be a drag but also McCain's relative strength in the GOP state primary. McCain's victory over Mitt Romney in the January 29, 2008, primary, which the Republicans counted and the Democrats did not, essentially ended Romney's presidential bid (though he did limp along for another week).

Because of the role Florida did *not* play in Obama's primary success and because it was essential to McCain's success, it appeared McCain started the general election with a leg up. But Obama's vast financial resources allowed him to compete in Florida at a time when McCain was trying to save money. At one point during the general election campaign, Obama had spent 8 million dollars in unanswered money on television in the state. In addition, Obama opened up a slew of offices and cobbled together a massive effort to turn out voters early. The voter registration drives the campaign sponsored helped propel turnout to a record number in the state. There's a saying among some successful elected officials in Florida that one should always treat every election as one with only new voters, because it seems there are 500,000 new voters every four years. Sure enough, turnout grew by just about that number from 2000 to 2004 and from 2004 to 2008.

McCain hadn't spent a dime in Florida for a good chunk of the campaign, hoping to live off the organization of a very successful state Republican Party. Toward the end, when the polls in Florida started drifting in Obama's direction, McCain started to take Obama's Florida challenge more seriously. By that point, the economic crisis had taken hold. For Florida, the economic downturn was a one-two punch as home building and tourism, two essential cogs in Florida's economic engine, broke down.

While we don't have data to back this up, it's pretty clear that Obama's success with the baby boomers can be explained by the economy. It's the baby boomers in Florida (a state both authors sort of call home) who were relying on equity in their homes and investment property, who have felt the most pain.

Geographically, Obama's victory can be explained quite easily. He improved upon Kerry's performance in the I-4 corridor (the area of the state that runs from Daytona to Tampa-St. Petersburg) and in South Florida. Two of the 10 biggest counties in the country that flipped from Bush 2004 to Obama 2008 were not only in Florida but in the I-4 corridor: Hillsborough and Pinellas Counties (both in the Tampa–St. Petersburg market). Moreover, the race that stuck out for just how tough it was to be a Republican in the swing areas of the state was the fight for the state's 8th Congressional District (encompassing much of Orlando). The Democratic upset of Republican Ric Keller can be explained by two causes: Bush and the Republican brand and the demographic changes taking place in Central Florida.

If Florida truly is trending blue or toward the Democrats, then keep an eye on this 8th Congressional District. If Democrats continue to hold on to it and carry it in future statewide races, it will probably mean they'll start winning statewide contests more consistently than they have for the last 20 years. If the 8th snaps back to the GOP, then perhaps 2008 was a onetime deal.

The 2010 political season is going to be a busy one in Florida with both Charlie Crist potentially seeking reelection and an open Senate seat being available. A Democratic win in either one will be a sign that something trendsetting was taking place in Florida and that a realignment is possible. The Democratic candidate bench in Florida has been thin for some time with much of the future of the state party resting on the shoulders of the state's lone Democrat in state government, Chief Financial Officer Alex Sink.

And what happens in 2010 in Florida will have 2012 implications. Republicans like Governor Charlie Crist and former Governor Jeb Bush are both considered national players, and Bush may run for the open Senate seat. How Crist does in 2010 will have a lot to say about his future in 2012. As for Bush, while his brother may have turned his last name into a four letter word in some circles, it's worth noting that the last time the Republicans elected a president without a Bush or a Nixon on the ballot was 1928. And while it's hard to imagine any political family could have a third act in presidential politics, never say never.

INDIANA
An Obama Phenomenon, or Is Something Else Happening?
11 ELECTORAL VOTES

Indiana has been a Republican state historically and is about as red as any state in the area. Only in the landslide of 1964 did Indiana turn blue. However, Obama was a senator from a neighboring state and campaigned here heavily in the primaries. In spite of its very red history, Indiana proved to be a very competitive state, surprisingly so because it didn't fit the pattern of other red states that have moved into the battleground. The polls showed a McCain lead until the end of October when the race tightened. At the end, the polls showed an extremely close race and while they had the wrong winner, they were well within the margin of error.

	2008		2004	
Obama	1,374,039	49.9%	Kerry	39.3%
McCain	1,345,648	48.9%	Bush	49.9%
Other candidates	31,251			
	2,750,938			

Note: 100% 5,230 of 5,230 precincts; 100% 92 of 92 counties. Chart based on final, official vote totals.

Obama squeaked out a 28,391 vote victory. Turnout jumped 4.5% to 59.3% of the eligible population, the ninth biggest jump among the 50 states.

The total number of votes cast jumped 282,979. That rise, in a slow growth state, masked a huge swing. The number of votes for McCain dropped 133,790 from Bush's 2004 total, while Obama's total, 405,028 more than Kerry's, won in the state. Obama swung Indiana 22 points from 2004 and needed this 500,000-plus vote swing. To pull this off in a Florida or a North Carolina, two fast-growing states, isn't a surprise. To do it in an Indiana, a state that fights every 10 years to prevent its population decline from costing it congressional seats during reapportionment, it's stunning. And early voting and absentee ballots accounted for about 25% of the vote, up from 10% in 2004.

Eleven of the 92 Indiana counties switched parties in 2008 and all went Democratic. Obama's strength in the cities was on display in Indiana. He won six of the ten biggest counties by vote, swinging four of them from the GOP side in 2004. Marion County, with Indianapolis, the biggest county in the state, continued its Democratic ways from 2004, giving Obama a 107,674 vote margin, after going

Democratic by only 6,000 votes in 2004. And Lake County, with a large African-American population, provided its usual big Democratic margin, 71,559 votes.

But St. Joseph County (South Bend and Notre Dame University), Vanderburgh County (Evansville), Porter County (Valparaiso), and Tippecanoe County (Lafayette and Purdue University) all went from Republican in 2004 to Democratic in 2008. Monroe County, home of Indiana University, remained Democratic and gave Obama a 33 point margin.

The remaining large counties—Allen (Fort Wayne), Elkhart, Hamilton, and Hendricks—all continued their Republican ways, but the GOP margin dropped by at least 12 points in each county. In the primary of May 6, 2008, Clinton received 50.7% of the vote and Obama received 49.3%.

| | 2008 | | | 2004 | | |
	TOTAL	OBAMA	McCAIN	TOTAL	KERRY	BUSH
GENDER						
MALE	47	47	52	48	37	62
FEMALE	53	52	47	52	41	58
AGE						
18–29	19	63	35	14	47	52
30–44	31	47	52	33	33	66
45–64	37	49	50	41	42	57
65+	13	37	61	12	37	63
RACE						
WHITE	88	45	54	89	34	65
BLACK	7	90	10	7	92	8
HISPANIC	4	77	23	3	–	–
PARTY						
DEMOCRAT	36	88	11	32	84	15
REPUBLICAN	41	13	86	46	5	95
INDEPENDENT	24	54	43	22	46	51
IDEOLOGY						
LIBERAL	20	87	12	14	79	21
♦ MODERATE	44	60	39	43	50	48
♦ CONSERVATIVE	36	16	83	42	14	85
EDUCATION BY RACE						
WHITE, COLLEGE DEGREE	32	43	56	–	–	–
WHITE, NO COLLEGE DEGREE	56	45	53	–	–	–
NONWHITE, COLLEGE DEGREE	4	83	17	–	–	–
NONWHITE, NO COLLEGE DEGREE	8	84	16	–	–	–

(continued)

	2008			**2004**		
	TOTAL	OBAMA	McCAIN	TOTAL	KERRY	BUSH
RELIGION						
PROTESTANT	64	42	57	69	33	67
WHITE PROTESTANT	58	37	62	62	29	71
WHITE EVANGELICAL PROTESTANT	38	29	70	36	20	80
WHITE PROTESTANT, NOT EVANGELICAL	20	54	45	26	40	59
BLACK PROTESTANT	4	–	–	5	–	–
HISPANIC PROTESTANT	2	–	–	1		
CATHOLIC	18	50	50	18	43	56
WHITE CATHOLIC	15	47	52	16	35	63
HISPANIC CATHOLIC	2	–	–	1	–	–
JEWISH	1	–	–	0	–	–
OTHER	6	81	17	5	–	–
NONE	11	76	21	7	58	40
NEW VOTER						
YES	13	67	32	–	–	–
NO	87	47	52	–	–	–
INCOME						
LESS THAN $50,000	46	56	42	42	48	52
$50–100,000	38	46	53	40	35	63
MORE THAN $100,000	16	45	54	18	29	71
WORRIED ABOUT THE NATIONAL ECONOMY						
WORRIED	87	52	47	–	–	–
NOT WORRIED	11	30	69	–	–	–
WAR IN IRAQ						
APPROVE	45	16	84	56	11	88
DISAPPROVE	54	78	20	36	80	19
BUSH JOB						
APPROVE	32	11	89	61	6	93
DISAPPROVE	67	68	30	35	94	5
WILL JOHN McCAIN						
♦ *CONTINUE BUSH'S POLICIES*	**51**	**87**	**12**	–	–	–
MOVE IN A DIFFERENT DIRECTION	47	11	88	–	–	–
CANDIDATE QUALITIES						
VALUES	32	29	70	–	–	–
CHANGE	32	90	9	–	–	–
EXPERIENCE	21	5	95	–	–	–
CARES	10	78	20	–	–	–
CONTACTED BY McCAIN'S CAMPAIGN						
♦ *YES*	**22**	**34**	**63**	–	–	–
NO	77	54	45	–	–	–

	2008			**2004**		
	TOTAL	OBAMA	McCAIN	TOTAL	KERRY	BUSH
CONTACTED BY OBAMA'S CAMPAIGN						
YES	37	62	36	–	–	–
NO	62	43	57	–	–	–
ATTACKED OTHER CANDIDATE UNFAIRLY						
McCAIN DID	66	59	40	–	–	–
McCAIN DID NOT	31	31	68	–	–	–
OBAMA DID	53	32	67	–	–	–
OBAMA DID NOT	44	71	28	–	–	–
HAS THE RIGHT EXPERIENCE						
McCAIN DOES	66	32	68	–	–	–
McCAIN DOES NOT	33	85	13	–	–	–
OBAMA DOES	50	89	10	–	–	–
OBAMA DOES NOT	49	10	88	–	–	–
OBAMA'S POSITIONS ON THE ISSUES ARE						
TOO LIBERAL	46	7	92	–	–	–
TOO CONSERVATIVE	4	–	–	–	–	–
ABOUT RIGHT	48	92	7	–	–	–

Indiana has been right-of-center politically in recent history, with conservatives outnumbering liberals by significant margins. Since conservatives usually vote Republican by wide margins, Republican presidential candidates can win without the moderate vote. Democrats, however, must carry the moderate vote decisively to prevail.

Democrats made a real effort in Indiana in 2008, beginning with a competitive Democratic primary in the state, which energized the party. Then during the fall, four in ten voters in Indiana said they were contacted by Obama's campaign, compared with one in five contacted by McCain's campaign.

Voters have been more conservative here than in the rest of the country. In 2004, 42% were conservative, compared with 34% nationally. Indiana had plenty of conservative voters in 2008, but the largest group identified with the political center. Conservatives made up just over a third, 36% of voters, outnumbering self-described liberals by almost two to one. But moderates were most numerous, accounting for more than four in ten Indiana voters in 2008, 44%. These moderate voters backed Obama by a margin of 21 points, 60% to 39%. In 2004, moderate voters in the Hoosier State divided about evenly, as 50% voted for Kerry and 48% voted for Bush.

Nine in ten Hoosiers called the economy not so good or poor, and just as many worried about the direction of the economy over the next year. Fifty-one percent believed John McCain would continue Bush's policies.

HOW HILLARY CLINTON WON INDIANA FOR OBAMA

There is one person, and one person only, to whom Barack Obama owes his victory in Indiana and that's Hillary Clinton.

If Clinton had not pressed on with what was a long-shot bid to catch up to Obama in the primary process after March, it's unlikely the Obama folks would have discovered the competitiveness of Indiana. Falling in early May, the Indiana primary proved to be Clinton's last stand. Coupled with North Carolina, these two key primary states in Obama's march to the nomination also ended up being key parts of Obama's electoral landslide.

But in the case of Indiana, the Obama camp never really believed the state was going to be competitive (despite some early 2008 polling evidence). After they spent a solid two weeks campaigning in the state, the team became convinced it was a state to watch.

But like many of Obama's attempts to put red states in play, the McCain campaign and the Republican National Committee (RNC) didn't buy into the idea that Indiana was endangered. Like the response that reporters received when they asked about North Carolina, the McCain folks would regularly respond to questions about the competition in Indiana with, "Well, if we're losing Indiana, this campaign is done."

Eventually, of course, out of pure necessity, the Republicans targeted Indiana with some TV ad money and a few campaign visits. But the campaign was halfhearted, unlike the Obama team's treatment of Indiana. The Democratic campaign spent a lot of time in the state. Obama even visited an Indiana polling site on Election Day as if to underscore how serious he was about his chances of carrying the state.

What's not clear after this election is whether Indiana is now a new member of the presidential battleground or simply a onetime phenomenon based on geography.

Obama's electoral strength in his home region is one part of his political prowess that often gets overlooked. But the strength is unmistakable. Obama overperformed John Kerry and Al Gore in every state that touches Illinois, aside from Kentucky. In fact, the importance of these states bordering Illinois is undeniable in both the primaries and the general. From Iowa at the start to Missouri and Wisconsin and Indiana, these states played important roles in electing Obama to the White House.

It's very possible that Indiana shifting to the battleground is simply due to Obama being from the region. This is similar to how Bill Clinton and Al Gore were able to put Arkansas and Tennessee in play when neither state was truly a battleground state, evidenced by what happened in 2004 and 2008 in those two states when neither was a national candidate.

For instance, if the state was truly seeing a major Democratic resurgence, the incumbent Republican governor would not have won by the margin he did, right? Republican Governor Mitch Daniels won by 17 points and one in four Daniels voters supported Obama.

But there is a case to be made that Indiana is simply late to the battleground game. Check out the states that surround it; all are either deep blue or battleground states, except for Kentucky, including Illinois, Michigan, and Ohio. And with the economy such a major focus of the 2008 campaign, it's no wonder Indiana voters ended up being more open-minded about their presidential candidates than in years past.

The state is the quintessential Midwestern Republican state, conservative, sure, but not Southern conservative. And as the party has shifted ideologically and geographically to the right and to the South, right-leaning Indiana voters may have felt the GOP has moved away from them. While they like their Indiana Republicans like Daniels or Senator Dick Lugar, they aren't as comfortable with the national party anymore.

One other thing to keep in mind: in every one of the new states that entered into the presidential battleground—including Indiana, Colorado, Virginia, and North Carolina—Democrats had found plenty of success winning statewide races; only victories on the presidential level had eluded them.

It may not be until 2016 or even 2020 that we know for sure whether Indiana is a permanent member of the battleground but for now and for 2012, it's clear it will be.

IOWA
Don't Take Your Hawkeye
Off This Battleground Ball
7 ELECTORAL VOTES

Iowa is a clear example of a battleground state. In 2004, Bush beat Kerry by less than 1% after a series of four straight Democratic victories. Before 1988, Iowa, like much of the Midwest, was a Republican state. The polls showed a significant Obama lead throughout the campaign, but the polls overestimated Obama's final margin.

	2008		2004	
Obama	**828,940**	**53.7%**	Kerry	49.2%
McCain	**682,379**	**44.2%**	Bush	49.9%
Other candidates	**32,343**			
	1,543,662			

Note: 100% 1,873 of 1,873 precincts; 100% 99 of 99 counties. Chart based on final, official vote totals.

Iowa was a classic swing state in 2000 and 2004 and received lavish attention from the presidential campaigns. In 2008, it was trending Democratic and got little love from the campaigns. Turnout was essentially level at just 70% of the voting eligible population. Vote totals dropped in 55 counties and rose in 44.

A total of 21 counties also switched from Republican in 2004 to Democratic in 2008. Overall the pattern was consistent: an increase in the Democratic vote in each county and a decline in the total GOP votes in the county. In the caucus of January 3, 2008, Obama received 37.6% of the vote, Edwards received 29.7%, and Clinton received 29.5%.

	2008			2004		
	TOTAL	OBAMA	McCAIN	TOTAL	KERRY	BUSH
GENDER						
MALE	47	50	47	46	47	52
FEMALE	53	55	43	54	51	49
AGE						
♦ *18–29*	17	61	36	17	53	46
30–44	27	48	50	26	44	55
45–64	38	54	44	38	49	51
65+	18	49	48	19	53	46
RACE						
WHITE	91	51	47	96	49	50
BLACK	3	93	6	1	–	–
HISPANIC	3	–	–	1	–	–

	2008			**2004**		
	TOTAL	OBAMA	McCAIN	TOTAL	KERRY	BUSH
PARTY						
DEMOCRAT	34	93	6	34	92	8
REPUBLICAN	33	9	90	36	7	93
INDEPENDENT	33	56	41	30	53	45
IDEOLOGY						
LIBERAL	19	89	8	19	86	13
♦ *MODERATE*	**44**	**63**	**36**	**45**	**59**	**40**
CONSERVATIVE	37	21	77	36	18	81
EDUCATION BY RACE						
WHITE, COLLEGE DEGREE	38	50	49	60	49	51
WHITE, NO COLLEGE DEGREE	54	52	46	37	49	50
NONWHITE, COLLEGE DEGREE	3	–	–	2	57	43
NONWHITE, NO COLLEGE DEGREE	6	76	23	0	–	–
RELIGION						
PROTESTANT	59	46	52	63	44	56
WHITE PROTESTANT	55	44	54	61	43	56
♦ *WHITE EVANGELICAL PROTESTANT*	**28**	**32**	**66**	**29**	**31**	**68**
WHITE PROTESTANT, NOT EVANGELICAL	27	57	40	32	53	46
BLACK PROTESTANT	1	–	–	1	–	–
HISPANIC PROTESTANT	2	–	–	0	–	–
CATHOLIC	26	59	41	23	53	46
♦ *WHITE CATHOLIC*	**24**	**57**	**42**	**23**	**52**	**47**
HISPANIC CATHOLIC	1			0	–	–
JEWISH	0	–	–	0	–	–
OTHER	5	80	18	5	67	29
NONE	10	68	30	9	69	30
NEW VOTER						
YES	9	67	32	11	50	49
NO	91	52	46	89	49	50
INCOME						
♦ *LESS THAN $50,000*	**43**	**61**	**36**	**51**	**56**	**43**
$50–100,000	37	50	48	37	44	55
MORE THAN $100,000	21	46	53	12	37	62
WORRIED ABOUT THE NATIONAL ECONOMY						
WORRIED	87	55	44	–	–	–
NOT WORRIED	12	36	60	–	–	–
WAR IN IRAQ						
APPROVE	42	15	84	52	16	83
DISAPPROVE	56	82	16	44	88	10

(continued)

71

	2008			**2004**		
	TOTAL	OBAMA	McCAIN	TOTAL	KERRY	BUSH
BUSH JOB						
APPROVE	29	9	89	53	9	90
♦ *DISAPPROVE*	**70**	**71**	**27**	**46**	**95**	**4**
WILL JOHN McCAIN						
CONTINUE BUSH'S POLICIES	49	88	10	–	–	–
MOVE IN A DIFFERENT DIRECTION	46	15	83	–	–	–
CANDIDATE QUALITIES						
VALUES	30	32	66	–	–	–
CHANGE	35	90	9	–	–	–
EXPERIENCE	19	5	94	–	–	–
CARES	11	74	23	–	–	–
CONTACTED BY McCAIN'S CAMPAIGN						
♦ *YES*	**30**	**42**	**57**	–	–	–
NO	67	58	40	–	–	–
CONTACTED BY OBAMA'S CAMPAIGN						
♦ *YES*	**41**	**68**	**30**	–	–	–
NO	56	42	56	–	–	–
ATTACKED OTHER CANDIDATE UNFAIRLY						
McCAIN DID	69	62	36	–	–	–
McCAIN DID NOT	27	29	70	–	–	–
OBAMA DID	54	40	58	–	–	–
OBAMA DID NOT	42	70	29	–	–	–
HAS THE RIGHT EXPERIENCE						
McCAIN DOES	64	33	66	–	–	–
McCAIN DOES NOT	35	89	8	–	–	–
OBAMA DOES	53	89	10	–	–	–
OBAMA DOES NOT	46	11	86	–	–	–

Obama's victory over Hillary Clinton and John Edwards in the Iowa Democratic caucuses launched his presidential campaign, and the campaign maintained a presence in the state from then on. Forty-one percent of voters said they had been contacted by the Obama campaign. Only 30% said they had been contacted by the McCain campaign.

Obama opened dozens of offices and actively courted farmers, while McCain opposed ethanol subsidies. Some 67% of Iowans supported federal government subsidies for ethanol production. Of those voters, 56% went for Obama and 42% for McCain.

A full 70% of Iowa voters disapproved of the job Bush has done as president. Of those voters, 71% voted for Obama and 27% for McCain. In 2004, 46% disapproved of Bush's job performance.

Groups who supported Obama at exceptionally strong levels included 63% of moderates, 61% of those earning less than $50,000, and 61% of voters under the age of 30. Both the Gen Y and baby boom generations swung by more than 12 points to give Obama the edge in Iowa but neither increased their share of the electorate.

White Evangelical Protestants were 28% of the vote and two-thirds voted for McCain—however, they were the only religious cohort with a majority voting for McCain as 57% of non-Evangelical white Protestants voted for Obama, as did 57% of white Catholics.

OBAMA'S LAUNCHING PAD

Considering how poorly McCain's politics matched Iowa's, the fact that he lost the state by less than 10 points is enough to convince many Republicans that Iowa will stay in the presidential battle-ground.

Obama's eventual victory in Iowa during the general election began early in 2007, as he started his path to the Democratic nomination using a victory in Iowa as a launchpad to overtake Clinton nationally. As for McCain, the Republican barely campaigned in the state during the caucuses and wouldn't budge on his views toward government subsidies on ethanol, putting him behind from the get-go.

McCain never fully pulled out of Iowa and that always made the Obama folks scratch their heads. The Obama team believed Iowa was put away in September, but the McCain camp continued to campaign in the state. It's a quirky state for Republicans compared to the rest of the Midwest. On one hand, it has a deep social conservative base, which is how a Republican like Mike Huckabee was able to do well in the Iowa caucuses during the primary campaign.

But the state also has a moderate Republican streak to it, which is why the Republicans that win statewide are ones who are more comfortable talking about farm policy than homeschooling.

Because of Iowa's importance in the nominating process, one should never assume the state is totally out of play. It's possible Obama will always have an advantage in the state since the state's voters feel a sense of loyalty to him, because they were the ones who launched his candidacy. But with Republicans likely to have the Iowa caucuses to themselves for 2012, and if the eventual GOP nominee is the person who wins the caucuses, the state's voters might feel the same sense of loyalty they showed Obama in 2008. Then the state could end up as tightly contested as it was in 2000 and 2004, rather than what it looked like in 2008.

But before the Republicans begin thinking about 2012, the party needs to rebuild its state apparatus. For the first time in his political career, Democratic Senator Tom Harkin was virtually unopposed for reelection in 2008. Not only that, but the Democrats hold three of the state's five U.S. House seats; just four years ago, the GOP had a four to one advantage. Democrats also have double-digit advantages in both the state house and senate. The 2010 cycle could tell us a lot about Iowa's future as a battleground state. If Democratic Governor Chet Culver somehow loses, that would be a sign that Iowa's swing state status is here to stay. But if Republican Senator Chuck Grassley doesn't seek or win another term in 2010, then the slow drift of the state toward the Democrats is something that won't be stopped in the near future.

MISSOURI
Is It a Battleground or Slipping Away from the Dems?

11 ELECTORAL VOTES

Missouri has been a true battleground state that normally votes for the winning candidate. However, in 2008, it missed, not by a lot, but a miss nevertheless. The most recent miss before this was 1956. The polls showed a McCain lead postconvention that narrowed to a virtual tie by the election.

	2008		2004	
McCain	1,445,814	49.4%	Bush	53.3%
Obama	1,441,911	49.3%	Kerry	46.1%
Other candidates	37,480			
	2,925,205			

Note: 100% 3,533 of 3,533 precincts; 100% 115 of 115 counties. Chart based on final, official vote totals.

Missouri, the classic swing state, was once again in that role in 2008. Missouri voters received a great deal of campaign attention and responded by turning out 7% more voters than in the 2004 presidential race. Turnout, as a percentage of the eligible population, was up 2.7 points to 68%. McCain won Missouri by the narrowest margin among all the states, both in terms of votes—3,903—and percentage of the vote, 0.133 of a percentage point. But Obama improved the Democratic showing in the Show Me State over 2004.

Only five of the 115 counties switched parties and all went Democratic. Most were small counties except for a St. Louis suburb, Jefferson County.

The vote total dropped from 2004 in 34 counties and all went Republican in both elections, except for Iron County, which narrowly went Democratic. Eighty-one counties had increases in total vote and eight were Democratic.

Obama's strength was centered in two places: St. Louis (city and county) and Kansas City and its surrounding Jackson County. His margin in those areas was just under 310,000 votes. In the primary of February 5, 2008, Obama received 49.3% of the vote and Clinton received 47.9%.

	2008			**2004**		
	TOTAL	OBAMA	McCAIN	TOTAL	KERRY	BUSH
GENDER						
MALE	46	48	50	47	47	52
FEMALE	54	50	48	53	45	54
AGE						
♦ *18–29*	21	59	39	20	51	48
30–44	27	49	50	29	43	56
45–64	39	47	52	–	45	54
♦ *65+*	13	43	56	11	52	48
RACE						
WHITE	82	42	57	89	42	57
BLACK	13	93	7	8	90	10
HISPANIC	2	–	–	1	–	–
PARTY						
♦ *DEMOCRAT*	40	89	11	35	89	11
REPUBLICAN	34	6	93	36	5	95
INDEPENDENT	26	45	51	29	46	52
IDEOLOGY						
LIBERAL	19	86	13	19	87	13
♦ *MODERATE*	45	61	38	45	54	46
CONSERVATIVE	36	16	83	36	16	83
EDUCATION BY RACE						
WHITE, COLLEGE DEGREE	31	43	55	57	43	56
WHITE, NO COLLEGE DEGREE	52	41	58	33	39	60
NONWHITE, COLLEGE DEGREE	6	83	16	7	82	16
NONWHITE, NO COLLEGE DEGREE	12	85	14	2	73	26
RELIGION						
PROTESTANT	65	42	57	60	36	63
WHITE PROTESTANT	54	34	65	55	32	67
♦ *WHITE EVANGELICAL PROTESTANT*	37	27	72	34	23	76
WHITE PROTESTANT, NOT EVANGELICAL	17	48	51	21	46	53
BLACK PROTESTANT	8	92	3	4	87	13
CATHOLIC	18	45	55	22	49	50
WHITE CATHOLIC	16	42	58	21	47	52
JEWISH	1	–	–	2	–	–
OTHER	7	75	24	6	69	29
NONE	10	79	18	9	72	26
NEW VOTER						
YES	10	61	38	11	58	41
NO	90	48	51	89	44	55

	2008			**2004**		
	TOTAL	OBAMA	McCAIN	TOTAL	KERRY	BUSH
INCOME						
♦ *LESS THAN $50,000*	**46**	**57**	**41**	**48**	**52**	**47**
$50–100,000	38	44	56	39	42	58
MORE THAN $100,000	17	46	54	13	40	59
UNION MEMBER						
YES	14	63	36	14	63	36
NO	86	47	52	86	43	56
WORRIED ABOUT THE NATIONAL ECONOMY						
WORRIED	89	50	48	–	–	–
NOT WORRIED	11	40	59	–	–	–
BUSH JOB						
APPROVE	28	9	90	54	5	94
♦ *DISAPPROVE*	**71**	**65**	**33**	**46**	**94**	**5**
WILL JOHN McCAIN						
CONTINUE BUSH'S POLICIES	49	88	10	–	–	–
MOVE IN A DIFFERENT DIRECTION	49	11	89	–	–	–
CANDIDATE QUALITIES						
VALUES	34	27	71	–	–	–
CHANGE	33	90	9	–	–	–
EXPERIENCE	19	2	98	–	–	–
CARES	10	82	17	–	–	–
CONTACTED BY McCAIN'S CAMPAIGN						
YES	37	36	63	–	–	–
NO	61	57	41	–	–	–
CONTACTED BY OBAMA'S CAMPAIGN						
YES	44	56	43	–	–	–
NO	53	44	54	–	–	–
ATTACKED OTHER CANDIDATE UNFAIRLY						
McCAIN DID	68	59	40	–	–	–
McCAIN DID NOT	29	28	70	–	–	–
OBAMA DID	53	31	68	–	–	–
OBAMA DID NOT	44	73	26	–	–	–
HAS THE RIGHT EXPERIENCE						
McCAIN DOES	65	29	71	–	–	–
McCAIN DOES NOT	34	88	10	–	–	–
OBAMA DOES	49	91	9	–	–	–
OBAMA DOES NOT	50	8	90	–	–	–

(continued)

	2008			2004		
	TOTAL	OBAMA	McCAIN	TOTAL	KERRY	BUSH
OBAMA'S POSITIONS ON THE ISSUES ARE						
TOO LIBERAL	46	5	94	–	–	–
TOO CONSERVATIVE	4	–	–	–	–	–
ABOUT RIGHT	47	94	6	–	–	–

In 2008, more Missouri voters identified themselves as Democrats compared to four years ago. In 2008, Democrats made up 40% of voters, Independents 26%, and Republicans 34%. In 2004, Democrats made up 35% of voters, Independents 29%, and Republicans 36%. Independents voted for McCain 51% to 45% over Obama, which was almost identical to the Bush-Kerry margins in 2004.

Seniors backed McCain 56% to 43%. One in eight voters was older than 65 and McCain was able to swing this age group 17 points from the Kerry margin over Bush, one of the biggest Republican swings in this state.

White Evangelical Protestants were 37% of the votes in 2008, up three points from 2004, and they voted for the McCain-Palin ticket by a three to one margin.

Obama made the race close by running up a big lead among moderates, young voters, and those earning less than $50,000. He was supported by nearly six in ten of each of these groups.

Seventy-one percent disapproved of Bush's job performance and two-thirds of those voted for Obama. Missouri was the only state Obama didn't carry where President Bush had a job rating of 35% or less. At the same time, only 49% thought Obama had the right experience to be president, while 65% thought that McCain did.

HOW COMPETITIVE IS THIS STATE REALLY?

The closeness of the McCain victory in this state demands that we call Missouri a battleground state, right? For now. Here's the thing, there is clearly a ceiling for Democrats in Missouri. After all, if a Democratic nominee can't carry Missouri in a year like 2008, when can a Democrat carry the state?

Obama had everything going his way in the state including a strong ticket down the ballot, an effective statewide organization, a GOP opponent who wasn't inspiring the base, and the fact that St. Louis voters had gotten to know Obama over a four year period, unlike most swing state voters. The St. Louis media market is a must buy for any politician running statewide in Illinois, so St. Louis voters got their share of Obama biography spots starting in 2004.

There has been a very slow drift away from the Democrats in Missouri for some time; it hasn't been dramatic but it's there nonetheless. This doesn't mean Democrats can't win in the state but it means nothing will ever come easy. The ceiling for a Democratic candidate in the state is much lower than the ceiling for a Republican candidate, at least when it comes to federal races like the presidential and Senate races.

Ideologically, Missouri falls in the middle of the rest of the country but with a slight tilt to the right. So if you believe the country is center-right, then Missouri is your bellwether. But if you believe the country is center-center, then Missouri is a *very*, very light shade of red. And if there was one piece of data that indicates why the state may have narrowly stuck with McCain over Obama, it's the fact that just 36% of the electorate were college-educated voters. Missouri falls in the bottom 10 of states in terms of the percent of college-educated voters, and McCain carried eight of those ten states, including Missouri.

The 2010 cycle will probably bring one nationally targeted race to the state as Republican Senator Kit Bond never has an easy time at reelection. The direction of the economy will probably dictate Bond's future more than anything else as Missouri is a key manufacturing state and could be hit hard over the next few years. As for 2012, nothing about these election returns indicates Obama *won't* target the state. But some Democrats may ask themselves if the effort is really worth it, since the trend line for the next 10 years isn't as favorable in Missouri as it is in a state like Arizona or even Texas.

NORTH CAROLINA
In the Battleground to Stay
15 ELECTORAL VOTES

North Carolina was a Democratic stronghold until the Civil Rights Act in the 1960s. It has voted Republican since, except for supporting a Southern Democratic nominee in 1976. It had been a strong Republican state in presidential elections until 2008. The polls showed a significant McCain lead until the end of September when the race tightened. From that point on, no candidate was able to open up a significant lead, and the final results reflected the virtual tie predicted by the polls.

	2008		2004	
Obama	2,142,651	49.7%	Kerry	43.6%
McCain	2,128,474	49.4%	Bush	56.0%
Other candidates	39,664			
	4,310,789			

Note: 100% 2,962 of 2,962 precincts; 100% 100 of 100 counties. Chart based on final, official vote totals.

Obama's campaign declared it could wrest the Tar Heel State from Republican control and they did. But he won by only three-tenths of a percentage point, 14,177 votes, the third closest win in terms of vote margins among the states after Missouri and Montana.

And the huge jump in turnout was not just because of the 2008 campaign. The 809,782 vote increase over 2004 followed a jump of 395,455 votes in 2000 and another 589,745 in 2004.

North Carolina elections are usually swung by the three urban conglomerations: Charlotte & Mecklenburg County; the Research Triangle counties of Durham, Orange, and Wake, containing Raleigh, Durham, and Chapel Hill; and the Triad of Guilford and Forsyth counties with Greensboro, High Point, and Winston-Salem. A Democrat must do well in these three areas to win; a Republican must score votes here to go with the votes from the rest of the state that is traditionally more Republican.

Obama won 33 counties, including all those in these three metro areas. Obama started with a 100,110 vote edge in Charlotte & Mecklenburg, up from only an 11,000 Kerry margin in 2004. Then he flipped Wake County (the biggest vote prize in the state) with nearly a 64,000 vote margin, running up a 168,000 vote edge in the Research Triangle. In the Triad, Obama flipped Forsyth County into the Democratic column and ran up a 62,000 vote margin in that area.

So that 330,000 vote edge from the metro areas added to flipping the Asheville area in the mountains (Buncombe County) and Fayetteville (home of the Fort Bragg U.S Army base in Cumberland County), and the Democrats were suddenly very competitive. McCain did win an easy victory in Onslow County, home of the Camp Lejeune U.S. Marine Corps base. In the primary of May 6, 2008, Obama received 56.2% of the vote and Clinton received 41.5%.

	2008			**2004**		
	TOTAL	OBAMA	McCAIN	TOTAL	KERRY	BUSH
GENDER						
MALE	46	43	56	41	38	60
FEMALE	54	55	44	59	46	54
AGE						
18–29	18	74	26	14	56	43
30–44	27	48	52	33	37	61
45–64	39	43	56	40	42	57
65+	16	43	56	13	44	55
RACE						
♦ *WHITE*	**72**	**35**	**64**	**71**	**27**	**73**
BLACK	23	95	5	26	85	14
HISPANIC	3	–	–	1	–	–
PARTY						
DEMOCRAT	42	90	9	39	84	16
♦ *REPUBLICAN*	**31**	**4**	**95**	**40**	**4**	**96**
INDEPENDENT	27	39	60	21	41	56
IDEOLOGY						
LIBERAL	19	87	13	17	80	18
MODERATE	44	63	37	44	50	49
CONSERVATIVE	37	15	84	40	18	81
EDUCATION BY RACE						
WHITE, COLLEGE DEGREE	32	38	61	35	20	80
WHITE, NO COLLEGE DEGREE	41	33	67	35	35	65
NONWHITE, COLLEGE DEGREE	10	92	8	20	81	18
NONWHITE, NO COLLEGE DEGREE	18	86	14	9	69	25
WHITE EVANGELICAL OR BORN-AGAIN						
YES	44	25	74	36	16	84
NO	56	68	31	64	58	40
NEW VOTER						
YES	13	68	32	12	58	41
NO	87	47	52	88	42	58

(continued)

	2008			**2004**		
	TOTAL	OBAMA	McCAIN	TOTAL	KERRY	BUSH
INCOME						
LESS THAN $50,000	50	57	42	50	55	44
$50–100,000	31	43	56	33	32	68
MORE THAN $100,000	19	44	56	17	31	68
WORRIED ABOUT THE NATIONAL ECONOMY						
WORRIED	85	49	51	–	–	–
NOT WORRIED	14	47	53	–	–	–
WAR IN IRAQ						
APPROVE	46	16	84	54	8	91
DISAPPROVE	53	78	21	42	89	9
BUSH JOB						
APPROVE	31	3	97	57	6	93
DISAPPROVE	68	69	30	42	94	5
WILL JOHN McCAIN						
CONTINUE BUSH'S POLICIES	47	90	10	–	–	–
MOVE IN A DIFFERENT DIRECTION	49	12	88	–	–	–
CANDIDATE QUALITIES						
VALUES	29	29	71	–	–	–
CHANGE	28	88	11	–	–	–
EXPERIENCE	20	5	94	–	–	–
CARES	20	73	27	–	–	–
CONTACTED BY McCAIN'S CAMPAIGN						
YES	26	41	58	–	–	–
NO	72	53	46	–	–	–
CONTACTED BY OBAMA'S CAMPAIGN						
YES	34	66	33	–	–	–
NO	64	41	58	–	–	–
ATTACKED OTHER CANDIDATE UNFAIRLY						
McCAIN DID	68	58	42	–	–	–
McCAIN DID NOT	29	35	64	–	–	–
OBAMA DID	52	31	68	–	–	–
OBAMA DID NOT	44	74	26	–	–	–
HAS THE RIGHT EXPERIENCE						
McCAIN DOES	61	23	76	–	–	–
McCAIN DOES NOT	37	94	6	–	–	–
OBAMA DOES	48	93	7	–	–	–
OBAMA DOES NOT	50	8	91	–	–	–

	2008			**2004**		
	TOTAL	OBAMA	McCAIN	TOTAL	KERRY	BUSH
OBAMA'S POSITIONS ON THE ISSUES ARE						
TOO LIBERAL	42	4	95	–	–	–
TOO CONSERVATIVE	3	–	–	–	–	–
ABOUT RIGHT	51	90	9	–	–	–

North Carolina has been one of the fastest growing states, but it retains solid conservative roots. In 2004, 40% of North Carolina voters were conservative compared to 34% nationally. In 2008, 37% of voters here were conservative, and there was no change to the 34% nationally. Over the last quarter century Tar Heel voters have been leaving the Democratic Party. In 1984, 50% identified themselves as Democrats, dropping to 39% in 2004. At the same time Republican party identification rose six points and Independents were up 5%. However, in 2008, the partisan makeup shifted dramatically and there was a nine point drop in Republican identification, while Democrats increased their share three percentage points and Independents by six points.

North Carolina has seen its share of racial turmoil including the momentous lunch counter protests in Greensboro in 1960. As the first African-American nominee of a major party, Obama could not have gotten as far as he did in the presidential campaign without attracting significant support among white voters. White men and women have voted overwhelmingly Republican here since at least 1984, when they supported Reagan over Mondale 76% to 24%.

Obama did better among North Carolina white voters than either Kerry or Gore did. Four years ago Kerry got just 27% of the white vote in North Carolina while Bush got 73%. Obama did a good deal better as more than one in three white voters, 35%, voted for him. However, the white proportion of the vote dropped from 83% in 1992 to 72% in 2008.

Black voters have been strongly in the Democratic camp for a long time. Obama captured an even greater share of the black vote than is typical for a Democratic candidate. In 2004, 85% of African-Americans voted for Kerry with Bush taking 14%. In 2008, Obama was supported by 96% of black voters while McCain was the choice of only 3%.

Evangelical white Protestants were 36% of the vote in 2004, and they broke for George Bush by an 84% to 16% margin, a 68 point spread. In 2008, they represented 44% of North Carolina voters, an eight point increase. However, while their share rose, the

Republican advantage within this group dropped significantly. McCain garnered 74% of the white Evangelical vote while Obama won 25%.

THE CAMPAIGN'S GREATEST ACCOMPLISHMENT?

There was a point during the campaign when the Obama folks were quietly telling reporters that they liked their chances better in North Carolina than Ohio. While Obama would eventually win Ohio by a larger margin, there was a reason the Obama folks believed this.

Obama only won Ohio because Republican turnout dropped dramatically. Contrast that with how Obama won North Carolina. The Obama campaign was always at its best when it could change the makeup of an electorate. In the case of North Carolina, this was definitely a state that had all the ingredients Obama was looking for: an under-registered African-American population, a slew of new voters who were nonnative North Carolinians, and a fairly youthful population.

And, like many of its successes in the general election, the Obama campaign's drive to win North Carolina began during the drawn-out Democratic nomination process. North Carolina's Democratic primary fell in May and it turned out to be one of Hillary Clinton's two last stands (the other was Indiana). The Obama camp knew it would win North Carolina in the primary but it needed a big win. And that need meant the campaign went overboard in its attempt to register new voters. That early organizational work in the primary paid real dividends in the general.

But the Obama victory would not have happened without the decision by the GOP, and the McCain campaign in particular, to disregard the warning signs in the state. For too long in the fall, the McCain campaign decided to ignore North Carolina and instead focus on other battleground states. When the McCain campaign finally decided to contest North Carolina, they were already behind, particularly in the drive to turn out the early vote.

Democrats have always been strong in statewide races and the party continued its dominance in gubernatorial elections with five straight wins. U.S. Senate elections regularly swing back and forth between the two parties, though it has been rare for the Democrats to win a Senate race in a presidential year. In fact, Kay Hagan's Senate win over Elizabeth Dole is the Democrats' first Senate victory in a presidential election since 1968.

By the way, it should not go unnoticed that there was not a white male in the top three spots on the 2008 Democratic ticket in North Carolina and all three of those Democrats, Obama, Hagan, and now Governor Bev Perdue, won.

Considering North Carolina's population boom, its stay in the presidential battleground will probably be a long one. The Republican Party is particularly weak in the state as evidenced by the party's inability to win a governor's race in nearly two decades. But one wonders what a little attention to the state might mean for the GOP by 2010 or even 2012. The one major race to keep an eye on in 2010 is the reelection bid by Republican Senator Richard Burr. He will be trying to do something that no senator holding that particular Senate seat has done in nearly 40 years—win a second term.

OHIO
Where Did All the Republicans Go?
20 ELECTORAL VOTES

Ohio is a battleground that has very close elections in a state rich with electoral votes. Ohio has been another bellwether state, not voting for the eventual winner only once in the last 50 years, 1960. The polls showed a close race that widened in October. The polls correctly predicted the final margin.

	2008		2004	
Obama	2,933,388	51.5%	Kerry	48.7%
McCain	2,674,491	46.9%	Bush	50.8%
Other candidates	90,381			
	5,698,260			

Note: 100% 11,156 of 11,156 precincts; 100% 88 of 88 counties. Chart based on final, official vote totals.

Ohio, the state no winning Republican has ever lost, was a central battlefield in 2008, but the outcome was a bit unexpected. Obama pulled off the victory by a relatively comfortable margin (at least in Ohio terms), but turnout was essentially stable in the state, to about an estimated 66.9% with about as many voting for president in 2008 as in 2004. In contrast to so many other states, this came despite an intense campaign.

The big get for Obama was Hamilton County (Cincinnati) in the southern part of the state, a reliable GOP bastion since 1968. Lake County, suburbs east of Cleveland, flipped as well.

Obama only won 22 of Ohio's 88 counties, owing his victory to the big cities and the populous counties, often with substantial concentrations of union members and African-Americans. To win, a Democrat must start in Cuyahoga County and that is what happened, with Obama winning nearly a quarter million vote majority in 2008. Then he picked up a 99,000 vote edge in Franklin County (Columbus) and a 60,000 vote margin in Lucas County (Toledo).

The Republican vote dropped by more than 130,000 in the raw vote from 2004 to 2008 in the counties won by the Democrats. Moreover, the Republican vote dropped in counties McCain won by an additional 140,000 in the raw vote. In the primary of March 4, 2008, Clinton received 54.3% of the vote and Obama received 44.0%.

	2008			**2004**		
	TOTAL	OBAMA	McCAIN	TOTAL	KERRY	BUSH
GENDER						
MALE	48	51	48	47	47	52
FEMALE	52	53	45	53	50	50
AGE						
♦ *18–29*	**17**	**61**	**36**	**21**	**56**	**42**
30–44	27	51	47	30	47	52
45–64	39	53	46	37	48	52
65+	17	44	55	12	42	58
RACE						
WHITE	83	46	52	86	44	56
BLACK	11	97	2	10	84	16
HISPANIC	4	–	–	3	65	35
PARTY						
DEMOCRAT	39	89	10	35	90	9
♦ *REPUBLICAN*	**31**	**8**	**92**	**40**	**6**	**94**
INDEPENDENT	30	52	44	25	59	40
IDEOLOGY						
LIBERAL	20	83	16	19	85	14
MODERATE	45	61	38	47	59	41
CONSERVATIVE	35	22	76	34	13	87
EDUCATION BY RACE						
WHITE, COLLEGE DEGREE	33	49	50	53	44	55
♦ *WHITE, NO COLLEGE DEGREE*	**50**	**44**	**54**	**34**	**41**	**58**
NONWHITE, COLLEGE DEGREE	6	69	30	9	77	22
NONWHITE, NO COLLEGE DEGREE	11	91	8	4	77	23
RELIGION						
PROTESTANT	58	48	52	57	44	56
WHITE PROTESTANT	48	39	61	49	38	62
WHITE EVANGELICAL PROTESTANT	27	25	74	25	24	75
WHITE PROTESTANT, NOT EVANGELICAL	20	57	43	24	50	49
BLACK PROTESTANT	9	96	3	7	82	17
HISPANIC PROTESTANT	1	–	–	1	–	–
CATHOLIC	23	47	52	26	44	55
WHITE CATHOLIC	20	46	53	24	41	59
HISPANIC CATHOLIC	2	–	–	1	–	–
JEWISH	2	–	–	1	–	–
OTHER	5	75	21	6	72	26
NONE	12	72	27	10	69	29

(*continued*)

	2008			2004		
	TOTAL	OBAMA	McCAIN	TOTAL	KERRY	BUSH
NEW VOTER						
YES	8	63	36	15	54	46
NO	92	51	48	85	47	52
INCOME						
LESS THAN $50,000	44	59	38	48	58	42
$50–100,000	36	52	47	38	43	56
MORE THAN $100,000	21	42	58	14	39	61
UNION MEMBER						
YES	15	58	41	17	60	39
NO	85	51	48	83	46	53
WORRIED ABOUT THE NATIONAL ECONOMY						
♦ *WORRIED*	86	54	45	–	–	–
NOT WORRIED	12	41	58	–	–	–
WAR IN IRAQ						
APPROVE	34	12	88	54	17	83
DISAPPROVE	64	74	24	40	90	10
BUSH JOB						
APPROVE	28	10	89	53	7	93
DISAPPROVE	71	69	30	46	94	5
WILL JOHN McCAIN						
CONTINUE BUSH'S POLICIES	47	92	7	–	–	–
MOVE IN A DIFFERENT DIRECTION	48	14	85	–	–	–
CANDIDATE QUALITIES						
VALUES	29	30	69	–	–	–
CHANGE	32	91	8	–	–	–
EXPERIENCE	21	5	95	–	–	–
CARES	14	80	19	–	–	–
CONTACTED BY McCAIN'S CAMPAIGN						
♦ *YES*	36	41	58	–	–	–
NO	61	58	41	–	–	–
CONTACTED BY OBAMA'S CAMPAIGN						
♦ *YES*	43	59	40	–	–	–
NO	54	46	53	–	–	–
ATTACKED OTHER CANDIDATE UNFAIRLY						
McCAIN DID	71	61	37	–	–	–
McCAIN DID NOT	27	28	71	–	–	–
OBAMA DID	53	38	61	–	–	–
OBAMA DID NOT	44	69	30	–	–	–

	2008			2004		
	TOTAL	OBAMA	McCAIN	TOTAL	KERRY	BUSH
HAS THE RIGHT EXPERIENCE						
McCAIN DOES	62	32	67	–	–	–
McCAIN DOES NOT	36	89	9	–	–	–
OBAMA DOES	51	92	7	–	–	–
OBAMA DOES NOT	48	11	88	–	–	–
OBAMA'S POSITIONS ON THE ISSUES ARE						
TOO LIBERAL	43	7	93	–	–	–
TOO CONSERVATIVE	3	–	–	–	–	–
ABOUT RIGHT	49	95	4	–	–	–
♦ *DEMOCRATIC HILLARY CLINTON SUPPORTER*						
	16	81	18	–	–	–

Economic issues were paramount in Ohio as the state suffered from the highest unemployment rate in 16 years, 7.2%. Nine out of ten said they were worried about the direction of the economy. Obama won those voters 54% to 45%.

In 2004, 40% of voters identified themselves as Republicans. In 2008 that dropped 10 points to 30%. Independents were 29% of the voters and Obama won them by a 52% to 45% margin.

Obama's victory in Ohio showed that his problems with working-class whites in the primaries did not continue in the general election. His problems with this group first became a focus of campaign coverage after the Ohio Democratic primary, when whites with no college education voted three to one in favor of Hillary Clinton. McCain courted working-class whites in the Buckeye State, home of "Joe the Plumber"—who became a symbol of these voters.

In November, Obama was able to secure 46% of the noncollege white vote, six points less than McCain's 52%. In fact, Obama did better with these voters than Kerry did four years earlier, when he lost this group to Bush by 18 points, 41% to 59%.

Could a black candidate relate to white voters as well as a white candidate? Obama had the best showing among whites in Ohio for a Democrat since 1996.

Three in ten voters live in a union household. They supported Obama over McCain by a 57% to 42% margin.

Young voters also played a major role in Ohio. Voters under the age of 30 were 17% of the electorate, down from 21% in 2004, and they gave Obama 63% of their votes, compared to 34% for McCain. In 2004, young voters also favored the Democrat, but only by a 14 point margin.

Both campaigns made a tremendous effort in Ohio, but more voters said they were contacted by the Obama campaign, 43%, than the McCain campaign, 36%.

SHOULD IT HAVE BEEN THIS CLOSE?

Ohio held an election and a bunch of Republican voters decided not to show up. There's no more stunning statistic from 2008 than this one: Obama received just 40,000 more votes than Kerry did in 2004, which by itself should not have been enough new votes to flip the state. But something funny happened in Ohio; the Republican vote from 2004 to 2008 dropped nearly 300,000. That's how a two point GOP victory in 2004 turned into a four point Democratic win in 2008.

So did Obama win Ohio or did McCain lose it? There's a strong case to be made that McCain did more to lose Ohio than Obama did to win it. Like Missouri, there's a sense among some Democrats that their support levels in the state have topped out on the presidential level. While the state is winnable, it will never be a landslide. With the state growing at a much slower rate than other battleground states, the lack of new voters isn't something that allows the Democrats to expand their opportunities.

Meanwhile, for all the talk about Obama's inability to connect with working-class voters in Ohio, it's McCain that seemed to have a hard time connecting with voters suffering from the economic downturn. In battleground state after battleground state, McCain underperformed with voters who were worried about the economy. While some of that can be blamed on Bush and his record, McCain also has to take some responsibility on this front. His "the fundamentals of the economy are strong" comment in mid-September was a phrase that McCain surely wishes he never uttered. McCain really did poorly in states hurting from the downturn in manufacturing, including Ohio, Indiana, and Michigan. Perhaps his "government isn't the answer" mantra wasn't playing well with these voters who were looking for government to provide a safety net, or for government to bail out, say, the automakers.

So while it isn't clear whether Obama did any better in Ohio than Kerry, clearly a big group of voters decided that McCain wasn't feeling their pain, but they weren't quite ready to support Obama. So, instead, they didn't show up. For the future's sake of the Republican Party in Ohio, it will be paramount to figure out who these voters were. Identifying these voters and their concerns will be key to the GOP's attempts to come back.

And while it appears Republicans have lost more than Democrats have won in Ohio, this isn't to say Democrats aren't finding plenty of success. Thanks to a weak economy, Democrats have been able to get a major foothold here, holding the governor's mansion, one of the state's two U.S. Senate seats, a one-seat advantage in the U.S. House delegation (based on a map that was drawn by Republicans), and control of half the state legislature (the Democrats won the state house in 2008; Republicans still control the state senate).

In 2010, Democratic Governor Ted Strickland and Republican Senator George Voinovich are both up for reelection. They could find themselves in tough fights as Republicans really want to get their mojo back in the state and Democrats are feeling overconfident about their ability to win.

For 2012, it's hard to imagine that Ohio's importance will be reduced at all. The only thing that will temper the importance of Ohio is the likelihood that its electoral vote total will be diminished by at least one vote, if not two, thanks to the state's very slow population growth compared to states in the Southwest and South.

VIRGINIA
The Country's New Perfect Bellwether?
13 ELECTORAL VOTES

Virginia voted Democratic from the Civil War through 1948. Since 1952, outside of 1964, Virginia has been a Republican stronghold. One great surprise in this election was the emergence of Virginia as a battleground state. The polls showed a narrow race until the end of September when Obama began to open up a lead. The polls correctly predicted the final Obama margin.

	2008		2004	
Obama	1,959,532	52.6%	Kerry	45.5%
McCain	1,725,005	46.3%	Bush	53.7%
Other candidates	38,723			
	3,723,260			

Note: 100% 2,487 of 2,487 precincts; 100% 134 of 134 counties and independent cities. Chart based on final, official vote totals.

Obama won 48 of the 134 Virginia counties and towns, flipping 18 of them from the Republicans compared to 2004.

To turn Virginia blue, at least for one election, the path for Obama was clear: win large majorities in northern Virginia with its close ties to Washington, dent the traditional GOP dominance in the Norfolk–Hampton Roads area, and then reduce GOP margins elsewhere.

In northern Virginia, the strategy was a huge success. From a mere 22,000 vote plurality for Kerry in 2004, Obama won a 234,079 vote majority in northern Virginia. He turned Loudoun County, poster child for fast growth and high income on the East Coast, and Prince William County, epicenter of the home foreclosure crisis, from the GOP. Both Loudoun and Prince William were prime examples of exurban success for Bush in 2004.

Virginia Beach still went Republican but by a narrow 1,434 votes. In that county alone, Democrats added 28,000 votes while the GOP lost 3,000 votes compared to 2004. Norfolk, Hampton, and Newport News all stayed Democratic but added more than 15,000 new Democratic votes each.

Henrico County, the suburban county that surrounds heavily African-American Richmond, had not voted Democratic since 1952. But it did in 2008, by a resounding 56% to 43% margin.

And despite campaigning in far southwestern Virginia, Obama did not win there. But through the mountainous westernmost counties of the state, Obama did manage to raise the Democratic share of the vote from 37% to 41%. In the primary of February 12, 2008, Obama received 63.7% of the vote and Clinton received 35.5%.

	2008			2004		
	TOTAL	OBAMA	McCAIN	TOTAL	KERRY	BUSH
GENDER						
MALE	46	51	47	46	40	59
FEMALE	54	53	46	54	50	50
AGE						
♦ *18–29*	21	60	39	17	54	46
30–44	30	51	47	32	40	59
45–64	38	51	48	41	45	55
65+	11	46	53	10	51	49
RACE						
♦ *WHITE*	70	39	60	72	32	68
♦ *BLACK*	20	92	8	21	87	12
HISPANIC	5	65	34	3	–	–
PARTY						
DEMOCRAT	39	92	8	35	92	8
REPUBLICAN	33	8	92	39	5	95
INDEPENDENT	27	49	48	26	44	54
IDEOLOGY						
LIBERAL	21	90	9	17	83	17
MODERATE	46	58	41	45	57	42
CONSERVATIVE	33	18	80	38	15	85
EDUCATION BY RACE						
WHITE, COLLEGE DEGREE	40	44	55	–	–	–
WHITE, NO COLLEGE DEGREE	30	32	66	–	–	–
NONWHITE, COLLEGE DEGREE	12	75	24	–	–	–
NONWHITE, NO COLLEGE DEGREE	18	88	12	–	–	–
WHITE EVANGELICAL OR BORN AGAIN						
YES	28	20	79	–	–	–
NO	72	64	35	–	–	–
NEW VOTER						
♦ *YES*	13	63	35	–	–	–
NO	87	50	49	–	–	–
INCOME						
LESS THAN $50,000	30	62	37	39	52	48
$50–100,000	35	52	48	38	44	56
MORE THAN $100,000	35	46	52	23	40	59

(*continued*)

	2008			**2004**		
	TOTAL	OBAMA	McCAIN	TOTAL	KERRY	BUSH
WORRIED ABOUT THE NATIONAL ECONOMY						
WORRIED	88	53	46	–	–	–
NOT WORRIED	11	43	55	–	–	–
WAR IN IRAQ						
APPROVE	41	13	86	51	13	86
DISAPPROVE	59	79	19	43	85	14
BUSH JOB						
APPROVE	27	10	90	55	8	92
DISAPPROVE	72	68	31	44	93	6
WILL JOHN McCAIN						
CONTINUE BUSH'S POLICIES	51	88	10	–	–	–
MOVE IN A DIFFERENT DIRECTION	46	12	87	–	–	–
CANDIDATE QUALITIES						
VALUES	32	34	65	–	–	–
CHANGE	35	92	7	–	–	–
EXPERIENCE	21	3	96	–	–	–
CARES	9	80	19	–	–	–
CONTACTED BY McCAIN'S CAMPAIGN						
♦ *YES*	**38**	**35**	**64**	–	–	–
NO	59	63	36	–	–	–
CONTACTED BY OBAMA'S CAMPAIGN						
♦ *YES*	**50**	**59**	**40**	–	–	–
NO	48	45	54	–	–	–
ATTACKED OTHER CANDIDATE UNFAIRLY						
♦ *McCAIN DID*	**69**	**61**	**38**	–	–	–
McCAIN DID NOT	28	31	68	–	–	–
♦ *OBAMA DID*	**47**	**34**	**65**	–	–	–
OBAMA DID NOT	50	69	30	–	–	–
HAS THE RIGHT EXPERIENCE						
McCAIN DOES	63	31	69	–	–	–
McCAIN DOES NOT	36	91	6	–	–	–
OBAMA DOES	55	90	10	–	–	–
OBAMA DOES NOT	43	6	92	–	–	–
OBAMA'S POSITIONS ON THE ISSUES ARE						
TOO LIBERAL	41	6	93	–	–	–
TOO CONSERVATIVE	4	–	–	–	–	–
ABOUT RIGHT	52	92	7	–	–	–

McCain did well among whites, winning them 60% to 39%, a 21 point margin. However, Obama's support among whites was higher than white Democratic candidates in recent elections. In 2004, Kerry lost the white Virginia vote to Bush by a whopping 36 points, 68% to 32%.

One in five Virginia voters was African-American and they broke 91% to 9% in favor of Obama. Black voters in Virginia backed Kerry 87% to 12% four years ago.

Obama's vaunted ground game lived up to its reputation in Virginia, far outpacing the McCain campaign's efforts to turn out his voters. The Obama campaign opened more offices around the state than any Democratic candidate in the past decade, while the McCain campaign put more effort into the final three days before the election to get their supporters to the polls.

The campaigns also covered a lot of ground in the Old Dominion. Half of all Virginia voters, 51%, were contacted by the Obama campaign, while less than four in ten, 37%, said the McCain campaign reached them. This advantage in campaign contact was important, since six in ten voters contacted by the Obama campaign voted for the Democrat, 61%, and six in ten of those contacted by the McCain campaign voted Republican, 63%.

McCain campaigned in Virginia during the final week to try to keep the state in the GOP column. His efforts seem to have had some success with the late deciders. Thirteen percent of Virginia voters waited until the last week to make their final decision, and they favored McCain by a significant margin, 57% to 41%, over Obama.

Neither candidate pulled many punches in this bruising campaign, particularly in battlegrounds like Virginia. However, the candidate who comes across as too negative can pay a real price on Election Day. Virginia voters were more critical of the tone of McCain's campaign. Over two-thirds of Virginia voters, 69%, believed McCain crossed the line and engaged in unfair attacks. This compares to less than half of voters, 46%, who said Obama was too negative or nasty toward McCain.

In Virginia, six in ten said the economy was their top voting issue. Iraq and terrorism were the major concern of just one in ten voters.

Many groups helped Obama to victory. This election also drew new voters into the process. New voters made up 13% of the electorate, and they went for Obama 63% to 35%. The Obama campaign targeted Virginia with its voter registration efforts and young voters were a significant part of that targeting. Young voters, 21% of the electorate, went for Obama 60% to 39%.

CAN REPUBLICANS STOP THIS SLIDE?

In 2004, the Kerry campaign flirted with the idea of targeting Virginia. But after a few weeks of TV ads, the campaign decided to save resources and hold off on its attempts to expand the battleground. Going into the 2008 presidential election, many observers believed Virginia would definitely be in the battleground.

The population growth and Democratic resurgence in the state has been unmistakable in the last five years. Starting with Mark Warner's gubernatorial victory in 2001, Democrats have now won five of the last seven major statewide campaigns. In addition, the Democrats have made a remarkable comeback in U.S. House races, going from an eight to three deficit to a six to five advantage.

For some time, Republicans had blinders on as to what was happening in Virginia, claiming that either candidate error (see George Allen and "macaca") to better candidate recruiting (see Mark Warner and Tim Kaine) were the explanations for its recent losses.

And like the Republicans' late start in North Carolina and Indiana, there was a slice of the GOP intelligentsia that was in denial about the competitiveness of Virginia. That led to a massive spending advantage by Obama over McCain in the early part of the general election. The Republican campaign went months without airing a single ad in the northern Virginia area (via the Washington, D.C., media market).

The fact that the Republicans overlooked Virginia is surprising. In 2004, Colorado and Virginia stuck out among the states that Bush carried. Both Colorado and Virginia were among the top 10 youngest states and top 10 highest educated states, according to the census. And of those top 10 states, Bush won just two in 2004, Virginia and Colorado.

So when Democrats were looking for new ways to get to 270 electoral votes, it is clear why Colorado and Virginia were likely targets.

Republicans are clearly behind the eight ball in Virginia. The party's ideological split is causing them major problems in statewide races. Republicans who might be able to compete in the fast-growing parts of the state (including northern Virginia and Hampton Roads) aren't viewed as the leading lights of the state GOP. Like a lot of states that have slipped from the grip of the GOP, the conservative tilt of the Republican brand has cost the party an opportunity to win over moderate and new voters. In state after state, one can look at conservative victories over moderates as an explanation for the GOP's problem in holding on in formally red states, from Colorado to Virginia to places like Nevada and New Mexico.

The big test for the GOP will come in 2009 when the party hopes the state's pattern of electing a governor opposite of the party in the White House holds. A GOP victory in the governor's race would be a reminder to Democrats that their hold on the state is tenuous. After all, take a look at Obama's margin of victory nationally and his margin in the state; they are virtually identical. This makes Virginia, potentially, the country's most perfect bellwether. In fact, check out the Democrat to GOP party identification split. Nationally, the number was 39% to 32%, Democrats over Republicans, compared to 39% to 33% in Virginia. So as Virginia goes, so goes the nation? It was that way when the country was founded and it may be that way some 230 years later.

Receding Battleground States

(7 States)

There are seven states that had been battlegrounds in the last few elections but which are now on the verge of losing their battleground status. Some have become more Democratic because of changes in demographics (see Nevada and New Mexico); others have become less of a battleground due to economic conditions (see Pennsylvania and Michigan). Some states were extremely close in the last couple of elections but are drifting consistently toward one party (see New Hampshire and Minnesota). Even though some were not close in 2008, all are still battlegrounds under different circumstances and none should be completely written off in 2012. However, it does appear that in the most competitive of environments, these seven states will still keep their same political shade.

MICHIGAN
Tough Year for Big Blue
but Not for Dem Blue
17 ELECTORAL VOTES

Michigan voted primarily Republican until the Great Depression. From the 1930s through the 1960s, the state was in contention. From 1972 through 1988 the state voted exclusively Republican but has voted Democratic ever since. The economic downturn hit Michigan very hard and has likely contributed to the Democratic margin. The polls showed a narrowing of the Obama margin after the Republican convention, but after the economic crisis began, the margin widened. The polls correctly predicted the Obama margin.

	2008		2004	
Obama	2,872,579	57.4%	Kerry	51.2%
McCain	2,048,639	41.0%	Bush	47.8%
Other candidates	80,548			
	5,001,766			

Note: 100% 5,763 of 5,763 precincts; 100% 83 of 83 counties. Chart based on final, official vote totals.

Just a shade over 5 million votes were cast in Michigan in the 2008 presidential race with turnout up two percentage points to 68.6% of the voting eligible population. Fully 20% of the votes were cast early or by absentee ballot. This is a gigantic development for future Michigan campaigns, because before 2008 Michigan was not known as an early voting state.

A total of 31 of the state's 83 counties flipped to Obama in 2008, after supporting Bush in 2004. And the pattern was almost uniformly consistent: the GOP vote dropped in actual numbers while the Democratic vote rose.

Two suburban counties outside Detroit, Macomb and Oakland, are the very heartland of the Reagan Democrats, the blue-collar workers who shifted away from the Democrats in 1980. Oakland has flipped back and forth between the parties by less than 10,000 votes in recent elections, but this time Obama won by 95,610 votes, even as turnout was virtually unchanged in the county. Macomb, which went narrowly for Bush in 2004, was solidly in the Democratic column by a 53% to 45% edge.

And even Kent County, home of Grand Rapids and long a GOP bastion, flipped from 57% to 40% in 2004 to an even split in 2008, with Obama squeaking out a 1,573 vote win. The change actually fits a pattern for Obama in the Midwest as he improved in many long-time Midwestern Republican strongholds. This may say more about the Republican Party's brand problem than anything about Obama.

In the primary of January 15, 2008, Clinton received 55.2% of the vote to 40.1% for uncommitted. Obama was not on the ballot.

	2008			**2004**		
	TOTAL	OBAMA	McCAIN	TOTAL	KERRY	BUSH
GENDER						
MALE	46	52	45	49	48	50
FEMALE	54	60	38	51	53	46
AGE						
♦ *18–29*	20	68	29	21	55	43
30–44	28	56	43	26	44	54
45–64	37	52	45	38	53	47
65+	16	53	45	15	51	48
RACE						
WHITE	82	51	47	82	44	54
BLACK	12	97	3	13	89	10
HISPANIC	3	64	33	2	62	36
PARTY						
DEMOCRAT	41	93	6	39	93	7
REPUBLICAN	29	10	89	34	6	94
INDEPENDENT	29	52	42	27	49	47
IDEOLOGY						
LIBERAL	25	88	11	22	89	10
MODERATE	43	63	34	44	56	42
CONSERVATIVE	32	22	75	34	20	79
EDUCATION BY RACE						
♦ *WHITE, COLLEGE DEGREE*	30	48	49	32	41	58
WHITE, NO COLLEGE DEGREE	52	52	46	50	47	52
NONWHITE, COLLEGE DEGREE	5	81	18	6	71	26
NONWHITE, NO COLLEGE DEGREE	13	86	13	12	82	17
RELIGION						
PROTESTANT	54	51	46	53	45	54
♦ *WHITE PROTESTANT*	43	42	55	40	34	65
WHITE EVANGELICAL PROTESTANT	27	33	63	20	24	75
WHITE PROTESTANT, NOT EVANGELICAL	19	56	43	32	59	40
BLACK PROTESTANT	8	97	3	5	89	11
CATHOLIC	26	52	46	29	50	49

	2008			**2004**		
	TOTAL	OBAMA	McCAIN	TOTAL	KERRY	BUSH
WHITE CATHOLIC	24	51	47	26	48	51
HISPANIC CATHOLIC	1	–	–	5	–	–
JEWISH	1	–	–	2	71	22
OTHER	6	5	1	6	66	32
NONE	12	79	12	10	69	26
NEW VOTER						
YES	12	77	21	12	65	31
NO	88	54	43	88	49	50
INCOME						
LESS THAN $50,000	43	61	36	46	59	40
$50–100,000	38	56	42	37	46	53
MORE THAN $100,000	19	47	52	17	40	59
UNION MEMBER						
YES	18	71	27	19	66	32
NO	82	54	44	81	47	52
WORRIED ABOUT THE NATIONAL ECONOMY						
WORRIED	89	59	39	–	–	–
NOT WORRIED	10	44	54	–	–	–
LOCAL JOB SITUATION, COMPARED TO FOUR YEARS AGO						
BETTER TODAY	1	–	–	14	20	78
WORSE TODAY	88	61	37	55	76	23
ABOUT THE SAME	10	31	67	31	24	75
WAR IN IRAQ						
APPROVE	35	14	83	49	18	81
♦ *DISAPPROVE*	**63**	**81**	**16**	**47**	**86**	**12**
BUSH JOB						
APPROVE	23	10	88	50	11	89
♦ *DISAPPROVE*	**76**	**72**	**26**	**49**	**92**	**5**
WILL JOHN McCAIN						
CONTINUE BUSH'S POLICIES	54	91	7	–	–	–
MOVE IN A DIFFERENT DIRECTION	43	15	83	–	–	–
CANDIDATE QUALITIES						
VALUES	30	35	62	–	–	–
CHANGE	38	91	8	–	–	–
EXPERIENCE	17	7	92	–	–	–
CARES	12	79	16	–	–	–
ATTACKED OTHER CANDIDATE UNFAIRLY						
McCAIN DID	67	66	31	–	–	–
McCAIN DID NOT	30	37	61	–	–	–

(*continued*)

	2008			2004		
	TOTAL	OBAMA	McCAIN	TOTAL	KERRY	BUSH
OBAMA DID	48	40	56	–	–	–
OBAMA DID NOT	49	74	24	–	–	–
HAS THE RIGHT EXPERIENCE						
McCAIN DOES	57	33	66	–	–	–
McCAIN DOES NOT	42	90	7	–	–	–
OBAMA DOES	57	91	8	–	–	–
OBAMA DOES NOT	41	10	86	–	–	–

The 12 point spread in party preference between Democrats and Republicans in 2008 is the widest in nearly two decades, eclipsing that of 1996, when Clinton headed the ticket. That year, 41% of Michigan voters said they were Democrats and 32% said they were Republicans.

But there are still some signs that Michigan is not a fully blue state: 44% described themselves as moderate, the same as in 2004. Only 24% labeled themselves liberal, up two points from 2004, while 32% said they were conservative, a two point decline.

The economy was the primary issue on voters' minds and more than eight in ten said the job situation in their community was worse than four years ago.

The partisan shift might have more to do with widespread distaste for President Bush. On Election Day, 76% disapproved of his job performance, and more than seven in ten of them voted for Obama.

Youth, new voters, and union members all broke heavily for Obama. He also narrowly secured the white Catholic vote, which a Catholic candidate, John Kerry, just missed doing in 2004.

DID ECONOMIC DOWNTURN MASK A GOP OPPORTUNITY? MAYBE NOT

From the day McCain announced his second bid for the presidency, Michigan was considered one of the candidate's most important states. As an early primary state (falling just after New Hampshire), the Wolverine State was a big part of McCain's plans as he plotted a course for the Republican nomination. In 2000, McCain won Michigan's Republican primary, and the fact that Michigan was even earlier on the primary calendar in 2008 was music to the candidate's ears. He saw a clear, easy path to the nomination. Skip Iowa, win New Hampshire and Michigan, and put the nomination away by winning South Carolina, a state that broke McCain's heart and candidacy in 2000. Well, it was Michigan that broke McCain's heart in 2008 as Mitt Romney won the state, but McCain was able to come back and win a *very* narrow primary victory in South Carolina and then knock out Romney and the rest of the GOP field in Florida 10 days later.

But just because McCain lost Michigan in the primary didn't mean he was counting the state out in his general election plan.

Michigan was one of two states where Obama never campaigned during the primary season. Michigan was one of two states that attempted to break the Democratic Party primary and caucus rules (the other was Florida); the primary didn't officially count for much in this contentious primary season. In fact, Obama's name never even appeared on the state's primary ballot. As a way to underscore the state's lack of importance (or so Obama hoped), Obama convinced three of his primary rivals—John Edwards, Joe Biden, and Bill Richardson—to join him in requesting that his name not even be on the ballot. This left Hillary Clinton (along with Chris Dodd and the two gadfly candidates) as the only names on the ballot. Of course, when the non-party-sanctioned primary was held on January 15, Clinton won going away. But as a way to keep the state potentially competitive if a delegate fight ensued (which, clearly, it did), there was an effort by supporters of both Obama and Edwards to get their supporters to vote "uncommitted"—an option in Democratic presidential primary and caucus contests. The uncommitted vote topped 40% and set the stage for a rules fight inside the party that would eventually be settled in favor of Obama and would cement his primary victory over Clinton.

Still, in all of the Michigan meshugas, Obama was doing very little to prepare to win Michigan in the general election—something the Obama campaign worried about.

There were a lot of intangibles that appeared to be working against Obama. One was the lack of time he'd spent in the state. He tried to make up for lost time by holding large campaign events, including the John Edwards endorsement announcement (held in Grand Rapids before Edwards's personal problems became public) and the Al Gore endorsement (held in Detroit). These very large events were designed to quickly identify volunteers for what became known as Obama's vaunted ground game.

Another anti-Obama intangible appeared to be the political trouble of Detroit's African-American mayor, Kwame Kilpatrick. The reasoning by some was that white swing voters in suburban Detroit would allow the Kilpatrick issue to skew their own views of another African-American politician, Obama. There was so much nervousness on this issue, in fact, that Obama's forces were thought to be against a Michigan primary revote solely because of the Kilpatrick issue. Kilpatrick ended up being forced out of office just before the November election, but that was after McCain had pulled out of the state so the story was only a minor blip on the presidential radar.

And the third intangible was McCain himself. McCain's ideology was very much in line with traditional Michigan Republicans. Many successful Michigan Republicans were conservatives with a slight moderate streak somewhere, either on social issues or labor issues. It had been a hallmark of Republican success in the state. In addition, there was much talk during the summer of 2008 that McCain might pick his chief primary rival, Mitt Romney, as his running mate. Romney's Michigan ties run deep, of course, as his father was governor of the state and ran one of the state's auto manufacturers, American Motors Corporation.

But McCain didn't pick Romney; the economic crisis hit (the state sported the nation's highest unemployment rate in the country in September 2008 and ranked fifth in home foreclosures), and Obama's overwhelming financial edge allowed the Democrat to put the state away much earlier than anyone anticipated.

The Republicans have stayed more competitive in the state over the last decade than they should have. There's been a clear trend to the Democrats statewide for nearly 10 years but Republicans have held up for so long, thanks mostly to their control of state government. Those advantages down the ballot transferred up at least to the congressional level as Republicans drew the state's political map. But the demographic drift toward the Democrats over the last eight years has allowed them to overcome what was a Republican-controlled, gerrymandered congressional and legislative map. The two parties have split control of the state's legislature (Democrats control the house, Republicans the state senate). And for the first time in over a decade, the Democrats control the state's 15 seat U.S House delegation, thanks to a two seat pickup in 2008.

The recipe for a Republican comeback in this state starts with better candidates. It's been quite a while since the Republicans have outdone the Democrats on the candidate-recruiting front. Moreover, the Republicans have struggled with connecting to the average economically challenged worker. As the party has been more associated with the rich over the last few years, the blue-collar, rank-and-file voter has been wooed back to his/her Democratic roots. George W. Bush proved that winning on the back of social issues just isn't enough in a place like Michigan. So until the Republicans figure out how to become competitive on the issue of the economy, it's possible the trend toward the Democrats in this state will continue.

The good news for the Republicans is that the party will get an early opportunity to start turning their fortunes around with the 2010 governor's race. Democrat Jennifer Granholm is term-limited, and there really isn't an heir apparent. Expect the Democratic primary to be very competitive (and potentially contentious, as Granholm's was in 2002), leaving the Republicans the opportunity to rally around a nominee. While gubernatorial races are rarely barometers for where a state is headed in a presidential year, it is a chance for the out-party to get its juice back and start the rebuilding process.

MINNESOTA
Republicans Lose in Their Convention Host State
10 ELECTORAL VOTES

Minnesota voted almost exclusively Republican from 1860 through the 1920s. After that, it normally voted Democratic except for the 1972 landslide. However, the 2000 election was unexpectedly close and gave Republicans hope that this was a state that was trending toward them. In 2008, the polls showed a lead for Obama with a significant narrowing in mid-September. After the financial crisis, the lead widened and the polls correctly predicted the final margin.

	2008		2004	
Obama	1,573,354	54.1%	Kerry	51.1%
McCain	1,275,409	43.8%	Bush	47.6%
Other candidates	61,606			
	2,910,369			

Note: 100% 4,130 of 4,130 precincts; 100% 87 of 87 counties. Chart based on final, official vote totals.

Turnout in Minnesota is traditionally among the highest in the country, but it sagged a bit in 2008. The high turnout is thanks to the fact that folks can register and vote on Election Day itself. Turnout ended up at 77.9%, down about half a point from 2004. A total of 18 Bush counties from 2004 flipped in 2008.

The most important of the counties to switch are Dakota and Washington, both suburbs of Minneapolis–Saint Paul. Both had gone narrowly Republican in 2004, after voting for Gore in 2000. Both went back in the Democratic column as the GOP vote totals fell.

In the caucus of February 5, 2008, Obama received 66.4% of the vote and Clinton received 32.2%.

	2008			2004		
	TOTAL	OBAMA	McCAIN	TOTAL	KERRY	BUSH
GENDER						
MALE	47	50	47	48	51	48
FEMALE	53	57	41	52	52	46
AGE						
♦ *18–29*	22	65	34	20	57	41
30–44	28	49	49	29	51	48

	2008			**2004**		
	TOTAL	OBAMA	McCAIN	TOTAL	KERRY	BUSH
45–64	37	51	47	39	50	49
♦ *65+*	**13**	**55**	**43**	**12**	**49**	**51**
RACE						
WHITE	90	53	46	93	50	49
BLACK	3	–	–	3	87	12
HISPANIC	3	–	–	1	–	–
PARTY						
DEMOCRAT	40	94	6	38	92	7
REPUBLICAN	36	8	91	35	6	94
INDEPENDENT	25	56	39	27	55	42
IDEOLOGY						
LIBERAL	26	92	7	24	91	7
MODERATE	44	58	40	45	57	42
CONSERVATIVE	30	15	83	31	12	87
EDUCATION BY RACE						
WHITE, COLLEGE DEGREE	40	56	43	44	54	45
WHITE, NO COLLEGE DEGREE	50	49	48	48	45	54
NONWHITE, COLLEGE DEGREE	4	–	–	3	–	–
NONWHITE, NO COLLEGE DEGREE	6	77	21	5	–	–
RELIGION						
PROTESTANT	54	47	51	53	43	56
WHITE PROTESTANT	50	46	52	50	42	58
WHITE EVANGELICAL PROTESTANT	25	33	65	–	–	–
WHITE PROTESTANT, NOT EVANGELICAL	25	60	38	–	–	–
BLACK PROTESTANT	2	–	–	5	–	–
CATHOLIC	27	47	52	28	50	49
WHITE CATHOLIC	25	47	51	26	48	50
HISPANIC CATHOLIC	1	–	–	5	–	–
JEWISH	1	–	–	2	–	–
OTHER	6	78	21	6	75	22
NONE	12	77	21	12	79	20
NEW VOTER						
YES	9	67	32	9	61	37
NO	91	52	46	91	50	49
INCOME						
LESS THAN $50,000	38	59	38	40	56	42
$50–100,000	39	53	45	39	50	49
MORE THAN $100,000	23	49	50	21	46	53

(*continued*)

	2008			**2004**		
	TOTAL	OBAMA	McCAIN	TOTAL	KERRY	BUSH
UNION MEMBER						
YES	17	59	40	17	62	37
NO	83	52	47	83	49	50
WORRIED ABOUT THE NATIONAL ECONOMY						
♦ *WORRIED*	**89**	**55**	**43**	–	–	–
NOT WORRIED	11	33	65	–	–	–
BUSH JOB						
APPROVE	25	8	91	49	7	93
♦ *DISAPPROVE*	**73**	**68**	**30**	51	94	4
WILL JOHN McCAIN						
♦ *CONTINUE BUSH'S POLICIES*	49	91	7	–	–	–
MOVE IN A DIFFERENT DIRECTION	49	17	82	–	–	–
CANDIDATE QUALITIES						
VALUES	37	36	62		–	–
CHANGE	36	91	8	–	–	–
EXPERIENCE	16	2	96	–	–	–
CARES	8	69	27	–	–	–
ATTACKED OTHER CANDIDATE UNFAIRLY						
McCAIN DID	64	63	36	–	–	–
McCAIN DID NOT	33	36	62	–	–	–
♦ *OBAMA DID*	**53**	**40**	**58**	–	–	–
OBAMA DID NOT	44	70	28	–	–	–

Minnesota has gone with the Democratic nominee the last nine elections, an unmatched streak nationwide for the party.

McCain spent a lot on ads (in one of the few states where he outspent Obama), but they did not do him any favors as 64% thought McCain attacked Obama unfairly and these voters favored Obama by 27 points. Among the 53% who believed Obama attacked McCain unfairly, McCain held a more narrow 18 point lead.

Three-quarters disapproved of how President Bush was handling his job. Half thought McCain would continue Bush's policies, and about nine in ten of those voters went for Obama. Among those who thought McCain would break with Bush, about eight in ten voted for the self-described maverick.

Minnesota voters were worried about the economy and looking for a president who could change things. Obama picked up support from both youth and seniors and from voters both rich and poor.

Obama won among the eight in ten voters from families making less than $100,000 year, and he was about tied among those who make $100,000 a year or more. Four years ago, Bush won that group.

Nine in ten voters were worried about the direction of the national economy next year.

Self-described Independents were about a quarter of the voters and in the presidential race they broke heavily for Obama.

DID HOSTING THE GOP CONVENTION ACTUALLY HURT THE PARTY?

So were 2000 and 2004 anomalies or not? That's what the Republican Party would like to know. In both of George W. Bush's successful presidential campaigns, he made Minnesota more competitive for a Republican on a presidential level than it had been in more than 30 years. He lost by two points in 2000 and by a shade under four points in 2004. And because of that competitiveness, the Republicans thought 2008 was the year to really put their foot on the gas and attempt to win this state by deciding to hold their national nominating convention in the Twin Cities. This decision, made by one of Bush's two political right hands, then RNC Chair Ken Mehlman, was an early indication that Republicans were bound and determined to make yet another run at turning Minnesota red.

There was stubbornness on the part of the Republicans—both in the McCain campaign and in the Republican Party as a whole—about their chances in Minnesota. Despite an enormous amount of evidence that Minnesota wasn't as competitive in 2008 as it was in 2004 or 2000, the party kept pouring resources into the state. Part of that stubbornness was born out of the fact that Minnesota was a battleground state on the Senate and House level as the Senate race ended up being the closest in the country (thanks to a third-party candidate). Moreover, Democrats were targeting a couple House seats in an attempt to increase their advantage in the state's U.S House delegation. So, the good news for the GOP: it wasn't wasted money as the party more than held its own on the House and Senate level.

But as a presidential battleground, it's hard to imagine that this state is somehow trending Republican. The Democratic lean of the state has been masked in recent years by outside events that have given the Republicans opportunities to win statewide. The death of Paul Wellstone (just a few weeks before Election Day) gave Norm Coleman his Senate seat in 2002. The one-term phenomenon of Jesse Ventura gave growth to a third party in the state that, while unsuccessful at winning without Ventura in 1998, does seem adept at picking off Independent voters. That allows the Republican Party to do what it does best, turn out its base and win elections on their backs.

In fact, Republican Governor Tim Pawlenty in his two successful bids for governor has never topped 47%, let alone 50%. The last Republican to win more than 50% in a major statewide race was Arne Carlson in 1994 when he won his second term for governor in a landslide. By the way, in a sign of how damaged the national Republican brand is in this state, Carlson endorsed Obama and has been rumored to be a potential future Democratic candidate.

Republicans have overperformed on the state level, and that's probably led to the false hope for the party in trying to win this state on a presidential level. With the right candidate (say a hometown boy like Pawlenty) on the national ticket, maybe Minnesota will sneak into the battleground in 2012. Absent that, it's hard to imagine Minnesota voting Republican on the national level in anything but a national Republican landslide. This doesn't mean the 2010 election cycle won't be interesting in Minnesota, but for now it's a state that remains more competitive on the state level than on the federal level.

NEVADA
Everything's Coming Up
Dem Gold in Silver State
5 ELECTORAL VOTES

Nevada has voted Republican in eight of the last ten elections. How-ever, this state has had significant population growth that first pushed it into battleground status and may, in fact, have pushed it all the way past it. Though, keep this in mind: Nevada has proven to be a reliable bellwether. It has been wrong in picking the president just once since 1912, when the Silver State sided with Ford over Carter in 1976. The polls showed a very close contest that widened in October, but the polls significantly underestimated Obama's victory margin.

	2008		2004	
Obama	**533,736**	**55.1%**	Kerry	47.9%
McCain	**412,827**	**42.7%**	Bush	50.5%
Other candidates	**21,285**			
	967,848			

Note: 100% 2,015 of 2,015 precincts; 100% 17 of 17 counties. Chart based on final, official vote totals.

Turnout rose in Nevada by more than two percentage points to 57.5% of the voting eligible population. The total number of votes in this fast-growing state jumped by more than 130,000 from 2004. That continued the rapid rise in the number of votes as 2004 was up 163,000 from 2000.

Fully two-thirds of all 2008 votes were cast early or absentee.

About two-thirds of Nevada's voters are in Clark County, home to Las Vegas. And Clark has been the only reliably Democratic county in the state since 1988. But in 2008, what had been a 26,000 vote Democratic margin in Clark ballooned into a 122,803 vote edge for Obama. And this year, Clark was joined by Washoe County, home to Reno and Carson City, the state capital, in pro-viding majorities to Obama. For both, it was the first time since 1968 that Democrats had won those counties. In the caucus of January 19, 2008, Clinton received 50.8% of the vote and Obama received 45.1%.

	2008			**2004**		
	TOTAL	OBAMA	McCAIN	TOTAL	KERRY	BUSH
GENDER						
MALE	48	51	47	48	44	54
♦ FEMALE	52	59	38	52	52	47
AGE						
18–29	17	67	31	16	56	42
30–44	33	60	37	28	47	51
45–64	36	51	46	39	46	53
65+	15	42	55	17	50	50
RACE						
WHITE	69	45	53	77	43	55
BLACK	10	94	5	7	86	13
♦ HISPANIC	15	76	22	10	60	39
PARTY						
DEMOCRAT	38	93	6	35	90	10
REPUBLICAN	30	11	88	39	7	93
♦ INDEPENDENT	32	54	41	26	54	42
IDEOLOGY						
LIBERAL	22	87	11	18	85	14
MODERATE	44	64	33	47	55	43
CONSERVATIVE	34	21	77	34	18	81
EDUCATION BY RACE						
WHITE, COLLEGE DEGREE	31	47	51	33	44	55
WHITE, NO COLLEGE DEGREE	38	43	54	44	43	56
NONWHITE, COLLEGE DEGREE	9	68	28	8	55	43
NONWHITE, NO COLLEGE DEGREE	22	83	17	15	71	28
RELIGION						
PROTESTANT	48	47	51	52	38	61
WHITE PROTESTANT	35	36	63	41	33	66
WHITE EVANGELICAL PROTESTANT	15	24	74	–	–	–
WHITE PROTESTANT, NOT EVANGELICAL	20	43	55	–	–	–
BLACK PROTESTANT	6	97	2	5	86	13
CATHOLIC	25	57	42	25	52	47
WHITE CATHOLIC	15	46	53	17	46	53
HISPANIC CATHOLIC	8	78	22	5	71	29
JEWISH	3	–	–	4	62	35
OTHER	7	68	29	5	71	26
NONE	17	72	23	14	63	34
NEW VOTER						
YES	14	77	23	14	57	41
NO	86	52	45	86	47	52

	2008			**2004**		
	TOTAL	OBAMA	McCAIN	TOTAL	KERRY	BUSH
INCOME						
LESS THAN $50,000	33	64	34	41	56	42
$50–100,000	40	54	43	38	46	52
MORE THAN $100,000	27	49	50	21	38	61
WORRIED ABOUT THE NATIONAL ECONOMY						
♦ *WORRIED*	**85**	**59**	**39**	–	–	–
NOT WORRIED	14	39	58	–	–	–
BUSH JOB						
APPROVE	27	8	89	53	8	91
DISAPPROVE	73	74	25	46	94	5
WILL JOHN McCAIN						
CONTINUE BUSH'S POLICIES	52	92	6	–	–	–
MOVE IN A DIFFERENT DIRECTION	44	15	83	–	–	–
IRAQ WAR						
APPROVE	40	14	84	53	14	85
DISAPPROVE	59	85	14	44	89	9
UNION MEMBER						
YES	12	67	31	14	56	43
NO	88	54	44	86	47	52
CANDIDATE QUALITIES						
VALUES	26	40	58	–	–	–
CHANGE	34	91	7	–	–	–
EXPERIENCE	20	5	95	–	–	–
CARES	15	75	22	–	–	–
CONTACTED BY McCAIN'S CAMPAIGN						
♦ *YES*	**29**	**43**	**55**	–	–	–
NO	69	62	36	–	–	–
CONTACTED BY OBAMA'S CAMPAIGN						
♦ *YES*	**50**	**66**	**33**	–	–	–
NO	48	46	51	–	–	–
ATTACKED OTHER CANDIDATE UNFAIRLY						
McCAIN DID	70	68	31	–	–	–
McCAIN DID NOT	27	27	69	–	–	–
OBAMA DID	53	41	57	–	–	–
OBAMA DID NOT	45	74	24	–	–	–
HAS THE RIGHT EXPERIENCE						
McCAIN DOES	61	34	65	–	–	–
McCAIN DOES NOT	38	90	6	–	–	–
OBAMA DOES	55	93	6	–	–	–
OBAMA DOES NOT	44	9	87	–	–	–

Hispanics were 15% of the electorate and voted 78% to 20% for Obama. This is a big shift from the Hispanic result in 2004 when President Bush won 39% of Hispanics. The shift came from the half of the Hispanics who don't identify themselves as Catholics.

In 2004, Independents were 27% of the electorate, and Bush received 45% of that vote. In 2008, the percentage identifying as Independents was up to 32% and 56% went for Obama, 40% for McCain.

Nevada has the highest foreclosure rate in the nation and is among the top 10 states in highest job losses. The economy was understandably the top issue, with 85% saying they were worried about the direction of the nation's economy. Some 59% of these voters went for Obama and 39% for McCain.

Women made up 52% of the voters in Nevada, and 59% went for Obama, 38% for McCain. In 2004, Bush received the support of 47% of women voters in Nevada.

Half the electorate said they were contacted by the Obama campaign, and two-thirds of those contacted voted for Obama. This is significantly more than the 29% who were contacted by the McCain campaign, among whom he was only able to garner a 12 point spread.

LATINO TURNOUT TURNS SWING STATE BLUE

For the first time ever, Nevada found itself in the mix for an early contest in the Democratic primary fight. One of the reasons Democrats gave for choosing Nevada (over Arizona among other states) as an early primary or caucus state was the fact that the state was becoming important in the general election battleground.

The organizations that both Clinton and Obama built in the state, in conjunction with the extra investment the unions made, clearly paid off in November. The 14 point jump in Democratic performance was among the biggest shifts of all the 2008 battleground states.

This Democratic surge helped the party down the ballot as well. The party netted another U.S House seat (and now controls the delegation, two to one) as well as two state senate seats that shifted state senate control from the Republicans to the Democrats. The Democrats already controlled the state assembly.

If there was one glaring advantage Obama had over McCain, it showed itself during the early vote. As was noted above, nearly two-thirds of the state voted early and Obama invested more money in this early vote than McCain. There seems to be an entire western bloc of states (California, Oregon, Washington, and Arizona) where early voters are consistently outnumbering Election Day voters. This trend will continue to transform strategies as more candidates are likely to spend more time in these western battleground states in September than they do in October.

The other thing working in the Democrats' favor in Nevada is the demographic trend. The jump in Hispanic voters continues, as the number in 2008 was higher than in either 2000 or 2004, years Bush carried the state. In addition, the economic downturn allowed Democrats to overcome what is perceived as a conservative bent in the state. Many residents move to Nevada to take advantage of the state's low tax laws, and that automatically makes these new voters susceptible to low tax arguments, a staple of any Republican campaign. But because of the tough economic times, it seems taxes were an argument that fell flat for McCain in Nevada and elsewhere.

But everything about Nevada comes back to demographics. In the 17 states that fell below the national average on the number of white voters, Obama carried 11 of them, including Nevada. Nationwide, 74% of the electorate was white; in Nevada, that number was 69%. In fact, Nevada was just one of four states where both blacks and Hispanics each made up 10% or more of the electorate. The other three are California, Florida, and Texas. Obviously, Obama carried three of these four states.

Some may argue with our designation of Nevada as a receding battleground, but it's hard to imagine how the Republicans recover from this drubbing in one election cycle. To overcome their brand problems with Hispanics, the GOP would need some unintentional help from the Democrats in alienating Hispanics and that doesn't seem plausible in the next four years.

The next election cycle does provide Republicans with some comeback opportunities. Democratic Senate leader Harry Reid is up for reelection, and it's possible his high-profile national leadership post could make him a marked man in Nevada. But that GOP opportunity is countered by a major drag on the Republican Party's brand in the state. Republican Governor Jim Gibbons is seen by many as an embarrassment to his party. His high profile divorce coupled with some ethical issues has made him untenable in some corners. In fact, McCain kept a major distance away from Gibbons to the point that he asked the state's Lieutenant Governor to be his state campaign chair, a departure from the norm. National nominees always ask the state party's highest-ranking officeholders to serve in those ceremonial posts. If Gibbons seeks reelection, it could cause the GOP further headaches in the state and set back the party's chances of keeping this state competitive in the near term.

NEW HAMPSHIRE
Four Year Republican Slide Continues
4 ELECTORAL VOTES

New Hampshire has been a true swing state, but it voted Democratic in three of the last four elections. Kerry won a very narrow victory in 2004, and so strategists on both sides viewed the state as still a part of the battleground in 2008. It now appears to be part of the reliably blue New England. Polls here showed a close race until October when Obama opened up a significant lead. The polls correctly predicted the final Obama margin.

	2008		2004	
Obama	384,826	54.4%	Kerry	50.2%
McCain	316,534	44.7%	Bush	48.9%
Other candidates	6,251			
	707,611			

Note: 100% 301 of 301 precincts; 100% 237 of 237 towns, townships, and cities. Chart based on final, official vote totals.

In every New Hampshire county but one, the number of votes in the presidential election increased from 2004. But because the state's population has been growing as well, the turnout was virtually unchanged at 71% of the voting eligible population.

Every county in New Hampshire cast a majority of its votes for Barack Obama in the 2008 election, which is the reason why we are calling New Hampshire a receding battleground, rather than treating it as a toss-up state in future years. Although most conversations about elections in the Granite State revolve around cities and towns, instead of counties, Obama did win all 10 counties, picking up four that went for Bush in 2004. For example in Hillsborough, which covers Manchester and Nashua, Obama won a 7,642 vote victory, compared to Bush's 5,603 vote edge in 2004.

In the primary of January 8, 2008, Clinton received 39.1% of the vote and Obama received 36.5%.

| | **2008** | | | **2004** | | |
	TOTAL	OBAMA	McCAIN	TOTAL	KERRY	BUSH
GENDER						
MALE	48	49	49	51	47	52
♦ FEMALE	52	61	38	49	54	45
AGE						
♦ 18–29	18	61	37	16	57	43
30–44	26	51	48	34	45	53
45–64	42	56	43	39	51	48
♦ 65+	14	56	43	11	54	46
RACE						
WHITE	94	54	44	95	50	49
BLACK	1	–	–	1	–	–
HISPANIC	2	–	–	1	–	–
PARTY						
DEMOCRAT	29	92	8	25	95	5
REPUBLICAN	27	11	89	32	8	91
♦ INDEPENDENT	45	59	39	44	56	42
IDEOLOGY						
LIBERAL	26	91	8	21	87	12
MODERATE	46	60	40	49	57	42
CONSERVATIVE	28	17	82	30	13	86
EDUCATION BY RACE						
WHITE, COLLEGE DEGREE	50	58	40	51	54	45
WHITE, NO COLLEGE DEGREE	45	50	49	44	45	54
NONWHITE, COLLEGE DEGREE	3	–	–	3	–	–
NONWHITE, NO COLLEGE DEGREE	3	–	–	2	–	–
RELIGION						
PROTESTANT	37	47	51	40	40	59
WHITE PROTESTANT	36	46	52	38	39	60
BLACK PROTESTANT	0	–	–	1	–	–
CATHOLIC	38	50	50	38	47	52
WHITE CATHOLIC	36	49	50	36	47	52
HISPANIC CATHOLIC	1	–	–	1	–	–
JEWISH	2	–	–	2	–	–
OTHER	7	76	22	6	79	21
NONE	16	76	24	14	69	30
NEW VOTER						
YES	9	61	39	9	54	46
NO	91	55	44	91	50	49
INCOME						
LESS THAN $50,000	33	59	39	33	55	44
$50–100,000	38	53	46	42	47	52
MORE THAN $100,000	30	56	43	25	50	49

	2008			**2004**		
	TOTAL	OBAMA	McCAIN	TOTAL	KERRY	BUSH
WORRIED ABOUT THE NATIONAL ECONOMY						
WORRIED	91	57	42	–	–	–
NOT WORRIED	8	30	69	–	–	–
IRAQ WAR						
APPROVE	32	13	86	48	13	86
DISAPPROVE	66	76	23	45	90	9
BUSH JOB						
APPROVE	21	7	92	50	6	94
♦ *DISAPPROVE*	78	68	31	49	96	3
WILL JOHN McCAIN						
♦ *CONTINUE BUSH'S POLICIES*	50	92	7	–	–	–
MOVE IN A DIFFERENT DIRECTION	48	17	82	–	–	–
CANDIDATE QUALITIES						
VALUES	34	46	53	–	–	–
CHANGE	34	92	8	–	–	–
EXPERIENCE	21	5	95	–	–	–
CARES	7	77	19	–	–	–
HAS THE RIGHT EXPERIENCE						
McCAIN DOES	66	38	62	–	–	–
McCAIN DOES NOT	32	88	9	–	–	–
OBAMA DOES	56	89	11	–	–	–
OBAMA DOES NOT	43	10	88	–	–	–
OBAMA'S POSITIONS ON THE ISSUES ARE						
TOO LIBERAL	41	7	91	–	–	–
TOO CONSERVATIVE	4	–	–	–	–	–
ABOUT RIGHT	52	94	6	–	–	–
DEMOCRATIC HILLARY CLINTON SUPPORTER						
	11	84	15	–	–	–

Obama had strong support from women, who voted 61% to 38% for Obama and made up 52% of New Hampshire voters. This is despite Hillary Clinton having won the New Hampshire primary in January. Democrats who wanted her to win the nomination ended up supporting Obama, 84% to 15%. These former Clinton voters made up 11% of New Hampshire voters. In 2004, women voted 54% for Kerry and 45% for Bush.

Young voters also were solidly behind the Democrat, 62% to 37%. But Obama also won seniors here, 56% to 43%.

The Republican share of the electorate was down five points, while the Democrats were up four, and Independents basically held steady. A 59% majority of Independents voted for Obama, while 39% went for McCain. New Hampshire prides itself on the idea that it's the most independently minded of the New England states, and so it sports the highest self-identified "independent" number of any state in the Union.

McCain was hurt by President Bush, whose job approval in the state is just 21% while 78% disapproved. Of those voters who disapprove of Bush, 68% voted for Obama. Half of the voters in New Hampshire believed McCain would continue Bush's policies.

THE END OF A LONG ERA?

Beginning with John Kerry's narrow victory in this state in 2004, there's a trend toward the Democrats that's been unmistakable. In 2006, one of the authors used to joke that the Democratic wave came ashore in Nashua, because no state saw as dramatic a Democratic turn as New Hampshire. In that year, Democrats swept the state in a way that they hadn't done in nearly a century. They took control of the entire state legislature, including the 400 member state house, an achievement that Democrats did not believe was possible. In fact, there were winners in 2006 that never even campaigned.

So, perhaps it should not have been a surprise that 2008 would continue the Democratic trend. Not only did Obama carry the state, his margin was bigger than anyone anticipated. In addition, the two Democratic members of the U.S. House solidified their holds on their seats by winning reelection, and the Democrats nabbed one of the state's U.S. Senate seats for only the third time in the last 150 years, and the first time since the 1970s.

Like other 2004 blue states where McCain was optimistic, Republicans were convinced of two things about the Granite State. 1) The voters here love McCain. After all, New Hampshire created the candidate that we all now know as John McCain. It was in New Hampshire in 1999 and 2000 that McCain made famous his Straight Talk Express and his penchant for town halls. 2) New Hampshire was a state that had a love affair with the Clintons, twice making a candidate named Clinton the comeback kid. In 1992, it was Clinton's strong second place showing in the New Hampshire primary that convinced Democrats around the country that the affair allegations wouldn't be enough to take down Bill Clinton. And it was Hillary Clinton's upset win in the 2008 Democratic primary that kept her hopes for the Democratic nomination alive. That started one of the most drawn-out primary processes in Democratic Party history. And that Clinton love, the McCain folks incorrectly believed, could be enough to convince some swing voters to pick McCain over Obama.

A few things have happened in New Hampshire, however, since McCain's first appearance on the Granite State's stage in 2000. The Republican Party's brand has gotten a lot more conservative while the state's own Republican Party brand has gotten more moderate. There was a time when the Republican brand in the state was very conservative thanks mostly to the reputation created by the state's leading conservative media voice, the *Manchester* (now *New Hampshire*) *Union Leader*. But there's been a dramatic demographic change in the state over the last few years. While it's still true that new voters flock to the state from "Taxachusetts," in order to avoid paying state income taxes, the issue isn't the be all and end all in the state's politics. And Democrats, in order to find success in state races, have done their best to agree with the Republicans on the tax issue. That is why the state has elected two Democratic governors in the last 10 years, something it hadn't done in more than a generation before then.

Much of southern New Hampshire has become an exurb of Boston and, as that population has gotten more affluent and more influential in the state's politics, the Democrats have seen their fortunes rise.

The state just doesn't look like a battleground state anymore. For instance, a majority of the 2008 electorate were college graduates, something that is usually a trademark of a solid blue state. Only a handful of so-called battleground states featured a similar electorate. Moreover, the self-described Republican number (at 28%) also puts it in the ranks of very solid blue states.

Bottom line: as the Republican Party has focused more on cultural and religious issues, it's turned off folks in this once proud Republican state. Because of its independent streak and status as an early presidential primary state, it will still be treated as a potential battleground in 2012. One thing New Hampshire voters do not like is to be taken for granted. So President Obama can't assume New Hampshire is a lock for his 2012 column, as he might believe for the rest of New England, but with just a little bit of care and feeding, it appears the Democrats have a pretty good hold on this state.

NEW MEXICO
Democrats Dominate
Up and Down Ballot
5 ELECTORAL VOTES

New Mexico has traditionally been a swing state, voting equally over the years for Democrats and Republicans. But if one looks at the last decade, the state has voted Democratic in three of the last four elections, and that fourth was almost a tie with Bush beating Kerry by less than 1%. The polls showed a comfortable lead for Obama throughout the campaign but significantly underestimated the final margin.

	2008		2004	
Obama	472,422	56.9%	Kerry	49.1%
McCain	346,832	41.8%	Bush	49.8%
Other candidates	10,904			
	830,158			

Note: 100% 1,498 of 1,498 precincts; 100% 33 of 33 counties. Chart based on final, official vote totals.

Turnout in New Mexico was up under one percentage point to 59.6%. Sixty percent of the votes were cast early or by absentee ballot, continuing a trend in the West and Southwest of more voting taking place before Election Day. Six of the 33 counties in New Mexico backed Obama after voting for Bush in 2004.

Rapid growth is a hallmark of New Mexico and much of the Southwest. Although turnout statewide was up only a trace as a percentage of the eligible population, the total number of votes was up, 73,854, a 10% increase from 2004.

Sandoval County cast only 19,011 votes in the 1988 presidential election. In 2008, it cast 58,798, with Obama winning this rapidly growing swing county, flipping it back to the Democratic column after it went for Bush in 2004.

In the primary of February 5, 2008, Clinton received 48.8% of the vote and Obama received 48.0%.

	2008			**2004**		
	TOTAL	OBAMA	McCAIN	TOTAL	KERRY	BUSH
GENDER						
MALE	48	54	45	45	48	51
FEMALE	52	59	39	55	49	49
AGE						
18–29	21	71	27	17	49	50
30–44	28	52	47	27	41	56
45–64	35	54	45	39	51	47
65+	16	53	46	17	52	47
RACE						
WHITE	50	42	56	57	43	56
BLACK	1	–	–	2	–	–
◆ *HISPANIC*	**41**	**69**	**30**	**32**	**56**	**44**
PARTY						
DEMOCRAT	44	91	9	40	84	15
REPUBLICAN	28	8	91	33	5	94
INDEPENDENT	28	56	41	27	52	45
IDEOLOGY						
LIBERAL	22	92	8	22	84	14
MODERATE	44	62	36	42	60	39
CONSERVATIVE	34	29	69	36	14	85
EDUCATION BY RACE						
WHITE, COLLEGE DEGREE	29	49	49	28	48	50
WHITE, NO COLLEGE DEGREE	21	36	62	29	38	61
NONWHITE, COLLEGE DEGREE	16	67	32	13	55	43
NONWHITE, NO COLLEGE DEGREE	34	74	25	31	58	41
RELIGION						
PROTESTANT	44	37	61	49	33	67
WHITE PROTESTANT	30	30	69	33	30	68
WHITE EVANGELICAL PROTESTANT	16	17	81	–	–	–
WHITE PROTESTANT, NOT EVANGELICAL	15	42	57	–	–	–
BLACK PROTESTANT	1	–	–	2	–	–
◆ *HISPANIC PROTESTANT*	**10**	**49**	**51**	**8**	**27**	**72**
CATHOLIC	35	71	28	32	61	38
WHITE CATHOLIC	7	42	56	8	46	52
◆ *HISPANIC CATHOLIC*	**27**	**76**	**23**	**21**	**67**	**33**
JEWISH	1	–	–	1	–	–
OTHER	6	84	12	8	70	27
NONE	13	74	25	10	67	32

(*continued*)

	2008			**2004**		
	TOTAL	OBAMA	McCAIN	TOTAL	KERRY	BUSH
NEW VOTER						
YES	13	74	24	12	51	49
NO	87	55	44	88	49	50
INCOME						
♦ *LESS THAN $50,000*	44	65	33	53	51	48
$50–100,000	38	52	47	33	48	51
MORE THAN $100,000	19	53	46	14	43	54
WORRIED ABOUT THE NATIONAL ECONOMY						
WORRIED	83	60	38	–	–	–
NOT WORRIED	16	41	56	–	–	–
WAR IN IRAQ						
APPROVE	37	15	85	49	12	87
DISAPPROVE	61	84	14	46	88	10
BUSH JOB						
APPROVE	26	11	88	53	10	89
DISAPPROVE	73	74	24	46	94	5
WILL JOHN McCAIN						
CONTINUE BUSH'S POLICIES	51	92	6	–	–	–
MOVE IN A DIFFERENT DIRECTION	44	18	80	–	–	–
CANDIDATE QUALITIES						
VALUES	30	35	63	–	–	–
CHANGE	32	93	6	–	–	–
EXPERIENCE	18	8	91	–	–	–
CARES	16	83	14	–	–	–
ATTACKED OTHER CANDIDATE UNFAIRLY						
♦ *McCAIN DID*	71	66	32	–	–	–
McCAIN DID NOT	25	35	64	–	–	–
♦ *OBAMA DID*	49	42	56	–	–	–
OBAMA DID NOT	48	74	24	–	–	–
HAS THE RIGHT EXPERIENCE						
McCAIN DOES	57	33	67	–	–	–
McCAIN DOES NOT	42	90	7	–	–	–
OBAMA DOES	57	94	5	–	–	–
OBAMA DOES NOT	42	8	90	–	–	–
DEMOCRATIC HILLARY CLINTON SUPPORTER						
	13	88	11	–	–	–

Hispanics were 41% of the New Mexico electorate (largest of any state in the Union), and they went 69% for Obama and 30% for McCain. In 2004, Hispanics made up 32% of voters and went 56% for Kerry and 44% for Bush.

Obama improved his margins over Kerry among both Protestant and Catholic Hispanics. Four years ago Protestant Hispanics were 8% of the New Mexico electorate, and three-quarters of them voted for Bush. In 2008, their share increased slightly and they split their vote 49% for Obama, 51% for McCain—a dramatic 43 point swing.

Forty-four percent of voters in New Mexico have a family income under $50,000; they voted 65% for Obama and 33% for McCain. More families in New Mexico live below the poverty line, 14%, than the national average, 9%.

Democrats who supported Hillary Clinton in the New Mexico Democratic primary voted 88% for Obama and 11% for McCain. These Democratic Clinton supporters made up 13% of voters.

Both campaigns ran attack ads in the state critical of each other's immigration policies. The voters of New Mexico came away believing that both candidates made unfair attacks, though many more said McCain did. Nearly half (49%) said Obama made unfair attacks while 71% said McCain did.

Seventy percent of voters in this border state said illegal immigrants should be given a chance to apply for legal status, while 23% of voters said illegal immigrants should be deported. Among those supporting legal status, 63% voted for Obama and 36% for McCain.

HISPANICS HELP TURN BATTLEGROUND INTO A LANDSLIDE

If there ever was a state that can serve as an example of the Republican Party's brand problem with Hispanics, it's New Mexico. Here's a state that the Hispanic-friendly George W. Bush carried in 2004 and nearly carried in 2000. It moved a whopping 15 points in the Democrats' direction in 2008. As the exit poll shows, there's really only one explanation: immigration.

During the very contentious national debate over the Iraq war in 2005 and 2006, one other issue bubbled up into the national debate and it was immigration. But the immigration debate wasn't one that took place between Democrats and Republicans but between Republicans and other Republicans. George W. Bush and John McCain were the two biggest proponents of an immigration policy that was perceived as friendly to Hispanics, while the rest of the party was against it. And it was the rest of the party that won the day. The Bush-McCain supported immigration reform (which Democrats also largely supported) went down thanks to a concerted effort by the Republican base (led by talk radio and conservative TV commentators). This campaign to stop the Bush-McCain immigration legislation had some very negative effects on how Hispanics viewed the Republican Party. The GOP wasn't helped by the Republican presidential primary debate in 2007 that also included a contentious back-and-forth on immigration. All of this appeared to drive Hispanics into the waiting arms of the Democrats.

McCain's campaign did hold out early hope that Obama's lack of success in wooing Hispanic Democrats during the primary fight with Clinton would translate into an opening for the Hispanic-friendly McCain. But it appears Hispanics held McCain's party label against him more than they held Obama's race. There had been some unproven conventional wisdom (based on the results of a couple of mayoral races) that claimed Hispanics wouldn't support an African-American candidate. Considering that Obama carried Hispanics in greater numbers than either Kerry or Gore received in 2004 and 2000, respectively, that assumption was clearly proven false.

Overall, the Democratic dominance in New Mexico didn't stop at the presidential level; the party swept all three of the state's U.S. House seats and one of the two U.S. Senate seats. Of the nine statewide elected officials in the state, the Republicans can lay claim to just one seat, the state land commissioner. The Democratic coattails also stretched down the ballot to the state legislative level as the party picked up three seats in both the state senate and the state house.

The Republican Party has a lot of rebuilding to do in New Mexico. And until the party begins to make inroads again with Hispanics, it's hard to imagine that New Mexico won't continue its Democratic shift. Remember, Republicans lost this state in 2008 in a landslide when the Republican candidate was from a neighboring state and was perceived as being friendly to Hispanics. Imagine how poorly a more conservative Republican not from the region who was perceived as more hostile to Hispanic immigrants would have done in New Mexico. It's that bad right now for Republicans and Hispanics.

PENNSYLVANIA
America's Most Overrated Battleground State?
21 ELECTORAL VOTES

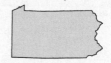

Pennsylvania has been considered a swing state for quite some time, despite the fact that it has voted Democratic in the last five elections. A Democrat hasn't won the presidency without Pennsylvania since Truman defeated Dewey in 1948. Polls showed Obama had a significant lead that narrowed after the conventions. In October, the lead widened even though the polls underestimated the final margin.

	2008		2004	
Obama	3,276,363	54.7%	Kerry	50.9%
McCain	2,651,812	44.4%	Bush	48.4%
Other candidates	64,209			
	5,992,384			

Note: 100% 9,284 of 9,284 precincts; 100% 67 of 67 counties. Chart based on final, official vote totals.

Turnout in Pennsylvania was up in 2008 by more than one percentage point to just under 64%.

Eleven counties switched sides from 2004, three from Kerry to McCain and eight from Bush to Obama. McCain spent a great deal of time and money in Pennsylvania but he lost the state. The three biggest counties to swing from Kerry to McCain were all in the southwest portion of the state, essentially the part of the state that borders on West Virginia: Beaver, Fayette, and Washington.

Obama won Chester, one of the big four suburban Philadelphia counties, completing his sweep of that area with wins in Bucks, Delaware, and Montgomery. Dauphin County, home to the state capital of Harrisburg, went Democratic for the first time since 1968, as was the case for nearby Berks County.

In the primary of April 22, 2008, Clinton received 54.6% of the vote and Obama received 45.4%.

	2008			**2004**		
	TOTAL	OBAMA	McCAIN	TOTAL	KERRY	BUSH
GENDER						
MALE	46	51	48	47	48	51
FEMALE	54	59	41	53	54	46
AGE						
18–29	18	65	35	21	60	39
30–44	28	51	47	28	48	51
45–64	39	55	43	37	48	52
65+	15	49	50	14	52	48
RACE						
WHITE	81	48	51	82	45	54
BLACK	13	95	5	13	84	16
HISPANIC	4	72	28	3	72	28
PARTY						
DEMOCRAT	44	90	10	41	85	15
REPUBLICAN	37	13	87	39	11	89
♦ *INDEPENDENT*	**18**	**58**	**39**	20	58	41
IDEOLOGY						
LIBERAL	23	91	9	22	88	12
MODERATE	50	58	41	48	57	43
CONSERVATIVE	27	19	79	30	13	86
EDUCATION BY RACE						
WHITE, COLLEGE DEGREE	44	52	47	31	44	56
♦ *WHITE, NO COLLEGE DEGREE*	**37**	**42**	**57**	**52**	**45**	**55**
NONWHITE, COLLEGE DEGREE	7	81	18	5	72	28
NONWHITE, NO COLLEGE DEGREE	13	89	10	12	79	20
RELIGION						
PROTESTANT	48	50	49	50	45	55
WHITE PROTESTANT	36	37	61	38	36	63
BLACK PROTESTANT	10	93	7	8	81	19
CATHOLIC	32	48	52	35	51	49
♦ *WHITE CATHOLIC*	**29**	**46**	**54**	**30**	**48**	**52**
HISPANIC CATHOLIC	2	–	–	1	–	–
JEWISH	4	–	–	2	–	–
OTHER	5	81	16	6	75	24
NONE	11	84	15	8	69	29
NEW VOTER						
YES	11	60	40	16	59	41
NO	89	55	44	84	49	51
INCOME						
LESS THAN $50,000	36	62	37	52	54	45
$50–100,000	34	52	47	33	49	50
MORE THAN $100,000	30	52	47	15	42	58

	2008			**2004**		
	TOTAL	OBAMA	McCAIN	TOTAL	KERRY	BUSH
UNION MEMBER						
♦ *YES*	**15**	**68**	**32**	**16**	**63**	**37**
NO	85	54	45	84	47	52
WORRIED ABOUT THE						
NATIONAL ECONOMY						
WORRIED	89	58	41	–	–	–
NOT WORRIED	10	40	60	–	–	–
WAR IN IRAQ						
APPROVE	36	13	87	49	16	84
DISAPPROVE	63	80	19	45	89	11
BUSH JOB						
APPROVE	25	10	89	50	8	92
DISAPPROVE	74	71	27	48	95	5
WILL JOHN McCAIN						
CONTINUE BUSH'S						
POLICIES	53	90	9	–	–	–
MOVE IN A DIFFERENT						
DIRECTION	44	14	85	–	–	–
CANDIDATE QUALITIES						
VALUES	33	40	58	–	–	–
CHANGE	35	91	8	–	–	–
EXPERIENCE	18	4	96	–	–	–
CARES	9	81	18	–	–	–
CONTACTED BY						
McCAIN'S CAMPAIGN						
YES	39	42	57	–	–	–
NO	57	64	35	–	–	–
CONTACTED BY						
OBAMA'S CAMPAIGN						
YES	50	71	28	–	–	–
NO	46	37	61	–	–	–
HAS THE RIGHT						
EXPERIENCE						
McCAIN DOES	61	35	65	–	–	–
McCAIN DOES NOT	38	91	7	–	–	–
OBAMA DOES	56	92	8	–	–	–
OBAMA DOES NOT	43	10	88	–	–	–
OBAMA'S POSITIONS						
ON THE ISSUES ARE						
TOO LIBERAL	41	8	91	–	–	–
TOO CONSERVATIVE	3	–	–	–	–	–
ABOUT RIGHT	53	95	4	–	–	–
DEMOCRATIC HILLARY						
CLINTON SUPPORTER						
	16	79	20	–	–	–

During the Democratic primary battle, Barack Obama had trouble winning certain groups of white voters who might have felt uncomfortable voting for an African-American candidate. Support from white working-class voters and white Catholics helped Hillary Clinton win Pennsylvania during the primaries.

In the general election, working-class whites—those who have no college degree—made up 37% of voters in Pennsylvania. This compares with just about one in five voters, 18%, nationwide, making the state a key target for McCain. But the white working-class vote was similar to four years ago. McCain beat Obama by 57% to 42%; four years ago Bush won the group 55% to Kerry's 45%, giving McCain no major advantage among a group that was commonly thought to be more race sensitive. And Kerry won the state despite this. The white Catholic vote was also almost the same as four years ago. Union voters made up slightly more than one-quarter of the electorate and voted for Obama, 62% to 37%. It was among union members, in particular, that McCain was hoping to cut into Obama's margin.

Obama was able to keep a large majority of Democrats who wanted Hillary Clinton to get the nomination. Those Clinton supporters stayed true to the party and gave Obama 79% of their votes; just 20% of them voted for McCain. That's approximately the number estimated to be Republicans who reregistered as Democrats to participate in the April 2008 primary. Independents gave Obama a 19 point margin, 58% to 39%.

FORGET IT, THE SUBURBS ARE JUST TOO BLUE FOR THE GOP TO WIN

McCain had quite the challenge on his hands when he made Pennsylvania his do-or-die state. He needed to figure out how to win over working-class white voters in *bigger* numbers than Bush did in 2004, while also trying to cut into Obama's likely margins in the Philadelphia suburbs. It turns out that wooing one type of voters didn't help woo the other. The campaign did a pretty good job at trying to take advantage of Obama's inability to connect with working-class white voters. Flipping the three counties in the southwest portion of the state—a.k.a. Joe the Plumber country—showed McCain did well on that front. But he was clobbered in the eastern part of the state. In fact, the loss wasn't just in the suburbs, it went all the way north to Scranton, a portion of the state where Obama was supposed to underperform.

The key mistake McCain made in Pennsylvania was treating the state as if it were made up of nothing but blue-collar voters. In fact, Pennsylvania, demographically, looks more like a Northeast or New England state than the industrial Midwest. Fully half of the state's electorate were college graduates, putting it closer to the education level in states that border it to the east (New York and New Jersey) and south (Maryland), than states that border it to the southwest (West Virginia) and west (Ohio).

It used to be said the key for Democrats was to win the east (Philadelphia) and west (Pittsburgh) and concede the middle. But the east has grown a lot bigger than just the Philadelphia area and now Obama has shown how a Democrat can simply run up huge margins in the entire eastern half of the state and win statewide. Republicans aren't going to win statewide in Pennsylvania anytime soon if they don't start making up for lost ground in the suburbs. In fact, this McCain deficit in the Philadelphia suburbs was mirrored in suburban communities all over the country; it wasn't just concentrated in Pennsylvania.

Democrats also had a huge advantage in party registration, one that some Republican strategists feared would make a Republican victory in the state nearly impossible. Democrats represented 44% of the 2008 electorate, making it among the most Democratic states in the Union. The only states with a higher Democratic Party identification that McCain carried were West Virginia and Kentucky. (That's a legacy relic in those two states, not some sort of sign that Republicans are winning over Democrats in general.) If anything, Pennsylvania has a Democratic tilt to it that looks a lot like the rest of the Northeast and not like an industrial Midwestern state.

Democrats netted another House seat in the state, giving them an 11 to 8 advantage in the state's 19 seat U.S. House delegation. While a three seat advantage may not seem like a lot, consider that Republicans controlled the entire redistricting process in Pennsylvania in 2001, and Democrats have found success based on a Republican-drawn map.

In 2010, the true blue nature of the state will be tested if moderate Republican Senator Arlen Specter seeks reelection. Specter is a relic of sorts in the U.S. Senate as the moderate wing of the Republican Party has been shrinking dramatically in these early twenty-first-century years. A Specter loss in 2010 would cement Pennsylvania's status as a Democratic stronghold. Should Specter prove that he can still win, it will at least give the GOP a blueprint for how to make a comeback in a state that is probably not nearly as competitive as its reputation.

WISCONSIN
An Obama-Illinois Phenomenon or a Trend?
10 ELECTORAL VOTES

Wisconsin was primarily Republican through the 1920s and voted Democratic through the Second World War. Then the state voted Republican most of the time through 1984. Since then, Wisconsin has voted Democratic, although the last two elections were very close. And 2008 makes six Democratic victories in a row. Wisconsin is one of just seven states to have voted Democratic six elections in a row and counting. The other six are Massachusetts, Minnesota, New York, Oregon, Rhode Island, and Washington. The Wisconsin polls showed a wide Obama lead, which narrowed after the conventions. Then, in October, the lead widened and the polls underestimated the final margin.

	2008		2004	
Obama	1,677,211	56.2%	Kerry	49.7%
McCain	1,262,393	42.3%	Bush	49.3%
Other candidates	43,813			
	2,983,417			

Note: 100% 3,621 of 3,621 precincts; 100% 72 of 72 counties. Chart based on final, official vote totals.

Turnout declined by 2.3 percentage points in Wisconsin in 2008, as compared with 2004, but the state still votes at one of the highest rates in the nation: 72.5% of the voting eligible population.

Wisconsin was one of the closest states in 2000 and 2004, with the Democrats winning both, but only by 4,000 votes in 2000 and 12,000 votes in 2004.

The total number of voters did not change much, but the outcome was certainly different. Obama won by 414,818 votes in the state. And there were only 17 counties where the vote totals increased. The picture for the GOP was worse: in each of the 72 Wisconsin counties, the total GOP vote for president in 2008 was lower than the vote for Bush in 2004. And 32 counties flipped from Bush in 2004 to Obama in 2008.

In the primary of February 19, 2008, Obama received 58.1% of the vote and Clinton received 40.8%.

	2008			**2004**		
	TOTAL	OBAMA	McCAIN	TOTAL	KERRY	BUSH
GENDER						
MALE	49	53	46	47	46	52
FEMALE	51	60	39	53	53	46
AGE						
♦ *18–29*	**22**	**64**	**35**	**20**	**57**	**41**
30–44	29	54	44	30	44	56
45–64	35	57	42	36	50	49
65+	14	50	50	14	54	46
RACE						
WHITE	89	54	45	90	47	52
BLACK	5	91	9	5	86	14
HISPANIC	3	–	–	2	51	47
PARTY						
DEMOCRAT	39	95	5	35	93	7
REPUBLICAN	33	10	89	38	8	91
♦ *INDEPENDENT*	**29**	**58**	**39**	**27**	**53**	**45**
IDEOLOGY						
LIBERAL	23	91	8	20	87	12
♦ *MODERATE*	**47**	**63**	**36**	**49**	**56**	**44**
CONSERVATIVE	31	20	79	32	17	82
EDUCATION BY RACE						
WHITE, COLLEGE DEGREE	35	56	44	33	50	49
WHITE, NO COLLEGE DEGREE	54	52	47	57	46	53
NONWHITE, COLLEGE DEGREE	3	–	–	3	–	–
NONWHITE, NO COLLEGE DEGREE	8	81	18	7	71	28
RELIGION						
PROTESTANT	45	47	53	50	40	59
WHITE PROTESTANT	42	43	56	44	38	61
WHITE EVANGELICAL PROTESTANT	23	30	69	–	–	–
WHITE PROTESTANT, NOT EVANGELICAL	19	59	40	–	–	–
BLACK PROTESTANT	2	–	–	2	–	–
CATHOLIC	33	53	47	32	52	48
WHITE CATHOLIC	30	52	48	29	50	50
HISPANIC CATHOLIC	1	–	–	1	–	–
JEWISH	0	–	–	1	–	–
OTHER	6	81	19	7	66	32
NONE	15	77	20	11	74	26
NEW VOTER						
♦ *YES*	**10**	**68**	**31**	**10**	**58**	**41**
NO	90	54	45	90	49	50

(*continued*)

135

	2008			**2004**		
	TOTAL	OBAMA	McCAIN	TOTAL	KERRY	BUSH
INCOME						
LESS THAN $50,000	42	65	35	51	55	44
$50–100,000	39	52	47	36	46	53
MORE THAN $100,000	19	48	51	13	40	60
UNION MEMBER						
YES	14	64	35	17	62	37
NO	86	54	45	83	48	52
WORRIED ABOUT THE NATIONAL ECONOMY						
WORRIED	90	58	41	–	–	–
NOT WORRIED	10	32	65	–	–	–
WAR IN IRAQ						
APPROVE	39	17	83	53	16	83
♦ *DISAPPROVE*	**59**	**81**	**17**	**44**	**89**	**10**
BUSH JOB						
APPROVE	27	11	89	54	10	89
DISAPPROVE	72	72	27	46	95	4
WILL JOHN McCAIN						
♦ *CONTINUE BUSH'S POLICIES*	**52**	**91**	**8**	–	–	–
MOVE IN A DIFFERENT DIRECTION	45	15	85	–	–	–
CANDIDATE QUALITIES						
VALUES	33	37	62	–	–	–
CHANGE	35	90	10	–	–	–
EXPERIENCE	17	5	94	–	–	–
CARES	11	84	15	–	–	–
CONTACTED BY McCAIN'S CAMPAIGN						
YES	39	47	52	–	–	–
NO	59	61	38	–	–	–
CONTACTED BY OBAMA'S CAMPAIGN						
YES	42	61	38	–	–	–
NO	56	51	47	–	–	–
ATTACKED OTHER CANDIDATE UNFAIRLY						
McCAIN DID	70	65	35	–	–	–
McCAIN DID NOT	28	33	65	–	–	–
OBAMA DID	54	40	59	–	–	–
OBAMA DID NOT	44	75	24	–	–	–
HAS THE RIGHT EXPERIENCE						
McCAIN DOES	62	34	65	–	–	–
McCAIN DOES NOT	37	90	8	–	–	–
OBAMA DOES	55	92	7	–	–	–
OBAMA DOES NOT	44	9	90	–	–	–

Obama was the choice of younger voters in Wisconsin; those 18 to 29 went for the Democrat 64% to 35%. Obama won heavily among first-time voters; 10% said this was the first year they had voted, and they went for Obama by more than two to one.

Obama did well with both sexes. He won among women 60% to 39% and among men 53% to 46%. Of the 47% of voters who called themselves moderates, Obama won 63% to 36%, and of those who called themselves Independents, he won 58% to 39%.

Only 27% approved of the way President Bush is doing his job. Fifty-two percent believed McCain would have continued the policies of Bush as president, and they went for Obama 91% to 8%. Among the 45% who thought McCain would go in different directions than Bush, McCain won 85% to 15%.

Fifty-nine percent of those polled said they disapproved of the war, and they voted for Obama 81% to 17%. Approval of the war was voiced by 39%, and they chose McCain by 83% to 17%. McCain fell short of Bush's results in 2004 among 30- to 44-year-olds in which group McCain got 44% of the vote compared to 56% for Bush.

African-Americans voted for Obama 91% to 9%. White voters went for Obama 54% to 45%.

Obama won among those with family incomes less than $100,000, 59% to 40%. Among those with family income of $100,000 or more, McCain narrowly won 51% to 48%. Seventy percent said McCain attacked Obama unfairly, and they voted for Obama 65% to 35%. Fifty-four percent said Obama attacked McCain unfairly, and they voted for McCain 59% to 40%.

FOR THE GOP, THE REBUILDING PROGRAM STARTS HERE

Talk to a rank-and-file Republican strategist who cares about the future of the Republican Party, and they'll lament the fact that the party ended up so noncompetitive in Wisconsin. After all, Wisconsin is the state where the Republican Party was founded. It must be frustrating for the Republican Party that in the twenty-first century, the party is nowhere to be found in the state where it was founded or in the home state (Illinois) of its first president, Abraham Lincoln.

Wisconsin is part of a new region that many readers probably didn't know existed; it is called the region of Illinois. Much has been made of Obama's skin color and age to explain his success, but one factor that is regularly left out of the analysis is his home state of Illinois. While Illinois itself is not a swing state, it is surrounded by swing states, including Wisconsin, Iowa, Indiana, and Missouri. Obama performed better than a typical Democrat in every one of these four states. Moreover, each state was critical to Obama during the primary season.

In fact, four of Obama's five most important primary or caucus performances came in states that border Illinois. There was his initial victory in Iowa that launched him. That was followed by his narrow win in Missouri on Super Tuesday, which gave Obama some swing-state bragging rights to compete with Clinton's big-state victories. Then came Wisconsin on February 19, 2008, which capped an 11 to 0 post–Super Tuesday winning streak that, in hindsight, cemented Obama's hold on the nomination. Finally, Obama's close finish in Indiana in early May ended whatever hopes Clinton had.

Bottom line: Wisconsin played a very prominent role in Obama's road to the Democratic nomination, and the affection the voters showed him in the primaries carried over into the general. The question for the GOP is whether 2008 is an anomaly or part of a trend in which the state is moving away from the GOP. If one were to graph Republican performance on the presidential and statewide levels over the last 20 years, a strong case could be made this is a trend and that Wisconsin ought to be erased from the battleground map. But if one only examined the election returns in the last 10 years, an argument for competitiveness still could be made.

The Obama coattails stretched down the ballot as Democrats were able to take control of the state assembly for the first time since 1994. In fact, Democrats control all of state government, both U.S. Senate seats, and hold a five to three advantage in the U.S. House delegation. Oh, and this was based on a map that was drawn by the Republicans.

The 2010 campaign could tell us a lot about the GOP's future in the state. With a competitive governor's race on the ballot in conjunction with Democratic Senator Russ Feingold's seat, it's a chance for the state GOP to wake from its slumber. Just winning one of these major two statewide offices would be a start for the party and could help determine whether the state ends up back in the battleground in 2012. Should Democrats hold both major races and if Obama remains as politically strong in this region of Illinois, then it wouldn't be a surprise to see Wisconsin missing from the GOP's initial presidential target list in 2012.

Emerging Battleground States

(5 States)

There are five new states that became potentially competitive in the 2008 election and are showing signs of staying competitive in the years to come. Some were the result of the Obama campaign targeting red states (see Georgia), others were the result of demographic changes (Arizona and Texas), and still others were the result of economic conditions (Montana and Nebraska). But all of these states moved from clearly red or blue into potential battlegrounds. Some became real battlegrounds while others tipped slightly into the battleground category. And in one case, Nebraska, only a part of the state became contested but because of the state's quirky electoral vote rules, it is worth inclusion.

ARIZONA
The Desert Sun Turning State
Purple Instead of Red?

10 ELECTORAL VOTES

Arizona has traditionally voted Republican. In fact, except for 1996, Arizona has voted Republican in every election since 1952. The rapidly changing composition of the population has made Arizona an emerging battleground state. And note that the margin of victory in 2008 represents a home state candidate. Without the presence of John McCain, it is likely Arizona would have been targeted in 2008. The polls showed a very close race but significantly underestimated the final margin.

	2008		2004	
McCain	1,230,111	53.6%	Bush	54.9%
Obama	1,034,707	45.1%	Kerry	44.4%
Other candidates	28,657			
	2,293,475			

Note: 100% 2,239 of 2,239 precincts; 100% 15 of 15 counties. Chart based on on final, official vote totals.

In fast-growing Arizona, turnout was up just under two percentage points to 55.9% of the voting eligible population. But because of the rapid growth, 280,868 more people cast ballots in the presidential race in 2008 than they did in 2004. And 45% of the votes were cast early or by absentee ballot.

No counties flipped in 2008, maintaining the same four Democratic counties and 11 Republican ones, which has been the pattern since Bill Clinton won the state in 1996. The county that counts is Maricopa, casting almost 60% of the votes in the state. This county that includes Phoenix and Tempe gave McCain an 11 point victory in 2008, down from Bush's 15 point margin in 2004. But that edge was about the same as Bush's win over Gore in Maricopa in 2000. In the primary of February 5, 2008, Clinton received 50.4% of the vote and Obama received 42.4%.

	2008			**2004**		
	TOTAL	OBAMA	McCAIN	TOTAL	KERRY	BUSH
GENDER						
MALE	49	45	53	47	41	58
FEMALE	51	45	54	53	47	52
AGE						
◆ *18–29*	17	52	48	15	48	50
◆ *30–44*	28	46	51	28	38	61
45–64	36	42	56	39	47	52
65+	18	43	56	18	43	56
RACE						
◆ *WHITE*	75	40	59	79	41	59
BLACK	4	–	–	2	–	–
◆ *HISPANIC*	16	56	41	12	56	43
PARTY						
DEMOCRAT	32	85	14	30	89	11
◆ *REPUBLICAN*	39	8	92	44	11	89
◆ *INDEPENDENT*	30	51	46	26	52	46
IDEOLOGY						
LIBERAL	21	75	24	19	86	13
MODERATE	42	52	46	43	52	47
CONSERVATIVE	36	17	82	38	15	84
EDUCATION BY RACE						
WHITE, COLLEGE DEGREE	38	41	58	37	48	52
WHITE, NO COLLEGE DEGREE	37	39	60	42	34	65
NONWHITE, COLLEGE DEGREE	9	54	41	7	59	39
NONWHITE, NO COLLEGE DEGREE	16	65	33	14	57	42
RELIGION						
PROTESTANT	55	35	63	53	32	67
WHITE PROTESTANT	44	31	68	45	28	71
WHITE EVANGELICAL PROTESTANT	20	16	84	–	–	–
WHITE PROTESTANT, NOT EVANGELICAL	24	45	53	–	–	–
BLACK PROTESTANT	3	–	–	–	–	–
HISPANIC PROTESTANT	4	–	–	5	44	56
CATHOLIC	24	49	49	23	47	52
WHITE CATHOLIC	15	40	55	15	39	61
HISPANIC CATHOLIC	8	–	–	7	–	–
JEWISH	2	–	–	2	–	–
OTHER	7	–	–	6	–	–
NONE	12	65	32	15	70	29

	2008			**2004**		
	TOTAL	OBAMA	McCAIN	TOTAL	KERRY	BUSH
INCOME						
LESS THAN $50,000	40	51	48	44	51	48
$50–100,000	38	40	60	36	41	58
MORE THAN $100,000	22	45	53	20	43	57
WORRIED ABOUT THE NATIONAL ECONOMY						
WORRIED	82	49	49	–	–	–
NOT WORRIED	16	30	69	–	–	–
WAR IN IRAQ						
APPROVE	42	8	91	55	10	90
DISAPPROVE	55	75	23	42	88	11
BUSH JOB						
APPROVE	37	8	91	57	7	92
♦ *DISAPPROVE*	62	68	30	42	94	5
CANDIDATE QUALITIES						
VALUES	29	31	66	–	–	–
CHANGE	31	86	13	–	–	–
EXPERIENCE	25	7	92	–	–	–
CARES	11	63	36	–	–	–

McCain definitely had a home court advantage as 60% thought favorably of their senator. However, as the Republican on the ticket he was still fighting against the 62% who disapproved of President Bush's job performance.

The Republican share of the electorate was down five points, while Independents were up four points, and Democrats basically held steady. Half of Independents, 51%, voted for Obama, while 46% went for McCain. This was about the same split as it was for Kerry four years ago. But considering that McCain was the state's "Mr. Independent," it was a disappointing result for him.

Most white voters favored McCain. Hispanics increased their share of the vote to 16%, up from 12% in 2004. Obama had a 15 point lead among Hispanic voters, just a couple of points more than Kerry. This was one of the slimmest Democratic increases among Hispanic voters in the country, probably due to McCain's home state advantage. A majority of voters said illegal immigrants should be offered a chance to apply for legal status and not be deported to the country they came from.

McCain and Obama were fairly even among voters in younger age groups, with only those 18–29 breaking for Obama. McCain held slight leads in older age groups. The biggest shifts were in the 30–44 age group, who had swung heavily to Bush four years ago, and started swinging back to the Democrats in this election.

Six in ten said the economy was the most important issue facing the country, and McCain and Obama split those voters evenly. McCain led among those who cited terrorism and energy policy. About four in five Arizonans said they're worried about the direction of the nation's economy in the next year, with most of those saying they're "very worried." Again, they split evenly between McCain and Obama.

OBAMA'S NUMBER ONE 2012 NEW TARGET?

In 2004, John Kerry toyed with targeting Arizona but as things started turning south for him in the Midwest, he pulled out of the state in order to concentrate on the Midwest and Rust Belt battleground states. Obama's campaign spent far fewer days and resources in Arizona in 2008 than Kerry in 2004, which makes Obama's improvement over Kerry all the more remarkable. Never mind the fact that McCain was the favorite son candidate and only won by single digits. No matter how one slices the results, there's plenty of evidence that 2008 is the last time for a while that Arizona will be on the sidelines in a presidential election.

According to the last census, Arizona has the fourth highest Hispanic population percentage-wise in the country. In fact, 10 states have a Hispanic population of 10% or more and Obama carried eight of those states. The only two he missed were Arizona and Texas, two of the five states we've included as emerging battlegrounds.

And it is this growth among Hispanics in general and Democratic dominance among Hispanics specifically that have many analysts convinced Arizona will be a major battleground in 2012.

Demographics in Arizona show the state looks more like the average battleground state than a base Republican state. Nearly half of the state's 2008 electorate, 47%, had a college education. Obama carried every single state (14 plus D.C.) that ranked higher than Arizona on this score. In fact, there were 23 states (plus D.C.) where college-educated voters made up 44% or more of the electorate. Obama carried all but three of those states: Arizona, North Dakota, and Texas. (See a pattern here?)

Then there is the state's ideological makeup compared to the rest of the battlegrounds. Obama carried six states that were *less* liberal than Arizona, including Ohio, Florida, Colorado, and North Carolina. Arizona falls into the range, ideologically, of many of the 2008 battleground states. Compare Arizona's 21% liberal, 42%

moderate, and 36% conservative breakdown to Colorado's 17% liberal, 46% moderate, and 36% conservative.

Hints of this shift in Arizona are emerging down the ballot as well. Democrats now control a majority of the state's eight member U.S. House delegation. It wasn't very long ago when Republicans held a consistent six to two margin. Now, it is the Democrats with a five to three advantage.

But the Republicans still have a built-in advantage: party registration. Republicans have a seven point margin that usually indicates a red state. In fact, Obama only carried one state where Republicans outnumbered Democrats and that was Indiana. In order for Democrats to put Arizona in play, they not only have to sweep Democrats, but they also have to take an even bigger chunk of the Independents than Obama did in 2008. Bottom line: as the 2008 presidential election demonstrates, it is a lot easier to carry a state when you aren't starting off behind in party registration.

Demographically, it appears Arizona is definitely headed for the battleground. But what's not clear is what the state will look like and what issues will matter. Arizona is an incredibly fast-growing state. By 2012, the state will probably be an even bigger electoral power. Right now, it's worth 10 votes in the Electoral College. Most demographers believe the state will pick up at least two congressional seats during the next reapportionment, which takes place in 2011, just one year before the 2012 presidential race.

Arizona's economy had been growing rapidly thanks mostly to a housing boom, based on the population growth. But what happens as the economy slows and the housing crisis persists? Dramatic economic downturns can have wild effects on a state's politics and trying to predict just where Arizona is going to fall on the political spectrum is very difficult.

As for 2010, if John McCain runs for reelection to his Senate seat, then we probably won't get any clues about the competitiveness of this state. But if McCain decides to retire and the Senate seat opens up, strategists will have an opportunity to test just how purple this state is turning going into 2012. One thing is clear, with the emergence of a Democratic resurgence all over the West, an Obama-run Democratic Party will probably do whatever it takes to lay the groundwork for making Arizona a battleground state by 2012.

GEORGIA
A Battleground on My Mind
15 ELECTORAL VOTES

Georgia, from the Civil War through 1960, was Democratic. The reaction to the Democratic-sponsored Civil Rights Act turned the state red. In 1968, Georgia voted for segregationist candidate George Wallace. The only times that Georgia has voted Democratic since is in 1976, 1980, and 1992 when the state supported a Southern Democratic nominee. With a sizable minority population and a changing population, Georgia is edging closer to battleground status. The polls showed a McCain lead that narrowed as the election approached. The small margin was reflected in the poll results.

	2008		2004	
McCain	2,048,744	52.2%	Bush	58.0%
Obama	1,844,137	47.0%	Kerry	41.4%
Other candidates	31,551			
	3,924,432			

Note: 3,303 of 3,303 precincts; 159 of 159 counties. Chart based on final, official vote totals.

Former Republican congressman turned Libertarian nominee Bob Barr won only 28,812 votes in his native state, out of 3.9 million cast. And with that, we've mentioned Bob Barr about one more time than we should have in this analysis. Though it was his presence on the ballot that had Republicans concerned about the state.

There was a major jump in turnout in 2008, rising to 61.1%, up nearly five percentage points from 2004. Georgia tied Maryland for seventh in terms of the biggest increases in turnout over 2004. The number of votes was up by 622,603 votes over 2004. And more than half of all votes, 53%, were cast early or absentee.

In contrast to many other states, the vote totals were up in almost every county.

Out of the state's 159 counties, Obama won 34 and McCain 125. And what is different from other states is that the total number of votes cast in the counties McCain won was up 382,000 from 2004, while the total number of votes in the counties Obama won was up 243,000. This relative advantage of increased turnout for McCain was not the case in other states. Elsewhere, the number of votes was more likely to drop in counties where the GOP won in 2008, but increase in the counties won by the Democrats. If it hadn't been for this phenomenon (perhaps driven by race?), McCain might have lost Georgia.

There were large victories for Obama in DeKalb and Fulton counties, which include Atlanta and the close-in suburbs. Turnout was up in both counties by hefty margins, but that was not just the Obama effect. Turnout was up dramatically in both counties from 2000 to 2004 as well. This is due, at least in part, to a population explosion that's taking place in Georgia.

But in the conservative suburbs north of Atlanta, McCain failed to get the big margins that Bush did, falling from a 35 point edge in 2004 in Cobb County to 9 points in 2008, and from 33 points to 11 points in Gwinett.

Tiny Webster County went Republican in 2008 after voting for Kerry in 2004. But nine relatively small counties did switch to the Democratic candidate in 2008. In the primary of February 5, 2008, Obama received 66.4% of the vote and Clinton received 31.1%.

	2008			2004		
	TOTAL	OBAMA	McCAIN	TOTAL	KERRY	BUSH
GENDER						
MALE	46	40	58	44	38	62
FEMALE	54	54	46	56	44	56
AGE						
♦ *18–29*	14	48	51	19	47	52
30–44	32	56	44	35	42	57
♦ *45–64*	42	42	58	38	38	61
65+	12	46	54	8	33	67
RACE						
WHITE	65	23	76	70	23	76
♦ *BLACK*	30	98	2	25	88	12
HISPANIC	3	–	–	4	–	–
PARTY						
DEMOCRAT	38	91	9	34	87	13
REPUBLICAN	35	6	94	42	3	97
♦ *INDEPENDENT*	28	40	57	24	39	60
IDEOLOGY						
LIBERAL	13	85	14	14	83	17
MODERATE	48	58	41	44	52	47
CONSERVATIVE	39	21	79	41	14	86
EDUCATION BY RACE						
WHITE, COLLEGE DEGREE	31	25	73	–	–	–
WHITE, NO COLLEGE DEGREE	34	22	78	–	–	–
NONWHITE, COLLEGE DEGREE	12	94	6	–	–	–
NONWHITE, NO COLLEGE DEGREE	23	93	7	–	–	–

(continued)

	2008			**2004**		
	TOTAL	OBAMA	McCAIN	TOTAL	KERRY	BUSH
WHITE EVANGELICAL OR BORN-AGAIN						
♦ YES	37	10	89	35	16	84
NO	63	67	32	65	55	45
NEW VOTER						
♦ YES	11	62	37	–	–	–
NO	89	44	55	–	–	–
INCOME						
LESS THAN $50,000	40	58	42	42	54	46
$50–100,000	38	46	53	36	34	66
MORE THAN $100,000	23	38	61	22	29	71
WORRIED ABOUT THE NATIONAL ECONOMY						
WORRIED	83	46	53	–	–	–
NOT WORRIED	17	49	50	–	–	–
BUSH JOB						
APPROVE	38	9	91	59	4	96
DISAPPROVE	60	69	30	41	93	6
CANDIDATE QUALITIES						
VALUES	33	28	71	–	–	–
CHANGE	30	86	13	–	–	–
EXPERIENCE	23	8	92	–	–	–
CARES	11	78	21	–	–	–

African-American turnout as a share of the electorate was up significantly. A full 30% of voters in Georgia were African-American (up five points from the 25% in 2004) and 97% backed Obama. Whites backed McCain by about the same margin they supported Bush in 2004.

McCain led among Independents 53% to 41% and among white Independents 66% to 27%. McCain also captured 28% of those who disapproved of Bush's job performance, a larger share than he won in most states.

One in ten voters were new to the process in 2008, and 62% of them supported Obama while McCain won 37%. As a proportion of the electorate, the under 30 vote actually declined five points from four years ago and their vote was almost evenly split, favoring McCain over Obama 51% to 48%. A bigger generational shift occurred among those in the 30- to 44-year-old age group and among seniors. Both groups were more than 25 points more Democratic. These Gen Xers in Georgia voted for Obama 56% to McCain's 44%, while seniors went for McCain 54% to 46%.

The white Evangelical vote came out strongly for the GOP

ticket, up two points as a share of the electorate to 37%, and voted nine to one for McCain-Palin.

TOO RACIALLY POLARIZED FOR DEMS TO MAKE INROADS?

When the general election began in earnest after the end of the primary race, Georgia was one of a handful of "new" states the Obama campaign was pushing as part of an expanded battleground. This distinction meant that Georgia would get a full share of resources (at least until Labor Day), including TV advertising and ground game resources.

For Team Obama, the thinking in Georgia was twofold: 1) they believed they could dramatically increase the share of African-Americans who would vote via massive voter registration and targeting. 2) Bob Barr's Libertarian candidacy could knock down the winning number from 50% plus 1 to 47% or 48%, a more realistic number for the Obama campaign to hit. As it turns out, the Obama folks, as they proved to be throughout the campaign, were dead-on in what they knew they could get in Georgia, which was 47%. What didn't happen: Barr never caught on as a conservative alternative, even in his home state.

Because Georgia was an on-again, off-again target for the Obama campaign, it's hard to fully appreciate just how "emerging" Georgia is as a battleground state. What if Team Obama had never pulled out of the state? What if the McCain campaign or the Republican Party as a whole had targeted the state sooner than they eventually did? What if McCain hadn't picked Sarah Palin?

There are a lot of unknowns when it comes to the competitiveness of Georgia. McCain lost the Georgia primary even when it was fairly clear he was the presumptive nominee. Had McCain not picked a running mate who was so popular with the base, it's possible GOP turnout in a place like Georgia would have been down and Obama could have closed the five point gap.

Obama never made a stop in the state during the heat of the fall campaign. His presence in a state seemed to make a difference in places like Indiana, Colorado, and Virginia. Could an Obama visit to Atlanta have stoked turnout even more?

Then there's the issue of whether African-American turnout was truly maximized. Georgia is one of three states (Louisiana and Mississippi are the other two) where Democratic demographers have argued that maximizing the registration and turnout of

African-Americans could turn this red state blue. There's a lot of evidence that suggests African-American turnout was maximized. Georgia ranked second among states in African-American turnout with 30% of the state's electorate in 2008 being black. Only Mississippi (and D.C., by the way) had a higher turnout at 33% and 56% respectively. Based on the 2006 U.S. census estimate, the 30% turnout figure matches the population breakdown. So it's hard to make the case that somehow African-Americans undervoted.

Ideologically, the state looks more like a red state than a battleground state as only 13% of voters describe themselves as "liberal," compared to 39% who call themselves "conservative." The most "conservative" state Obama carried was North Carolina, which featured 37% of the electorate calling themselves conservative. More striking is the fact that Georgia is the second least "liberal" state at 13%, with only Alabama featuring fewer liberal voters.

But if you examined Georgia based on the amount of voters who were college-educated, the state would look more like a swing state. At 43% of the electorate, Georgia's college-educated turnout puts it in the swing state range. Obama carried 20 of the 23 states in 2008 that featured a college-educated electorate of 44% or more.

Georgia is experiencing a population boom that's been ongoing for a couple decades, and it's these new voters that the Democrats will have to hope to woo in order to make up the last three points they need to turn this state blue. Perhaps it's the surprisingly fast-growing Hispanic population, or the nonnative white voters moving into the state for jobs, which could turn the tide.

As it stands now, there's more evidence that Georgia will stay red in the next election than turn purple and become a true battleground. But because of the growth factor and because the state will gain at least one more congressional seat by 2012 (which means one more electoral vote), the folks charged with setting up Obama's reelection apparatus will likely spend more time cultivating Georgia and attempting to keep it just as competitive, if not more so, in 2012.

The Republicans, led by former Christian Coalition head Ralph Reed, built a very strong state party, the fruits of which were seen in 2002 when the GOP pulled two major upsets in the race for governor and U.S. Senate. The strength the GOP showed that year has paid dividends for the party ever since, as the party has continued to dominate local elections. The 2010 campaign for governor could tell us a lot about how competitive the Democrats will be in statewide elections going forward.

MONTANA
Big Sky, Big Battleground
3 ELECTORAL VOTES

Montana has been reliably Republican, voting for only two Democrats since 1952. But the politics of the state seem to have changed in recent years as Obama made a surprisingly strong race in this state. While some polls actually had Obama ahead in Montana, most showed a very narrow McCain lead through the campaign and the polls correctly predicted the narrow McCain final margin. Montana is one of just three states featuring two Democratic U.S. senators and a Democratic governor that wasn't carried by Obama. The other two were Arkansas and West Virginia.

	2008		2004	
McCain	242,763	49.5%	Bush	59.1%
Obama	231,667	47.3%	Kerry	38.6%
Other candidates	15,679			
	490,109			

Note: 863 of 863 precincts; 56 of 56 counties. Chart based on final, official vote totals.

Ron Paul got 10,638 votes or 2.2% of the vote here, proving the state still has a Libertarian streak, and making McCain's margin as small as it was.

Turnout was up about 1.5 percentage points to an estimated 65.9% of the voting eligible population. Nearly two in five of the ballots were cast early or via absentee voting.

Seven of Montana's 56 counties switched to the Democratic side of the ledger in the 2008 presidential election, and most of Obama's county wins were by narrow margins.

Gallatin (home of Bozeman) swung from a 15 point GOP victory in 2004 to a three point Obama win in 2008. In Lewis and Clark County (where Helena is located), Bush won by 12 points in 2004, compared to a six point Democratic win this time. Targeting such areas as college campuses, the Obama campaign did well in Missoula County, where the state university is located, with the 2,994 vote margin four years ago expanding to a 15,788 vote victory. In the primary of June 3, 2008, Obama received 56.4% of the vote and Clinton received 41.2%.

	2008			**2004**		
	TOTAL	OBAMA	McCAIN	TOTAL	KERRY	BUSH
GENDER						
MALE	49	44	53	51	41	57
♦ *FEMALE*	**51**	**51**	**47**	**49**	**38**	**58**
AGE						
18–29	22	61	37	21	43	52
30–44	23	36	60	23	29	69
45–64	37	47	52	41	39	59
65+	18	45	49	15	56	39
RACE						
WHITE	90	45	52	95	39	58
BLACK	0	–	–	2	–	–
HISPANIC	4	–	–	1	–	–
PARTY						
DEMOCRAT	33	92	7	32	78	21
REPUBLICAN	33	10	89	39	3	95
♦ *INDEPENDENT*	**35**	**41**	**53**	**29**	**46**	**46**
IDEOLOGY						
LIBERAL	21	90	8	18	77	19
♦ *MODERATE*	**46**	**56**	**41**	**46**	**48**	**49**
CONSERVATIVE	34	10	87	36	11	86
EDUCATION BY RACE						
WHITE, COLLEGE DEGREE	38	48	50	–	–	–
WHITE, NO COLLEGE DEGREE	52	43	53	–	–	–
NONWHITE, COLLEGE DEGREE	3	–	–	–	–	–
NONWHITE, NO COLLEGE DEGREE	8	–	–	–	–	–
WHITE EVANGELICAL OR BORN-AGAIN						
YES	32	23	75	29	19	78
NO	68	59	38	71	48	49
INCOME						
♦ *LESS THAN $50,000*	**50**	**56**	**41**	**61**	**44**	**53**
$50–100,000	37	41	56	29	33	65
MORE THAN $100,000	14	42	57	10	33	64
WORRIED ABOUT THE NATIONAL ECONOMY						
WORRIED	85	50	47	–	–	–
NOT WORRIED	13	33	66	–	–	–
BUSH JOB						
APPROVE	37	6	93	56	8	91
DISAPPROVE	63	71	25	39	84	10

	2008			**2004**		
	TOTAL	OBAMA	McCAIN	TOTAL	KERRY	BUSH
CANDIDATE QUALITIES						
VALUES	32	28	70	–	–	–
CHANGE	31	92	6	–	–	–
EXPERIENCE	20	4	94	–	–	–
CARES	11	64	29	–	–	–

In just four years, women showed a significant swing in their preference for president. In 2004, 58% backed Bush, while only 38% voted for Kerry. In 2008, they split their vote almost evenly with 51% of women voting for Obama and 47% voting for McCain. Men backed McCain almost as strongly as they had backed Bush.

Montana is not as red as people think; a third are Democrats, a third Republicans, and 35% are Independents. (They've elected a Democratic governor and two Democratic senators. Democrats control the state house and almost split the state senate. The state's lone congressman is Republican.) About half, 46%, describe themselves as moderate rather than liberal or conservative. In 2008, Independents shifted 12 points more to the GOP side than they had four years ago.

Economic worries are the biggest issue for Montana voters. More than eight in ten are worried about the direction of the nation's economy in the next year, which was of particular concern to those earning less than $50,000 a year. These voters switched support in 2008 as more than half, 56%, voted for Obama and 41% voted for McCain. Four years ago, 53% of them voted for Bush.

About nine in ten voters who felt the most important quality in a president is that he can bring about change voted for Obama. He also got the votes of about two-thirds of those who said it's important that a presidential candidate "cares about people like me."

More than a third of voters said they had been impressed by Barack Obama's visits to the state.

Nine in ten voters who said experience was important voted for McCain, and he also was supported by about two-thirds of those who said it was important that the presidential candidate share their values.

The National Rifle Association (NRA) told Montana voters that Obama was a "poster child of the extremist, elitist gun-control movement," while Governor Brian Schweitzer, a Democrat, told them Obama "ain't ever going to take your gun away." Gun rights are an important issue in the state as 75% of voting households own a gun. McCain won these voters 57% to Obama's 40%. Among the 25% of voters in households not owning a firearm, Obama won by a 70% to 28% margin.

TOO CLOSE NOT TO TARGET

Early on, the Obama campaign believed it could put Montana in play. For one thing, there was a belief inside the campaign's Chicago headquarters that the Libertarian candidacy of Bob Barr would do well in this state, which has a history of giving a small but sizable chunk of support to Libertarian candidates. It turns out, of course, that it wasn't Barr who did well in Montana but Ron Paul, whose supporters got him on the ballot here.

But what made Montana so enticing to the Obama campaign team was the fact that it wouldn't take a big turnout of voters to flip the state. And they were right. Obama lost the state by a mere 11,000 votes. Only the raw vote in Missouri was closer.

Obama spent a lot of time cultivating his chances in the state while McCain's campaign decided to simply let the state be. The assumption by McCain's folks was, "If we're losing Montana, we've lost the election." But that wasn't the assumption the Obama folks made. The campaign made a surprising number of stops in the state, including one just before Obama made his way to Denver to officially accept the Democratic nomination.

Obama was also helped by the very long primary campaign. Montana's primary was on the last day of the Democratic primary season. And when given the choice of campaigning in Montana or South Dakota, Team Obama decided to spend more time in Montana since they figured they'd win the state primary and that time spent in the state could pay dividends for the general. It turned out the Obama folks were right on both counts as the race in Montana got close enough at the very end that the Republican National Committee decided to buy TV time to hold off the late Democratic surge.

The campaign's dominance on the radio airwaves was one other key advantage that paid dividends for Obama in Montana. While much has been made of Obama's TV ad budget, the amount of ad time he purchased on radio has been largely overlooked. But as veterans of Montana campaigns know, radio can be more effective than TV in this state whose voters spend a lot of time in their cars.

Of course, it wasn't just numbers that lured Team Obama into the state; it was the recent success of the Democratic Party. In a very short period of time, the Democrats, down the ballot at least, have shifted this state from deep red in the mid- to late-1990s to fairly blue. The state has a very popular two-term governor who won reelection in 2008 by a huge margin, two Democratic U.S. senators, and split control of the state legislature. Republicans won control of the state senate in 2008, but Democrats nabbed control of the state house.

Bottom line: Montana is a very competitive two-party state down the ballot and, at least in 2008, proved to be a competitive two-party state on the presidential level as well.

NEBRASKA
Omaha or Obama-ha?
5 ELECTORAL VOTES

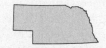

Nebraska is strongly Republican as it has not voted Democratic since the election of 1964. But Nebraska and Maine are the only two states that split electoral votes by the winner of the congressional district. And, for the very first time, the losing candidate in the state won an electoral vote. On a statewide basis, the polls showed a significant McCain lead throughout the campaign. But the public polls underestimated Obama's strength in the 2nd Congressional District.

	2008		2004	
McCain	452,979	56.5%	Bush	65.9%
Obama	333,319	41.6%	Kerry	32.7%
Other candidates	14,983			
	801,281			

Note: 100% 1,708 of 1,708 precincts; 100% 93 of 93 counties. Chart based on final, official vote totals.

Obama won one electoral vote because of the split electoral vote system. Turnout slid just about half a percentage point to 62.5% of the voting eligible population. One in five voters voted early.

The GOP won the state, but it was not pretty. Republican vote declined in every county in Nebraska, compared to 2004. This is an issue Republicans are experiencing all over the Plains and Midwest.

Democratic votes rose by 33,480 votes in Douglas County, home to Omaha. And it was up 10,000 voters or more in Lancaster and Sarpy. Neither Douglas nor Lancaster had voted Democratic since 1968.

And it was in the 2nd Congressional District, made up of Douglas and Sarpy, where Obama snared that solo electoral vote by a 3,313 vote margin, just over one percentage point, and potentially forever changed the battleground map yet again. In the caucus of February 9, 2008, Obama received 67.6% of the vote and Clinton received 32.2%.

	2008			2004		
	TOTAL	OBAMA	McCAIN	TOTAL	KERRY	BUSH
GENDER						
MALE	47	43	55	48	33	66
FEMALE	53	40	58	52	34	66
AGE						
♦ *18–29*	17	54	43	17	38	60
30–44	27	39	60	25	27	72

	2008			**2004**		
	TOTAL	OBAMA	McCAIN	TOTAL	KERRY	BUSH
45–64	38	39	60	41	34	64
65+	18	38	61	17	36	64
RACE						
WHITE	92	39	59	95	33	66
BLACK	4	–	–	2	–	–
HISPANIC	2	–	–	2	–	–
PARTY						
DEMOCRAT	29	84	16	24	80	18
REPUBLICAN	48	11	88	53	5	95
INDEPENDENT	22	51	43	22	50	46
IDEOLOGY						
LIBERAL	17	78	21	13	83	16
MODERATE	48	50	48	46	41	57
CONSERVATIVE	36	13	85	41	8	91
EDUCATION BY RACE						
WHITE, COLLEGE DEGREE	39	44	55	–	–	–
WHITE, NO COLLEGE DEGREE	53	36	62	–	–	–
NONWHITE, COLLEGE DEGREE	3	–	–	–	–	–
NONWHITE, NO COLLEGE DEGREE	6	–	–	–	–	–
WHITE EVANGELICAL OR BORN-AGAIN						
YES	31	25	74	31	18	81
NO	69	49	50	69	40	59
INCOME						
LESS THAN $50,000	42	46	52	47	34	65
$50–100,000	42	40	59	39	36	63
MORE THAN $100,000	16	38	60	14	29	70
WORRIED ABOUT THE NATIONAL ECONOMY						
WORRIED	88	43	56	–	–	–
NOT WORRIED	11	26	72	–	–	–
BUSH JOB						
APPROVE	38	9	90	65	5	95
♦ *DISAPPROVE*	**61**	**61**	**37**	**34**	**92**	**7**

While McCain won, Obama was able to improve over Kerry's performance across the board. The 18–29 share of the electorate did not increase but did swing 33 points more Democratic in 2008, favoring Obama over McCain 54% to 43%.

Eighty-eight percent were worried about the direction of the national economy and 56% of these voters went with the GOP.

McCain was also able to garner the support of 37% who disapproved of Bush's job performance.

Going forward, if the 2nd Congressional District ends up as competitive as it was in 2008, look for more extensive study of that electorate.

WHAT WILL HAPPEN WHEN THE GOP TRULY ENGAGES?

While the Republicans tried to pretend to be dismissive of the Obama campaign's rhetoric about targeting places like Montana and North Carolina (two states the party finally conceded would be competitive), the party truly was dismissive of the Obama camp's efforts to target one electoral vote in Nebraska.

And what did the Obama folks prove: half of politics is showing up and the Obama campaign showed up in Omaha, while the McCain camp did not. Is that the sole explanation for Obama's win? No, but it's an important one. Consider the following things about the one vote Obama won in Nebraska.

1) Omaha is a media market that bleeds into western Iowa. Obama started campaigning in Iowa in early 2007 and ran TV ads throughout the entire state, including buying time in Omaha.

2) Omaha is home to virtually all of the state's African-American population. While they are 4% of Nebraska's population, African-Americans make up nearly 13% of the population in Douglas County (home of Omaha).

3) Warren Buffett, perhaps Omaha's most famous living resident, supported Obama, and that intangible couldn't have hurt.

Nebraska, taken in whole, is not an emerging battleground state. But because of the state's quirky rules, which split their electoral votes by congressional district, the state won't be totally ignored in the future. In fact, don't be surprised if Obama's success in winning one vote out of very red Nebraska leads other either very red or very blue states to consider similar proposals. Republicans in California have attempted to rally support for a referendum that, if passed, would split California's electoral votes by congressional district. The Democratic Party out there has had success in stopping that movement, but who knows if Nebraska's results will motivate more states to ponder this change in their laws.

As many veterans of the 2000 presidential election are aware, the federal government does not mandate how states split their electoral votes. And as more states attempt to garner the attention of the presidential campaign, many changes are possible.

For the time being, Nebraska is now part of the battleground (sort of). At least Omaha is in the battleground. And, who knows, the state's 1st Congressional District, which mostly encompasses Lincoln, is not *that* much more Republican than the 2nd. One thing we've learned over the years is when a state is treated like a battleground, voters in that state suddenly find themselves acting like swing voters.

TEXAS
Maybe Not Today, Maybe Not Tomorrow, but Someday?
34 ELECTORAL VOTES

Texas went Democratic most of the time from after the Civil War until 1976. Since 1980, however, Texas has been Republican. Some of this may be due to the fact that a native Bush was on the ticket in all those elections except for 1996. The changing population is likely to make this state more competitive. The polls showed a significant McCain lead throughout the campaign and correctly predicted the final margin.

	2008		2004	
McCain	**4,479,328**	**55.5%**	Bush	61.1%
Obama	**3,528,633**	**43.7%**	Kerry	38.2%
Other candidates	**69,834**			
	8,077,795			

Note: 100% 8,466 of 8,466 precincts; 100% 254 of 254 counties. Chart based on final, official vote totals.

Texas is home to George W. Bush and gave him two big victories in 2000 and 2004. Obama cut the margin but still did not make it close in 2008, but there were many changes in the state's voting patterns. First, turnout was up about a point in terms of voting eligible population to 54.5%. But the total number of votes was up much more due to population growth in the state, rising more than 667,000 since 2004, quite a change for a state that was not a battleground in any shape or form.

Second, early and absentee voting passed 60% of the total in 2008, making Election Day quieter than one might expect in many precincts. If one were to map out the early voting, one would notice that from Washington state south through Nevada to Arizona and east to Colorado and Texas, there's a solid bloc of states that now have more votes cast before Election Day than on Election Day.

Eleven of the state's 254 counties switched to voting Democratic in 2008 from 2004. And following the pattern of Obama's support across the country, three of the biggest counties in the state with large urban areas switched: Harris (Houston), Dallas (Dallas), and Bexar (San Antonio).

Turnout was up in all three counties, as it was in 2004 over 2000. But this time it was the Democratic vote that soared, while the total number of Republican votes in each county fell.

And finally, in McLennan County, where Bush maintains a home in Crawford, McCain did win an easy victory by a 62% to 38% margin. But turnout was virtually unchanged in the county as the GOP vote dropped by more than 3,000, while the Democratic rose by a similar amount. In the primary of March 4, 2008, Clinton received 50.9% of the vote and Obama received 47.4%. And in the caucus, also of March 4, 2008, Obama received 56.2% of the vote and Clinton received 43.7%. Texas holds both a Democratic primary and caucus on the same day.

	2008			**2004**		
	TOTAL	OBAMA	McCAIN	TOTAL	KERRY	BUSH
GENDER						
MALE	47	39	59	45	40	60
FEMALE	53	47	52	55	37	63
AGE						
♦ *18–29*	16	54	45	20	41	59
30–44	31	46	52	29	31	68
45–64	39	41	58	40	37	62
65+	14	32	66	11	48	52
RACE						
♦ *WHITE*	63	26	73	66	25	74
BLACK	13	98	2	12	83	17
♦ *HISPANIC*	20	63	35	20	50	49
PARTY						
DEMOCRAT	33	89	10	32	90	10
REPUBLICAN	34	6	93	43	3	97
INDEPENDENT	33	36	62	24	31	67
IDEOLOGY						
LIBERAL	15	86	12	14	68	32
MODERATE	39	53	45	40	51	48
♦ *CONSERVATIVE*	46	21	78	45	17	83
EDUCATION BY RACE						
WHITE, COLLEGE DEGREE	33	25	74	–	–	–
WHITE, NO COLLEGE DEGREE	30	26	72	–	–	–
NONWHITE, COLLEGE DEGREE	14	70	29	–	–	–
NONWHITE, NO COLLEGE DEGREE	23	77	23	–	–	–
WHITE EVANGELICAL OR BORN-AGAIN						
♦ *YES*	34	16	83	–	–	–
NO	67	57	42	–	–	–

(continued)

	2008			**2004**		
	TOTAL	OBAMA	McCAIN	TOTAL	KERRY	BUSH
INCOME						
LESS THAN $50,000	37	56	42	44	50	50
$50–100,000	35	38	61	39	34	65
MORE THAN $100,000	29	34	65	17	22	78
WORRIED ABOUT THE NATIONAL ECONOMY						
WORRIED	81	46	53	–	–	–
NOT WORRIED	18	39	59	–	–	–
BUSH JOB						
APPROVE	41	6	93	64	6	94
DISAPPROVE	58	71	27	36	94	6

John McCain did not do as well as George Bush did among Hispanics and young voters. Still, he won by commanding margins among those over 65, conservatives, white men, white women, and white Evangelicals.

The youth share of the electorate was down, while the senior share was up, and those voters swung in opposite directions. Texans under 30 swung 27 points from four years ago to give majority support to Obama, 54%, while seniors moved the other way. In 2004, they split their vote almost evenly between Bush and Kerry, 52% to 48%. In 2008, two-thirds voted for McCain.

While Obama didn't do particularly well among the 63% of voters in Texas who are white, he did better than either John Kerry or Al Gore. There was no notable shift in the racial composition of those who came out to vote in Texas. But Obama did increase the Democratic margins among both blacks and Hispanics by more than 25 points.

In Texas, there's a seven point gender gap with 59% of men supporting McCain and only 52% of women.

THE GOP'S NIGHTMARE SCENARIO

How red is Texas? That's a question strategists from both parties are trying to figure out. In 2012 (barring a George P. Bush election in Texas somewhere or a Jeb Bush candidacy for president), there will not be a Bush in office or a Bush on the Texas ballot. It will be the first pure test of whether the Republican Party is stronger than Bush or whether the Bush brand is stronger than the GOP.

Demographically, it's pretty clear that Texas is going to be a battleground state in the next 10 years. The question is whether it will be in the next four years. On paper, one can see that, with *a lot* of care and feeding, Texas could be made competitive by the Democrats. But it would be very expensive, and it's not clear whether there is a payoff for the party in 2012.

Like Georgia, there's data that proves Texas is moving to the battleground, and there's data that indicates it may be further away than some might believe.

On the battleground side of the argument is this fact: of the 15 largest Hispanic turnout states, Obama carried 13 of the 15. The only two he missed were Arizona and Texas. And Texas had the second highest Hispanic turnout; only New Mexico (with 41% of the electorate calling themselves Hispanic) reported a higher Hispanic proportion of the electorate in 2008. Texas is also among the top 15 states in African-American turnout. In fact, of the four states that featured double-digit Hispanic and black electorates, Obama carried three of them (California, Florida, and Nevada); the lone exception was Texas.

Finally, on the battleground side of the argument is the fact that Obama carried every single state that featured a higher college-educated electorate than Texas. At 47%, Texas is in the upper half of states when it comes to college-educated voters. Overall, Obama carried 20 of the 23 states that featured an electorate with at least 44% of college-educated voters. The three he lost were Arizona, North Dakota, and Texas. Two of these three states are in our emerging battleground section.

But while there is a lot of evidence on that side of the argument, there's still plenty of reasons to consider Texas a red state. For instance, ideologically, the state looks more red than purple.

Texas is the eighth least "liberal" state and McCain carried the top 17 least liberal states. Texas falls smack in the middle of the list of 17 states. Moreover, Texas is the fourth most "conservative" state, trailing only Alabama, Utah, and Mississippi in the percentage of voters who called themselves conservative in the 2008 election.

Finally, there's the fact that Obama received only 26% of the white vote in Texas. Consider that Obama didn't carry a single state where he didn't receive at least 35% of the white vote. That's a lot of ground for Obama (or any Democrat) to make up among white voters in order to turn this state competitive.

The 2010 election cycle is going to be a real test for the Democratic Party. There will be plenty of opportunities to prove they are not dead in the state. If they can win the governor's race (or even come very close) and pick off a couple of statewide down-ballot races, they could be on their way to making this a competitive two-party state again.

The state's growing like crazy and becoming less white, which means it will demographically end up becoming less Republican (unless Hispanics swing dramatically toward the Republicans). But the question is: how fast is this state moving? Did Bush mask the movement or not? Consider that the last time a Bush was not on the Texas ballot or in office was 1976. Actually, if you exclude a couple of years in the early 1970s, you'd have to go back to the 1962 election cycle to find an election year in Texas without a Bush in office or on the ballot. The 2010 and 2012 election cycles will be worth watching to see where Texas really is headed and how fast it's getting there.

Red and Blue States

(30 States Plus D.C.)

Over the past few elections, particularly in 2000 and 2004, the United States appeared to be the "divided" states, split into two groups: "red" states and "blue" states. The red states voted Republican in presidential races virtually all of the time and the blue states voted Democratic virtually all of the time. With the exception of the elections involving a Southern Democrat in 1976, 1992, and 1996, this pattern seemed to persist. Reflective of the divide in the country and exacerbated by politicians, these states were basically uncontested. While the election of 2008 broke that pattern in some places, these red and blue states stayed clearly in one camp or the other. In fact, in many of these states, there was almost no presidential campaign activity by either party. This doesn't mean the parties don't compete over these states on some level, but as of the 2008 election, it's going to take serious efforts by either party to move them into the presidential battleground by 2012.

ALABAMA
The Tide Stays Deep Crimson
9 ELECTORAL VOTES

Alabama joined the Union in 1819. Typical of the Deep South, Alabama was Democratic from Reconstruction through the 1950s. Now the state is reliably Republican. This change was caused by white conservative voter reaction to the Democratic-sponsored civil rights legislation pushed by Lyndon Johnson. This was the beginning of the Republicans' "Southern strategy." Polling in 2008 showed this state was never in doubt, and the polls were accurate here.

	2008		2004	
McCain	1,266,546	60.3%	Bush	62.5%
Obama	813,479	38.7%	Kerry	36.8%
Other candidates	19,794			
	2,099,819			

Note: 100% 2,843 of 2,843 precincts; 100% 67 of 67 counties. Chart based on final, official vote totals.

Turnout soared in Alabama, jumping nearly five points to 61.8% of the voting eligible population. That is the eighth biggest jump in turnout among all 50 states, and Alabama was not a battleground state.

Only two counties switched allegiance from 2004 to 2008. In Jefferson County, anchored by Birmingham, Bush won by a 26,000 vote margin; Obama turned that around to win the county by 16,172 votes. Marengo County, halfway between Birmingham and Mobile, went narrowly for Bush in 2004 and narrowly for Obama in 2008.

In the primary of February 5, 2008, Obama received 56% of the vote and Clinton received 41.6%.

	2008			2004		
	TOTAL	OBAMA	McCAIN	TOTAL	KERRY	BUSH
GENDER						
MALE	46	36	62	46	30	69
FEMALE	54	42	58	54	43	57
AGE						
◆ 18–29	22	50	49	18	41	57
30–44	29	41	56	28	40	58
45–64	35	36	64	38	37	63
◆ 65+	13	22	78	16	28	72

(continued)

	2008			**2004**		
	TOTAL	OBAMA	McCAIN	TOTAL	KERRY	BUSH
RACE						
WHITE	65	10	88	73	19	80
♦ *BLACK*	29	98	2	25	91	6
HISPANIC	4	–	–	1	–	–
PARTY						
DEMOCRAT	37	85	14	34	92	7
REPUBLICAN	45	3	97	48	1	99
INDEPENDENT	18	33	64	18	29	66
IDEOLOGY						
LIBERAL	12	77	20	15	72	27
MODERATE	41	49	50	40	44	53
CONSERVATIVE	47	16	83	44	19	81
EDUCATION BY RACE						
WHITE, COLLEGE DEGREE	24	13	85	–	–	–
WHITE, NO COLLEGE DEGREE	41	9	90	–	–	–
NONWHITE, COLLEGE DEGREE	14	93	7	–	–	–
NONWHITE, NO COLLEGE DEGREE	20	93	7	–	–	–
BUSH JOB						
APPROVE	41	7	93	62	5	94
DISAPPROVE	58	61	38	35	91	7
WORRIED ABOUT THE NATIONAL ECONOMY						
WORRIED	85	38	61	–	–	–
NOT WORRIED	14	51	49	–	–	–

Not surprisingly, the share of the youth vote and the black vote both went up from 2004. In both groups, Obama improved upon Kerry's percentages. Of course, if the young voter number went up, something had to go down; and in this state it was proportional turnout among seniors, a group that went more heavily for McCain in 2008, 78%, than for Bush in 2004, 72%. Interestingly, despite a drop in other states, the white Evangelical share of the vote in Alabama actually increased from 2004, and these folks voted for the McCain-Palin ticket, 92%, at an even higher rate than they had for Bush-Cheney in 2004, 88%. Could this Palin effect help her in 2012?

DESPITE BEING BLOWN OUT, OBAMA
DID HAVE COATTAILS

Obama never really had a chance when you consider he could only carry 10% of the white vote. While there is no direct evidence, many hypothesize that race played a very important role in Obama's poor performance among white voters in Alabama. It was Obama's worst showing among white voters of any state in the Union. But while the state's high black population didn't translate into making the state more competitive on the presidential level, it did help Democrats down the ballot. Not only did Democrats hold one of their rare open House seats (the state's 5th District), but also the party picked up a House seat they haven't held since 1962. The narrow Democratic victory in the state's 2nd District (which sports a black population of approximately 30%) can be credited to two factors: better candidate recruiting (the Democrats had the mayor of Montgomery running) and also the spike in black turnout thanks to Obama. One of the real tests of this new Democratic coalition that Obama is attempting to build will be the turnout of these voters when Obama's name is *not* on the ballot. In 2010, the reelection chances of the Democrat in the 2nd District (Bobby Bright) depend a great deal on Obama voters showing up. The election will be an indication whether there is a true realignment taking place.

ALASKA
One Wacky Year Ends
with Presidential Stability
3 ELECTORAL VOTES

Alaska became a state in January 1959. Since then it has only voted Democratic once and that was in 1964. The presence of Sarah Palin, governor of Alaska, on the ticket did not produce much change from the 2004 results. Reliably Republican, polls never showed a close race here and may have underestimated the final McCain margin.

	2008		2004	
McCain	193,841	59.4%	Bush	61.1%
Obama	123,594	37.9%	Kerry	35.5%
Other candidates	8,762			
	326,197			

Note: Chart based on final, official vote totals.

As close followers of the state's heavily contested U.S. Senate race between eventual winner, Democrat Mark Begich, and Republican incumbent Ted Stevens, are painfully aware, it took weeks, not days, for the final vote count to be produced in this state. Needless to say, after showing a dip in turnout from 2004, when *all* the early vote was counted, the state sported a rise in total votes, which was expected. However, as a percentage of the eligible population, turnout was down slightly. Alaska does not have counties as local government units, making voting comparisons across the election at smaller geographic levels more difficult. In the caucus of February 5, 2008, Obama received 75.2% of the vote and Clinton received 24.7%.

	2008			2004		
	TOTAL	OBAMA	McCAIN	TOTAL	KERRY	BUSH
GENDER						
MALE	47	32	64	49	29	67
FEMALE	53	41	57	51	41	57
AGE						
18–29	21	37	61	21	37	59
30–44	31	33	64	33	33	64
45–64	37	41	57	38	37	63
65+	11	38	60	8	30	67
RACE						
WHITE	78	33	65	83	33	64
BLACK	3	–	–	4	–	–
HISPANIC	6	–	–	3	–	–

	2008			2004		
	TOTAL	OBAMA	McCAIN	TOTAL	KERRY	BUSH
ASIAN	2	–	–	2	–	–
ALASKA NATIVE	11	52	46	8	51	45
PARTY						
DEMOCRAT	20	84	15	19	84	14
REPUBLICAN	37	6	93	41	5	94
INDEPENDENT	43	43	52	40	41	53
IDEOLOGY						
LIBERAL	15	80	17	18	79	16
MODERATE	46	44	54	45	39	57
CONSERVATIVE	38	12	84	38	9	90
EDUCATION BY RACE						
WHITE, COLLEGE DEGREE	33	44	53	–	–	–
WHITE, NO COLLEGE DEGREE	45	25	73	–	–	–
NONWHITE, COLLEGE DEGREE	6	–	–	–	–	–
NONWHITE, NO COLLEGE DEGREE	16	53	46	–	–	–
BUSH JOB						
APPROVE	38	4	94	62	4	94
DISAPPROVE	60	58	38	37	86	8
WORRIED ABOUT THE NATIONAL ECONOMY						
WORRIED	85	40	58	–	–	–
NOT WORRIED	14	19	76	–	–	–

There was apparently a Palin effect. In one of the states bucking the national trend, Republicans were able to increase their margin a couple points, and the youth vote share did not increase. One reason why Democrats struggle so much in this state is the fact that nearly three-fourths of Alaska voters are gun owners and two-thirds of them voted for McCain-Palin. Palin does return to her state sporting a very high approval rating; 73% of those who voted in 2008 approved of the job she was doing as governor.

THE LAST FRONTIER IS STILL VERY RED

What a year for Alaska politics! The presidential contest started with the entrance of the state's last Democratic senator, Mike Gravel (who served two terms from 1968 to 1980), making a near mockery of himself in the Democratic primaries and the campaign ended with the state's formerly unknown Republican governor finding herself on the Republican ticket. In between, the state's most powerful politician, Ted Stevens, became a convicted felon and found himself out of the U.S. Senate for the first time in 40 years. There was a time (pre-Palin) when the Obama campaign thought they could put Alaska in play. The campaign bought TV time in the state; the thinking was that the state's penchant for supporting third-party candidacies (particularly Libertarians) could hold McCain's numbers down. Of course, once Palin was named to the GOP ticket, the Obama campaign abandoned its efforts. Stevens, as a convicted felon, came quite close to winning reelection, a sign of just how Republican this state really is. The state's new senator, Democrat Mark Begich (son of a former congressman from the state), ought to be glad he has six years to build a political constituency as nothing comes easy for Democrats in this state.

ARKANSAS
Clinton's Home State Is Redder Than Ever
6 ELECTORAL VOTES

Arkansas voted Democratic from Reconstruction until 1964. As with other Deep South states, this pattern changed as a result of Democratic support for civil rights legislation. In 1968, the state voted for third-party candidate George Wallace. Since then, it has usually voted Republican, with the exception of voting Democratic twice for fellow Arkansan Bill Clinton and once for Jimmy Carter. While Arkansas votes Republican for president, both U.S. senators and the governor are Democrats (one of only three states with this distinction, the other two being Montana and West Virginia). The polls never showed a narrow race here, but they seriously underestimated McCain's margin.

	2008		2004	
McCain	638,017	58.7%	Bush	54.3%
Obama	422,310	38.9%	Kerry	44.6%
Other candidates	26,290			
	1,086,617			

Note:100% 2,588 of 2,588 precincts; 100% 75 of 75 counties. Chart based on final, official vote totals.

McCain won the state easily, taking 66 of the state's 75 counties. Twelve counties switched to Republican in this election from 2004, more than a quarter of the 44 counties nationwide that switched in that direction. It matched Tennessee on this dimension.

Obama was only able to run up substantial majorities in Little Rock and Pulaski County, and in Pine Bluff and Jefferson County.

Turnout was down slightly in Arkansas, sinking to 53.4% of the voting eligible population.

As with Alabama, Arkansas was not a battleground focus of the campaigns. In the primary of February 5, 2008, Clinton received 70.2% of the vote and Obama received 26.1%.

	2008			2004		
	TOTAL	OBAMA	McCAIN	TOTAL	KERRY	BUSH
GENDER						
MALE	45	40	58	44	40	59
♦ *FEMALE*	55	39	58	56	49	50
AGE						
18–29	17	49	49	16	51	47
30–44	27	39	60	29	39	60

(continued)

	2008			2004		
	TOTAL	OBAMA	McCAIN	TOTAL	KERRY	BUSH
45–64	37	40	57	39	43	55
65+	19	32	65	16	54	46
RACE						
WHITE	83	30	68	83	36	63
BLACK	12	95	5	15	94	6
HISPANIC	3	–	–	1	–	–
PARTY						
◆ DEMOCRAT	36	77	21	41	82	18
◆ REPUBLICAN	32	7	93	31	3	97
◆ INDEPENDENT	31	30	67	29	38	60
IDEOLOGY						
LIBERAL	14	76	20	13	79	19
MODERATE	41	52	46	45	58	40
CONSERVATIVE	45	16	82	42	18	82
EDUCATION BY RACE						
WHITE, COLLEGE DEGREE	32	31	67	–	–	–
WHITE, NO COLLEGE DEGREE	50	30	68	–	–	–
NONWHITE, COLLEGE DEGREE	4	–	–	–	–	–
NONWHITE, NO COLLEGE DEGREE	13	89	10	–	–	–
BUSH JOB						
APPROVE	35	7	92	55	7	93
DISAPPROVE	63	57	40	44	92	6
WORRIED ABOUT THE NATIONAL ECONOMY						
WORRIED	85	40	58	–	–	–
NOT WORRIED	14	32	67	–	–	–

Arkansas is a solidly Democratic state at the state level (from governor to the state legislature and everything in between). But in this election, Democratic partisanship decreased five points from 2004, down to 36% from 41%. Republicans and Independents split the gain. Also, McCain was able to improve over Bush's performance among both Democrats and Independents. Was there a Hillary Clinton backlash in this state? Maybe. Women swung 18 points toward Republican McCain. In 2004 women split 49% for Kerry, 50% for Bush, but in 2008, 39% of women voted for Obama. However, only 28% of Democrats who supported Hillary Clinton in the primaries voted for McCain in the general.

OBAMA WAS NOT NATURAL FIT
IN NATURAL STATE

Arkansas was one of just four states where McCain improved his margin over Obama, compared to Bush v. Kerry. And Arkansas borders on the other three states, Louisiana, Oklahoma, and Tennessee, where McCain increased his victory margins over what Bush did in 2004. But despite this Republican dominance on the national level, the party is a mess down the ballot. Republicans didn't even recruit a candidate to challenge Democrat Senator Mark Pryor, who sailed into a second term. Things might have been different in Arkansas for Democrats at the presidential level had Hillary Clinton been on the ballot; then again, Republicans might have found more success down the ballot had once (and future?) presidential candidate Mike Huckabee been on the national ticket.

CALIFORNIA
A Golden Shade of Blue
55 ELECTORAL VOTES

California became part of the Union in September 1850. The state has continuously increased in population and electoral votes. With its 55 electoral votes, the state represents more than 10% of the country and 20% of what a candidate needs to win the presidency. The state was once Republican, believe it or not, but now California is a reliably Democratic state and has been since 1992. Republicans carried the state in every presidential election from 1952 through 1988, except for the landslide loss in 1964. In 2008, the polls never showed a narrow race here and accurately predicted the margin.

	2008		2004	
Obama	8,274,473	61.0%	Kerry	54.3%
McCain	5,011,781	37.0%	Bush	44.4%
Other candidates	275,646			
	13,561,900			

Note: Chart based on final, official vote totals.

California alone provided more than one-third of Obama's national vote margin of 9 million votes, giving him an edge of almost 3.2 million in the Golden State.

Despite the lack of campaigning in the state, preliminary estimates put turnout at 61.8%, up a full three percentage points from 2004, assuming that the state's slow vote count reaches expected totals.

The number of votes cast in the presidential race rose in only three counties and dropped in 55. But the slump was relatively one-sided, as the number of GOP votes dropped more or less across the board.

Ten counties went from Republican to Democratic, including such GOP bastions as San Diego and San Luis Obispo. San Diego, home to many active and retired military men and women, went for Obama by 10 percentage points, as the number of GOP votes dropped by more than 130,000 from 2004. In the primary of February 5, 2008, Clinton received 51.5% of the vote and Obama received 43.2%.

	2008			**2004**		
	TOTAL	OBAMA	McCAIN	TOTAL	KERRY	BUSH
GENDER						
MALE	46	58	40	49	50	47
FEMALE	54	64	35	51	57	41
AGE						
♦ 18–29	20	76	23	22	58	39
30–44	28	59	39	28	52	46
45–64	36	60	38	34	51	46
♦ 65+	15	48	50	16	55	43
RACE						
WHITE	63	52	46	65	47	51
BLACK	10	94	5	6	81	18
HISPANIC	18	74	23	21	63	32
PARTY						
DEMOCRAT	42	92	8	39	87	12
REPUBLICAN	30	14	85	33	9	89
INDEPENDENT	28	64	31	27	59	36
IDEOLOGY						
LIBERAL	25	91	8	26	88	10
MODERATE	44	67	31	46	56	41
CONSERVATIVE	30	23	74	28	19	80
EDUCATION BY RACE						
WHITE, COLLEGE DEGREE	36	57	42	33	54	43
WHITE, NO COLLEGE DEGREE	27	46	52	33	38	61
NONWHITE, COLLEGE DEGREE	13	70	28	13	74	23
NONWHITE, NO COLLEGE DEGREE	24	79	18	21	62	35
BUSH JOB						
APPROVE	21	14	85	46	9	90
DISAPPROVE	77	71	27	52	91	6
WORRIED ABOUT THE NATIONAL ECONOMY						
WORRIED	28	33	63	–	–	–
NOT WORRIED	14	–	–	–	–	–

California has a way of exaggerating conventional wisdom. For instance, while we know Obama did well among voters under 30 everywhere, he simply killed it among this age group on the Left Coast, carrying 75%. This easily offset the fact that McCain improved on Bush's share among seniors by a whopping 14 points. And while the Hispanic share of the vote decreased slightly, Obama's margin widened dramatically compared to Kerry's in 2004. While whites with college degrees turned out in greater numbers and at higher rates than they did for Kerry, working-class whites without a college degree backed McCain 52% to Obama's 46%.

GOP HAS NOWHERE TO GO BUT UP

As it has been for the last 20 years, California has simply become the ATM of presidential politics. Presidential candidates (even during the primaries) never traveled to the state without accomplishing one of two things: holding a major fund-raiser and appearing on some L.A.-based daytime or late-night talk show. The numbers show it: residents of the state gave a combined $108.7 million to the presidential candidates during the 2007 to 2008 cycle. The downward trend for the Republican Party in this vote-rich state can't be ignored, and yet the state is so much more left of center compared to the rest of the country that it's not clear how Republicans can both appeal to Californians and, say, Georgians at the same time. The good news for the GOP: the party now knows what bottom in this state looks like. Despite Obama's enormous win statewide, it did not trickle down (as some Republicans feared), since the party split in Congress remained unchanged. Keep an eye on the state's 2010 governor's race. Without Arnold Schwarzenegger on the ballot, the campaign should be a free-for-all on either side and whoever gets elected (particularly if it's a Republican) instantly becomes a player in national politics.

CONNECTICUT
A Darker Shade of Blue
7 ELECTORAL VOTES

Connecticut is now a reliably Democratic state, but like much of New England, it had been Republican. Democrats have won the state in the last four elections, but Republicans had won the five previous ones. In this election, the last Republican congressman from New England, Chris Shays, lost his seat. Polling here showed a significant Obama lead throughout the campaign and accurately predicted the final margin.

	2008		2004	
Obama	**1,000,994**	**60.7%**	Kerry	54.3%
McCain	**628,873**	**38.1%**	Bush	44.0%
Other candidates	**18,693**			
	1,648,560			

Note: 100% 759 of 759 precincts; 100% 169 of 169 towns, townships, and cities. Chart based on final, official vote totals.

Despite the drama of the state's sometimes Democratic U.S. senator traveling with the Republican presidential nominee, Connecticut drew almost no attention from the campaigns. And that support from Joe Lieberman didn't help McCain much. In 2004, Kerry carried all but one of the state's counties. In 2008, the last of the Nutmeg State's eight counties, Litchfield, voted Democratic, making the choice for Obama unanimous. In fact, McCain struggled to get above 40% of the vote in most of the counties. In the primary of February 5, 2008, Obama received 50.7% of the vote and Clinton received 46.7%.

	2008			2004		
	TOTAL	OBAMA	McCAIN	TOTAL	KERRY	BUSH
GENDER						
MALE	47	53	43	47	52	47
FEMALE	53	66	32	53	57	42
AGE						
18–29	18	79	18	16	70	29
30–44	25	61	38	27	56	43
45–64	44	53	42	43	50	49
65+	13	–	–	14	49	51

(continued)

	2008			**2004**		
	TOTAL	OBAMA	McCAIN	TOTAL	KERRY	BUSH
RACE						
WHITE	78	51	46	86	51	48
♦ *BLACK*	12	93	7	6	–	–
HISPANIC	8	–	–	7	75	25
PARTY						
DEMOCRAT	43	90	7	37	89	11
REPUBLICAN	27	15	83	30	10	89
INDEPENDENT	31	57	39	33	58	41
IDEOLOGY						
LIBERAL	29	90	6	26	92	8
MODERATE	44	63	34	50	54	45
CONSERVATIVE	27	27	70	24	18	82
EDUCATION BY RACE						
WHITE, COLLEGE DEGREE	46	52	44	–	–	–
WHITE, NO COLLEGE DEGREE	32	51	47	–	–	–
NONWHITE, COLLEGE DEGREE	9	–	–	–	–	–
NONWHITE, NO COLLEGE DEGREE	13	89	10	–	–	–
BUSH JOB						
APPROVE	18	–	–	46	10	90
DISAPPROVE	82	74	22	52	95	4
WORRIED ABOUT THE NATIONAL ECONOMY						
WORRIED	92	63	34	–	–	–
NOT WORRIED	7	–	–	–	–	–

In one of the more dramatic jumps in black proportion of the electorate anywhere in the country, Connecticut saw the black share of the vote increase to 12% in 2008, double the 6% four years ago. That spike in black turnout helped the Democrats increase their partisan split in the state by seven points.

NEW ENGLAND'S LAST REPUBLICAN LOSES

One wonders if Obama's vote total would have changed all that much had McCain decided to tap Senator Lieberman, a self-described independent Democrat, as his running mate rather than Sarah Palin. Honestly, there's little evidence Lieberman would have helped McCain. But the big story in the state was the Chris Shays loss. Just two years ago, Republicans held three of the state's five congressional districts. Now the GOP holds none, and it's not just Connecticut where the GOP is shut out on the House level. The Shays defeat in 2008 means the GOP doesn't hold a single congressional seat in all of New England. The party still remains relatively competitive in gubernatorial races in this state, but one wonders when this dramatic partisan shift that has buried the GOP in House, Senate, and presidential races will also begin hurting the GOP on the state level. We'll find out in 2010.

DELAWARE
They're Not Known as Blue Hens
for Nothing
3 ELECTORAL VOTES

From 1952 to 2000, Delaware correctly picked the winner of the presidential race (at least in terms of national popular vote). The streak was broken in 2004 when the state stayed Democratic despite the country's tilt toward Bush. As if the Democrats needed any help, the addition of Joe Biden to the ticket helped make Delaware one of the Democrats' five largest margins of victory in all 50 states. Polling here always showed a significant Obama lead and accurately predicted the margin.

	2008		2004	
Obama	255,459	61.9%	Kerry	53.4%
McCain	152,374	36.9%	Bush	44.8%
Other candidates	4,579			
	412,412			

Note: 100% 339 of 339 precincts; 100% 3 of 3 counties. Chart based on final, official vote totals.

With Biden on the ticket, the one county (of three) that had voted Republican in 2004 shifted. Kent County, including Dover and the giant air base there, moved easily into the Democratic column.

Turnout statewide also edged up slightly to 65.9%, up about 1.7 percentage points from 2004. In the primary of February 5, 2008, Obama received 53.1% of the vote and Clinton received 42.3%.

	2008			2004		
	TOTAL	OBAMA	McCAIN	TOTAL	KERRY	BUSH
GENDER						
MALE	45	52	46	43	48	52
FEMALE	55	70	29	57	58	41
AGE						
♦ *18–29*	20	71	25	16	54	45
30–44	28	64	35	32	57	43
45–64	38	59	41	36	51	48
65+	14	–	–	16	54	46
RACE						
♦ *WHITE*	77	53	45	76	45	55
BLACK	17	99	1	20	82	17
HISPANIC	3	–	–	2	–	–

	2008			**2004**		
	TOTAL	OBAMA	McCAIN	TOTAL	KERRY	BUSH
PARTY						
DEMOCRAT	48	91	9	41	88	12
REPUBLICAN	31	18	80	32	13	87
♦ *INDEPENDENT*	21	61	39	26	52	47
IDEOLOGY						
LIBERAL	23	95	5	21	84	16
MODERATE	50	67	33	48	62	37
CONSERVATIVE	27	25	72	31	21	79
BUSH JOB						
APPROVE	24	12	85	46	10	90
DISAPPROVE	75	77	22	53	94	6
EDUCATION BY RACE						
WHITE, COLLEGE DEGREE	39	55	45	–	–	–
WHITE, NO COLLEGE DEGREE	37	52	45	–	–	–
NONWHITE, COLLEGE DEGREE	10	–	–	–	–	–
NONWHITE, NO COLLEGE DEGREE	13	98	2	–	–	–
WORRIED ABOUT THE NATIONAL ECONOMY						
WORRIED	90	62	37	–	–	–
NOT WORRIED	10	–	–	–	–	–

There was a four point increase in the proportion of the youth vote in 2008 and a huge 37 point swing in their vote margin as 71% of those under 30 voted for Obama-Biden. And the addition of Biden may have also contributed to the fact that white voters swung 18 points from the Republican to the Democratic column in this election, giving Obama a majority of the white vote. In more evidence of the Biden enthusiasm, Democratic identification among voters was up seven points, while the share of voters calling themselves Independents was down five points.

ANOTHER BIDEN ON THE RISE?

Even had Biden not been on the Democratic ticket, Delaware wasn't going to go red. Over the past 20 years, the share of the Democratic vote has dramatically increased. What remains of the state's onetime swing-voting roots will be put to the test in 2010 when Ted Kaufman, appointed to fill Biden's seat, may not run for election, potentially paving the way for Biden's son, Beau, to run when he returns from his Iraq tour of duty. He could find himself in a potentially tough contest against the state's lone member of Congress, Republican Mike Castle (assuming Castle does run). By the way, the Democratic landslide produced some coattails, as the Democrats were able to get full control of the state legislature. Before 2008, Republicans held the state house and Democrats the state senate.

DISTRICT OF COLUMBIA
The Only Vote D.C. Gets Is a Blue One
3 ELECTORAL VOTES

Washington, D.C., the nation's capital, is heavily African-American and has voted Democratic ever since it has been allowed to cast ballots in the presidential elections in 1964. And it did so again in 2008, by a margin of about thirteen to one. It was easily Obama's biggest margin, even though D.C. does not count as a state in anything but electoral terms.

	2008		2004	
Obama	**245,800**	**92.5%**	Kerry	89.2%
McCain	**17,367**	**6.5%**	Bush	9.3%
Other candidates	**2,686**			
	265,853			

Note: 100% 143 of 143 precincts; not reported by county. Chart based on final, official vote totals.

Reflecting the demographics and the views of D.C., turnout was up a surprising 6.6 percentage points to 60.9%. In the primary of February 5, 2008, Obama received 75.4% of the vote and Clinton received 23.8%.

	2008			2004		
	TOTAL	OBAMA	McCAIN	TOTAL	KERRY	BUSH
GENDER						
MALE	43	91	6	44	86	12
FEMALE	57	93	6	56	92	7
AGE						
18–29	25	95	5	23	90	8
30–44	30	90	7	34	89	10
45–64	36	92	6	31	90	8
65+	9	–	–	12	88	12
RACE						
WHITE	35	86	12	38	80	19
♦ *BLACK*	56	97	3	54	97	3
HISPANIC	5	–	–	5	–	–
PARTY						
DEMOCRAT	78	98	1	74	97	2
REPUBLICAN	6	–	–	8	23	75
INDEPENDENT	16	–	–	18	85	10
IDEOLOGY						
♦ *LIBERAL*	46	98	1	45	96	3
MODERATE	43	92	7	43	89	10
CONSERVATIVE	11	–	–	12	66	33

(continued)

	2008			**2004**		
	TOTAL	OBAMA	McCAIN	TOTAL	KERRY	BUSH
EDUCATION BY RACE						
WHITE, COLLEGE DEGREE	32	88	10	–	–	–
WHITE, NO COLLEGE DEGREE	3	–	–	–	–	–
NONWHITE, COLLEGE DEGREE	26	93	5	–	–	–
NONWHITE, NO COLLEGE DEGREE	39	97	2	–	–	–
BUSH JOB						
APPROVE	8	–	–	13	33	67
DISAPPROVE	91	96	3	86	98	1
WORRIED ABOUT THE NATIONAL ECONOMY						
WORRIED	89	93	6	–	–	–
NOT WORRIED	11	–	–	–	–	–

The vote in Washington, D.C., is officially the most liberal in the country as nearly half of all voters, 46%, use that label to describe their own ideology. D.C. also has the highest percentage of African-American voters, 56%.

HAS DISTRICT'S BLUE STREAK AFFECTED VIRGINIA?

About the only thing in doubt was whether McCain would break 5% in the District. He did . . . barely. Not surprisingly, just 8% of all District voters approved of the job President Bush was doing, meaning that McCain couldn't even get 100% of Bush approvers. The thing that ought to worry the GOP is that this Democratic bent in the District is bleeding into the suburbs and has turned once swing areas of suburban Maryland and northern Virginia into Democratic bastions as well.

HAWAII
Obama's *Other* Home State
4 ELECTORAL VOTES

Hawaii was the last state to join the Union in 1959. Hawaii is a blue state, having voted Democratic in every election except the 1972 and 1984 contests. Polls never showed anything but a significant Obama lead. Hawaii was home to Obama during many of his formative years (he was born just two years after the state joined the Union). His grandmother, who raised him, lived there until she died just before the 2008 election.

	2008			2004	
Obama	**325,871**	**71.8%**	Kerry	54.0%
McCain	**120,566**	**26.6%**	Bush	45.3%
Other candidates	**7,131**			
	453,568			

Note: 100% 338 of 338 precincts; 100% 5 of 5 counties. Chart based on final, official vote totals.

There was little remarkable to talk about in the vote returns from the five counties, except that Honolulu, which flirted with the GOP in 2004, was solidly back in Democratic arms in 2008.

In the caucus of February 19, 2008, Obama received 75.7% of the vote and Clinton received 23.6%.

	2008			2004		
	TOTAL	OBAMA	McCAIN	TOTAL	KERRY	BUSH
GENDER						
MALE	48	72	26	45	51	49
FEMALE	52	72	26	55	57	43
AGE						
18–29	16	82	18	15	61	39
30–44	24	75	21	26	54	46
45–64	46	68	30	45	53	47
65+	14	69	30	14	55	45
RACE						
WHITE	41	70	27	42	58	42
BLACK	1	–	–	1	–	–
HISPANIC	8	–	–	10	54	46
♦ *ASIAN*	30	**68**	**30**	26	52	**48**
♦ *NATIVE HAWAIIAN*	19	80	18	22	48	52

(*continued*)

	2008			**2004**		
	TOTAL	OBAMA	McCAIN	TOTAL	KERRY	BUSH
PARTY						
DEMOCRAT	45	95	4	40	83	17
◆ *REPUBLICAN*	20	22	76	24	7	93
INDEPENDENT	34	72	25	36	54	46
IDEOLOGY						
LIBERAL	28	91	6	29	82	18
MODERATE	48	75	23	48	55	45
◆ *CONSERVATIVE*	24	41	57	23	19	81
EDUCATION BY RACE						
WHITE, COLLEGE DEGREE	20	77	21	–	–	–
WHITE, NO COLLEGE DEGREE	21	64	34	–	–	–
NONWHITE, COLLEGE DEGREE	26	71	26	–	–	–
NONWHITE, NO COLLEGE DEGREE	33	74	25	–	–	–
BUSH JOB						
APPROVE	23	31	67	49	13	87
DISAPPROVE	76	84	14	50	96	4

All voting blocs shifted toward the Democrats—even Republicans and conservatives swung closer to the blue column. Conservatives voted 57% for McCain, 41% for Obama, a 46 point shift in the vote margin from four years ago. Asian turnout was up four points. While they narrowly supported Kerry four years ago, they preferred Obama over McCain 68% to 30%. One in five voters were Native Hawaiians. In 2004, 52% voted for Bush; in 2008, 80% voted for Obama, a 66 point swing.

HOME IS WHERE THE BLOWOUT IS

Other than the margin in the District of Columbia, no actual state gave Obama a wider victory margin than Hawaii. Forget the pride those in Illinois had for their adopted favorite son, Hawaii swung an astounding 45 points from Kerry's margin in 2004. The coattails were apparent down the ballot as the already enormous Democratic advantages the party held in the state legislature were exaggerated. Ready for this, out of 25 members of the state senate, the GOP claims just two seats now, down from five pre-2008.

IDAHO
The State May Be Surrounded
by Battlegrounds but . . .
4 ELECTORAL VOTES

Idaho was Democratic until 1952 when the state voted for Dwight Eisenhower. Idaho voted Republican in every election other than the 1964 landslide and, unlike some of its neighbors to the north, south, and east, isn't showing any signs of movement left. It remains one of the reddest states. Polls never showed a narrow race. It's worth noting that Idaho will always be known as the birthplace of Sarah Palin, although she seldom advertised this fact.

	2008		2004	
McCain	403,012	61.5%	Bush	69.4%
Obama	236,440	36.1%	Kerry	30.3%
Other candidates	15,580			
	655,032			

Note: 100% 954 of 954 precincts; 100% 44 of 44 counties. Chart based on final, official vote totals.

Of the 44 counties, only three—Blaine, Latah, and Teton—gave a majority to Obama in 2008. And Latah and Teton both switched from voting GOP for the past two elections to do so. Turnout was down a bit in Idaho from 2004 at just under 63% of the voting eligible population. In the caucus of February 5, 2008, Obama received 79.5% of the vote and Clinton received 17.2%.

	2008			2004		
	TOTAL	OBAMA	McCAIN	TOTAL	KERRY	BUSH
GENDER						
MALE	48	32	65	46	28	70
FEMALE	52	41	58	54	32	67
AGE						
18–29	26	41	56	24	35	65
30–44	29	35	63	26	23	74
45–64	34	34	64	36	31	68
65+	11	–	–	14	34	65
RACE						
WHITE	90	33	65	93	29	69
BLACK	1	–	–	1	–	–
HISPANIC	6	–	–	4	–	–
PARTY						
DEMOCRAT	24	89	10	22	80	19
♦ *REPUBLICAN*	48	5	95	50	4	96
INDEPENDENT	28	45	48	27	39	58

(continued)

	2008			**2004**		
	TOTAL	OBAMA	McCAIN	TOTAL	KERRY	BUSH
IDEOLOGY						
LIBERAL	16	82	18	17	75	23
MODERATE	40	48	48	44	34	65
CONSERVATIVE	43	6	93	39	7	93
EDUCATION BY RACE						
WHITE, COLLEGE DEGREE	31	40	56	–	–	–
WHITE, NO COLLEGE DEGREE	59	30	69	–	–	–
NONWHITE, COLLEGE DEGREE	3	–	–	–	–	–
NONWHITE, NO COLLEGE DEGREE	7	–	–	–	–	–
BUSH JOB						
APPROVE	45	6	93	69	4	95
DISAPPROVE	54	60	37	30	89	8
WORRIED ABOUT THE NATIONAL ECONOMY						
WORRIED	91	38	61	–	–	–
NOT WORRIED	9	–	–	–	–	–

A third of the Idaho vote is white Evangelical, and 82% voted for McCain. With Republicans representing 48% of the vote, Idaho is officially one of the reddest states in the country.

MOSTLY RED STATE ELECTS RARE DEMOCRAT

The importance of Idaho in this election cycle will forever be etched in the minds of those who were charged with securing delegates for Hillary Clinton's ill-fated bid for the Democratic nomination. Idaho was the best example of how Obama's team exploited the caucus process in the Democratic primary fight. Obama's campaign netted more delegates for the Idaho caucus victory than Clinton did for her New Jersey primary victory. It's among the facts that, to this day, befuddle many of the supposed political geniuses that were charged with winning Clinton the Democratic nomination. Democrats did win back one of the state's two U.S. House seats for the first time in 16 years, thanks mostly to the Republicans nominating someone who was painted as too conservative, even for Idaho. Democrat Walt Minnick's victory over Republican Bill Sali in that House race is being credited by some GOP strategists as a gift of the brand of conservatism preached by the Club for Growth. Let's see if Minnick can survive in 2010 if the GOP nominates a less purified Republican.

ILLINOIS
Home Cookin'
21 ELECTORAL VOTES

Illinois was mostly a Republican state after the Civil War until the 1920s. After that, it voted Democratic until 1952 when it became Republican for eight out of ten elections until 1988. Illinois has voted Democratic in the last four elections. Not only is Illinois now considered reliably Democratic, but also it is the home state of Barack Obama. Polls never showed a narrow race here and correctly predicted the Obama margin.

	2008		2004	
Obama	3,419,673	61.9%	Kerry	54.8%
McCain	2,031,527	36.8%	Bush	44.5%
Other candidates	71,851			
	5,523,051			

Note: 100% 11,585 of 11,585 precincts; 100% 102 of 102 counties. Chart based on final, official vote totals.

There was no doubt that the Land of Lincoln would back favorite son Barack Obama and it did so solidly, giving him nearly 1.4 million of his more than 9 million vote margin nationwide. That margin came on the back of a turnout rate of 62.7%, up just a bit more than one percentage point from 2004.

Thirty-one of the state's 102 counties switched to back the Democratic standard-bearer, joining the 15 counties that previously voted Democratic in the 2004 race. Some of those counties had not voted for a Democratic presidential candidate in more than half a century: DuPage, Kendall, and McHenry counties last voted for a Democratic president in 1948.

Discussions of Illinois elections always start in Cook County, where more than 2.1 million votes were cast in 2008. Chicago has been a staunch Democratic redoubt for decades, while the surrounding suburbs in Cook County have tended to be a bit more Republican. And it was a fairly small bit in 2008, since Obama won by 84% to 14% in Chicago and a mere 67% to 32% in the suburbs.

In the primary of February 5, 2008, Obama received 64.7% of the vote and Clinton received 32.8%.

	2008			**2004**		
	TOTAL	OBAMA	McCAIN	TOTAL	KERRY	BUSH
GENDER						
MALE	47	57	42	46	54	46
FEMALE	53	64	35	54	56	43
AGE						
18–29	20	71	27	21	64	35
30–44	26	66	33	30	52	47
45–64	41	54	45	39	51	48
65+	13	55	45	10	59	41
RACE						
WHITE	73	51	48	78	48	51
♦ *BLACK*	17	96	3	10	89	10
HISPANIC	7	72	27	8	76	23
PARTY						
DEMOCRAT	47	91	8	39	93	7
REPUBLICAN	28	15	84	34	11	89
INDEPENDENT	26	55	43	27	57	41
IDEOLOGY						
LIBERAL	22	92	7	23	91	9
MODERATE	48	67	32	50	58	41
CONSERVATIVE	30	29	71	27	20	79
EDUCATION BY RACE						
WHITE, COLLEGE DEGREE	37	50	50	–	–	–
WHITE, NO COLLEGE DEGREE	36	53	46	–	–	–
NONWHITE, COLLEGE DEGREE	9	82	17	–	–	–
NONWHITE, NO COLLEGE DEGREE	18	91	8	–	–	–
BUSH JOB						
APPROVE	21	–	–	47	12	88
DISAPPROVE	77	70	29	51	93	6
WORRIED ABOUT THE NATIONAL ECONOMY						
WORRIED	85	62	37	–	–	–
NOT WORRIED	14	–	–	–	–	–

Relative to how the boomers and seniors voted, the proportion of those under the age of 45 was down in 2008. And while all ages voted for their native son, the margin among seniors was somewhat narrower than it had been for Kerry. So even in Obama's home state, the hesitance toward Obama among older voters was apparent. The African-American share of the vote was up seven points, and 96% voted for Obama. And that spike in black voters helped push the Democratic partisan identification advantage in the state up another eight points.

OBAMA'S SURPRISINGLY SHORT COATTAILS

While there was never a doubt about Obama, there was hope among some state Democrats that Obama's coattails would help bring his party two to four new U.S. House seats. Those coattails never materialized as Democrats netted just one new House seat, indicating the party probably has maxed out in its efforts to turn any more congressional districts blue. Democrats should not rest on their laurels in 2010. If the GOP is ever to make a comeback in this once key state to the party, it all starts with the two big races on the docket in 2010: the special election to fill out the rest of Obama's Senate term and the open governor's seat. Despite what happens in the state, there's no doubt that the new power center of politics is in Chicago. And if the so-called second city gets the 2016 Olympics, it'll be quite the comeback for a city that has forever been stuck in the East and West Coast shadows of New York and L.A.

KANSAS
Democrats May Not Care
What the Matter Is Here
6 ELECTORAL VOTES

Kansas hasn't voted for a Democrat since 1964 and continues to be a Republican state. In fact, the state is so Republican, it's worth noting that the Democrats haven't even held one of the state's two Senate seats in nearly 80 years. Polls never showed a narrow race here and correctly predicted the McCain margin.

	2008		2004	
McCain	**699,655**	**56.6%**	Bush	62.0%
Obama	**514,765**	**41.7%**	Kerry	36.6%
Other candidates	**21,452**			
	1,235,872			

Note: 100% 3,298 of 3,298 precincts; 100% 105 of 105 counties. Chart based on final, official vote totals.

In 2008, only three counties of 105 voted for Obama. Obama did crack 40% of the vote in Kansas, a feat matched recently only by Michael Dukakis in 1988 and Jimmy Carter in 1976. Turnout was up one percentage point from 2004 at just over 62%.

In the caucus of February 5, 2008, Obama received 74.0% of the vote and Clinton received 25.8%.

	2008			2004		
	TOTAL	OBAMA	McCAIN	TOTAL	KERRY	BUSH
GENDER						
MALE	48	39	60	45	34	64
FEMALE	52	46	53	55	38	62
AGE						
♦ 18–29	19	51	47	17	44	55
30–44	30	37	61	30	27	72
45–64	36	44	56	36	34	64
♦ 65+	15	34	66	17	48	51
RACE						
WHITE	90	40	59	90	34	64
BLACK	3	–	–	3	–	–
HISPANIC	4	–	–	5	–	–
PARTY						
DEMOCRAT	26	88	12	27	84	16
REPUBLICAN	49	12	87	50	5	94
♦ INDEPENDENT	25	52	44	23	46	52
IDEOLOGY						
LIBERAL	16	83	13	14	76	22

	2008			2004		
	TOTAL	OBAMA	McCAIN	TOTAL	KERRY	BUSH
◆ MODERATE	45	52	47	48	45	54
CONSERVATIVE	38	11	89	38	10	88
EDUCATION BY RACE						
WHITE, COLLEGE DEGREE	40	44	55	–	–	–
WHITE, NO COLLEGE DEGREE	50	37	62	–	–	–
NONWHITE, COLLEGE DEGREE	4	–	–	–	–	–
NONWHITE, NO COLLEGE DEGREE	6	–	–	–	–	–
BUSH JOB						
APPROVE	36	8	92	62	2	96
DISAPPROVE	63	58	41	37	95	4
WORRIED ABOUT THE NATIONAL ECONOMY						
WORRIED	93	41	58	–	–	–
NOT WORRIED	7	–	–	–	–	–

Obama showed some improvement over Kerry among several voting groups, narrowing the vote in several categories. Independent, moderate, and the youth votes all swung narrowly into the Democrat column. But like the pattern in many states, seniors swung 29 points more Republican, with 66% supporting John McCain.

REPUBLICAN UNITY IS THE KEY

As the Democrats have plotted their comeback nationally over the last decade, one book had become the mantra for many liberals, *What's the Matter with Kansas?* The idea being if the Democrats can figure out how to sell themselves again in Kansas, they can win anywhere. Well, Democrats have seen mild success in Kansas, but only after Republicans overreached with too conservative candidates either for Congress or governor. Republicans did win one of their four U.S. House seats, gained nationwide right here in Kansas, and it was won only after a less conservative Republican won the GOP primary. Perhaps the GOP needs its own *What's the Matter with Kansas?* to figure out its ideological future? Stay tuned as a couple big-ticket races are on the docket for 2010, including a potentially open Senate seat if once (and future?) GOP presidential candidate Sam Brownback decides to run for governor.

KENTUCKY
Only the Grass Is Blue
8 ELECTORAL VOTES

Kentucky is not a part of the Deep South geographically but it sure votes like it. It was Democratic like most Southern states until World War II. Since then, it has been a reliably Republican state with the exception of voting for two Southern governors in 1976, 1992, and 1996. Polls never showed a narrow race here, but they underestimated the McCain margin.

	2008		2004	
McCain	1,048,462	57.4%	Bush	59.6%
Obama	751,985	41.2%	Kerry	39.7%
Other candidates	26,061			
	1,826,508			

Note: 100% 3,541 of 3,541 precincts; 100% 120 of 120 counties. Chart based on final, official vote totals.

Kentucky was the site of a hot U.S. Senate contest in 2008, but little attention was paid by the presidential campaigns.

Just eight of 120 counties voted for Obama, although the largest counties in the state, Jefferson (with Louisville) and Fayette (with Lexington), did vote Democratic. That was a switch for Fayette, which went narrowly for Obama after decent margins in the past two presidential races for Bush. In the primary of May 20, 2008, Clinton received 65.5% of the vote and Obama received 29.9%.

	2008			2004		
	TOTAL	OBAMA	McCAIN	TOTAL	KERRY	BUSH
GENDER						
MALE	46	40	58	46	38	61
FEMALE	54	44	56	54	41	58
AGE						
♦ 18–29	18	51	48	19	45	54
30–44	27	43	54	28	41	58
45–64	41	39	61	39	38	61
65+	14	40	59	14	36	64
RACE						
WHITE	85	36	63	90	35	64
BLACK	11	90	8	8	87	12
HISPANIC	2	–	–	1	–	–
PARTY						
DEMOCRAT	47	69	30	44	71	28
REPUBLICAN	38	10	90	40	7	92
INDEPENDENT	15	38	58	17	41	56

	2008			**2004**		
	TOTAL	OBAMA	McCAIN	TOTAL	KERRY	BUSH
IDEOLOGY						
LIBERAL	17	74	26	15	78	21
MODERATE	45	53	46	46	49	50
CONSERVATIVE	39	15	83	39	16	84
EDUCATION BY RACE						
WHITE, COLLEGE DEGREE	32	38	60	–	–	–
WHITE, NO COLLEGE DEGREE	53	34	65	–	–	–
NONWHITE, COLLEGE DEGREE	4	–	–	–	–	–
NONWHITE, NO COLLEGE DEGREE	11	86	12	–	–	–
BUSH JOB						
APPROVE	35	7	93	60	7	93
DISAPPROVE	64	63	35	39	92	7
WORRIED ABOUT THE NATIONAL ECONOMY						
WORRIED	88	44	55	–	–	–
NOT WORRIED	12	37	62	–	–	–

Fitting a pattern we saw in other states, 45% of the electorate were white Evangelicals, and 74% of them supported McCain-Palin. The under 30 vote narrowly supported Obama 51% to 48%, a 12 point swing from Bush four years earlier.

NOT A FRIENDLY ILLINOIS NEIGHBOR TO OBAMA

For Obama, Kentucky was not an easy state despite the economic hard times hitting many of Kentucky's neighbors. It's the only state that borders Illinois where Obama was not competitive in either the primary or the general. There's a question of whether any Democrat could win the state nationally or if Kentucky was particularly race sensitive.

As was hinted at, most of the hot political action was down the ballot as Senate Republican leader Mitch McConnell had to once again sweat a reelection. The sometimes polarizing Republican has never had an easy time winning reelection but always does manage to survive. Some of his protégés have not been so lucky; as the now former Republican Governor Ernie Fletcher can tell you, and the incredibly vulnerable Republican Senator Jim Bunning will attest to, should he even decide to seek reelection in 2010. Had McConnell not survived, it would have provided an incredible exclamation point to what's been an incredible four year slide for the GOP nationally. McConnell, recognized by many of his colleagues in the Senate and in the state as one of the savviest politicos in elective office, has seen his state Republican Party struggle and presided over the Senate when his party lost more than a dozen seats in two elections. If McConnell's Senate Republicans don't make gains in 2010, his time as leader might come to an end.

LOUISIANA
Those Born on the Bayou Are Now Voting Republican
9 ELECTORAL VOTES

Like the rest of the solid South, Louisiana voted Democratic from Reconstruction through World War II. It voted for Democratic Southern presidential nominees in 1976, 1992, and 1996. However, Louisiana now seems reliably Republican. This drift was accentuated by the loss of African-American population after the hurricanes over the last few years. The drop in population in the Democratic areas around New Orleans was most acute. The polls significantly underestimated the McCain margin in Louisiana.

	2008		2004	
McCain	1,148,275	58.6%	Bush	56.7%
Obama	782,989	39.9%	Kerry	44.2%
Other candidates	29,497			
	1,960,761			

Note: 100% 3,956 of 3,956 precincts; 100% 64 of 64 parishes. Chart based on final, official vote totals.

Four parishes (the label for what are counties in other states) switched columns in 2008, with Caddo and East Baton Rouge going Democratic and the small parishes of Assumption and Pointe Coupee going to the GOP.

New Orleans, with Orleans Parish, saw its total votes drop by nearly 50,000 from 2004, as the voters have not returned after the storm. Major turnout drops were also seen in Jefferson Parish and St. Bernard Parish. In the primary of February 9, 2008, Obama received 57.4% of the vote and Clinton received 35.6%.

	2008			2004		
	TOTAL	OBAMA	McCAIN	TOTAL	KERRY	BUSH
GENDER						
MALE	42	34	64	45	39	60
FEMALE	58	42	56	55	45	54
AGE						
18–29	23	48	49	20	45	53
30–44	27	44	55	30	42	56
◆ 45–64	38	33	65	37	44	56
◆ 65+	13	29	69	13	34	66

(continued)

	2008			**2004**		
	TOTAL	OBAMA	McCAIN	TOTAL	KERRY	BUSH
RACE						
♦ *WHITE*	65	14	84	70	24	75
♦ *BLACK*	29	94	4	27	90	9
♦ *HISPANIC*	4	–	–	2	–	–
PARTY						
DEMOCRAT	42	75	24	42	78	21
REPUBLICAN	38	3	96	40	5	95
INDEPENDENT	21	32	62	18	39	58
IDEOLOGY						
LIBERAL	16	77	19	17	74	25
MODERATE	42	45	54	44	47	51
CONSERVATIVE	42	18	80	40	19	80
EDUCATION BY RACE						
WHITE, COLLEGE DEGREE	28	18	80	27	25	74
♦ *WHITE, NO COLLEGE DEGREE*	38	11	87	44	24	75
NONWHITE, COLLEGE DEGREE	10	81	17	8	82	17
NONWHITE, NO COLLEGE DEGREE	25	87	11	21	79	18
BUSH JOB						
APPROVE	43	5	94	58	8	92
DISAPPROVE	56	63	34	41	91	8
WORRIED ABOUT THE NATIONAL ECONOMY						
WORRIED	86	37	62	–	–	–
NOT WORRIED	13	47	51	–	–	–

Big swings for John McCain in Louisiana: among boomers, McCain was able to widen the lead Bush had four years ago by another 20 points. Seniors also supported him at a higher rate—69% voted for McCain. Black and Hispanic share of the vote were each up a couple points over four years ago, with white turnout down five points. However, the Republican margin among whites widened considerably, especially among non-college-educated whites. There was a 25 point swing toward McCain among these white working-class voters.

THE DEMOCRATS HAVEN'T RETURNED

Before there was a hurricane known as Katrina, Louisiana was one of those Southern states that Democratic demographers swore they could turn blue if the right Democratic candidate could maximize both voter registration among African-Americans and turnout. Well, Obama was the perfect test case for this and, well, it's clear the numbers just aren't there in Louisiana anymore to somehow turn this very red state blue. In fact, Louisiana ended up being one of just four states (Arkansas, Oklahoma, and Tennessee were the others) where McCain improved on Bush's 2004 performance. If that's not evidence of a missing vote, we don't know what is. The lack of Obama coattails cost Democrats at least one House seat; Obama was strong enough not to damage the reelection chances of Democratic Senator Mary Landrieu, who has put together one of the more remarkable electoral runs. As one Republican joked, "She ought to be chairwoman of the 'I can't believe she's a three-term Senator' caucus."

MAINE
As Maine Goes, So Goes Maine
4 ELECTORAL VOTES

Like the rest of New England, Maine was normally Republican from the Civil War (going blue only in 1912, 1964, and 1968) through the 1980s. But now Maine, which has voted Democratic in the last five elections and along with the rest of New England, seems reliably Democratic. Maine is one of only two states (the other is Nebraska) that awards electoral votes to congressional district winners. There has never been a split of Maine electoral votes. The polls always showed a significant Obama lead and accurately predicted the Obama margin.

	2008		2004	
Obama	421,923	57.7%	Kerry	53.6%
McCain	295,273	40.4%	Bush	44.6%
Other candidates	13,967			
	731,163			

Note: 100% 613 of 613 precincts; 100% 519 of 519 towns, townships, and cities. Chart based on final, official vote totals.

It was an easy win for Obama; the fifth time in five elections a Democrat has won the state. But turnout was down to 71%, a drop of 2.7 percentage points. In the caucus of February 10, 2008, Obama received 59.4% of the vote and Clinton received 39.9%.

	2008			2004		
	TOTAL	OBAMA	McCAIN	TOTAL	KERRY	BUSH
GENDER						
MALE	46	52	46	47	48	49
FEMALE	54	64	34	53	57	42
AGE						
♦ *18–29*	16	67	30	17	48	50
30–44	27	59	39	28	48	50
45–64	42	58	39	41	57	41
♦ *65+*	14	45	53	14	56	43
RACE						
WHITE	96	58	40	97	53	45
BLACK	1	–	–	1	–	–
HISPANIC	1	–	–	1	–	–
PARTY						
DEMOCRAT	35	89	10	31	86	13
REPUBLICAN	26	14	84	30	15	85
INDEPENDENT	39	60	36	38	56	40

	2008			**2004**		
	TOTAL	OBAMA	McCAIN	TOTAL	KERRY	BUSH
IDEOLOGY						
LIBERAL	27	86	11	26	81	17
MODERATE	44	63	35	47	55	43
CONSERVATIVE	29	23	73	27	20	77
EDUCATION BY RACE						
WHITE, COLLEGE DEGREE	40	61	37	–	–	–
WHITE, NO COLLEGE DEGREE	57	56	41	–	–	–
NONWHITE, COLLEGE DEGREE	1	–	–	–	–	–
NONWHITE, NO COLLEGE DEGREE	2	–	–	–	–	–
BUSH JOB						
APPROVE	23	14	85	46	7	92
DISAPPROVE	76	72	25	53	91	6
WORRIED ABOUT THE NATIONAL ECONOMY						
WORRIED	92	60	37	–	–	–
NOT WORRIED	8	35	62	–	–	–

Most in Maine swung toward Obama. Voters under 30 had the largest shift—swinging 39 points from having slightly favored Bush in 2004 to giving Obama a two-thirds' majority. Only seniors swung the other way; 56% had favored Kerry in 2004, but in 2008 they swung 21 points to favor McCain with 53%.

BLUE STATE WILL STILL ELECT REPUBLICANS

Very late in the campaign, as the McCain folks were counting on an increased push in the more rural parts of the battleground states, there was some thought he could win the state's 2nd Congressional District and snag one of the state's four electoral votes. The district is the most rural district; the campaign even sent Sarah Palin's husband, Todd, to campaign there. But, alas, it seemed a bit far-fetched. Obama had minimal coattails in the state; he was no help to Democrats' hopes of knocking off Republican incumbent Senator Susan Collins (she won a third term handily), but the increased Democratic vote did help the party win more seats in the state legislature, giving the party some padding where they needed it in the state senate.

MARYLAND
The Crabs Aren't the Only Thing Blue
10 ELECTORAL VOTES

Maryland has been reliably Democratic since the Civil War. Since 1960, Maryland has voted Republican only in the landslide wins of 1972, 1984, and 1988. Polls always showed a significant Obama lead and correctly predicted the margin.

	2008			2004	
Obama	**1,629,467**	**61.2%**	Kerry	55.9%
McCain	**959,862**	**36.6%**	Bush	42.9%
Other candidates	**32,884**			
	2,622,213			

Note: 100% 1,829 of 1,829 precincts; 100% 24 of 24 counties. Chart based on final, official vote totals.

No one contested Maryland at the presidential level, but you would not know that from the turnout. It was up an amazing 4.9 percentage points to an estimated 67.8%, tied for sixth with Georgia for increased turnout. It's possible part of Maryland's electorate was influenced by the fact that the state shares a battleground TV media market with northern Virginia.

Obama and the Democrats won only six of the 24 counties, but they were most of the large counties. Only one large county, suburban Anne Arundel County with Annapolis on the Chesapeake Bay, was in the GOP fold. In the primary of February 12, 2008, Obama received 60.7% of the vote and Clinton received 35.8%.

	2008			2004		
	TOTAL	OBAMA	McCAIN	TOTAL	KERRY	BUSH
GENDER						
MALE	45	59	39	46	54	45
FEMALE	55	64	35	54	58	41
AGE						
♦ *18–29*	20	70	26	14	62	35
30–44	30	65	35	30	52	48
45–64	39	55	43	44	56	43
65+	11	–	–	12	60	40
RACE						
♦ *WHITE*	64	47	49	71	44	55
BLACK	25	94	6	24	89	11
♦ *HISPANIC*	7	–	–	2	–	–
PARTY						
DEMOCRAT	51	88	10	48	89	11
REPUBLICAN	28	15	84	30	8	92
INDEPENDENT	21	57	36	22	50	47

	2008			2004		
	TOTAL	OBAMA	McCAIN	TOTAL	KERRY	BUSH
IDEOLOGY						
LIBERAL	26	91	9	24	88	10
MODERATE	52	64	34	49	61	39
CONSERVATIVE	23	24	74	28	20	79
EDUCATION BY RACE						
WHITE, COLLEGE DEGREE	36	52	45	–	–	–
WHITE, NO COLLEGE DEGREE	28	42	55	–	–	–
NONWHITE, COLLEGE DEGREE	15	86	14	–	–	–
NONWHITE, NO COLLEGE DEGREE	21	85	14	–	–	–
BUSH JOB						
APPROVE	22	–	–	43	6	93
DISAPPROVE	76	70	29	56	96	3
WORRIED ABOUT THE NATIONAL ECONOMY						
WORRIED	89	64	36	–	–	–
NOT WORRIED	11	–	–	–	–	–

A couple of significant increases in voting blocs: the youth vote was up six points to 20% of the electorate, and the proportion of the vote that is Hispanic increased five points and now is 7%. Of the states Obama won by 25 points or more, Maryland may have been the only one where he lost the white vote; he did so narrowly in Maryland, 49% to 47%.

GOP HITS ALL-TIME LOW

There's nothing like sharing a media market with a battleground state to help push turnout up. Add in the fact that the state has one of the larger non-Southern African-American populations and the recipe for a larger than expected turnout was all in place. The GOP used to be nominally competitive in this state, winning the occasional statewide office and holding its own in U.S. House races. But Democrats now hold seven of the eight U.S. House seats and hold huge majorities in the state legislature. This state is getting as blue as some of the New England states.

MASSACHUSETTS
The Only Red in This State Are the Sox

12 ELECTORAL VOTES

Massachusetts has been reliably Democratic since 1928. The state has voted Republican only four times since: 1952, 1956, 1980, and 1984. Massachusetts was the only state to vote Democratic in the 1972 Republican landslide. It is an example of the solidly Democratic New England. Polls never showed anything but a solid Obama lead here and accurately predicted the margin.

	2008		2004	
Obama	**1,891,083**	**62.0%**	Kerry	61.9%
McCain	**1,104,284**	**36.2%**	Bush	36.8%
Other candidates	**53,071**			
	3,048,438			

Note: 100% 2,168 of 2,168 precincts; 100% 351 of 351 towns, townships, and cities. Chart based on final, official vote totals.

Turnout rose about two percentage points to nearly 67% of those eligible, to give Obama about a 26 point win over McCain. In the primary of February 5, 2008, Clinton received 56.2% of the vote and Obama received 40.8%.

	2008			2004		
	TOTAL	OBAMA	McCAIN	TOTAL	KERRY	BUSH
GENDER						
MALE	50	56	42	48	57	41
FEMALE	50	68	30	52	66	33
AGE						
18–29	17	78	20	16	72	26
30–44	26	57	39	30	59	40
45–64	42	59	39	39	61	38
65+	15	–	–	15	56	43
RACE						
WHITE	79	59	39	87	59	40
BLACK	9	–	–	4	–	–
HISPANIC	6	–	–	6	80	18
PARTY						
DEMOCRAT	43	88	11	39	94	6
◆ *REPUBLICAN*	**17**	**9**	**90**	**16**	**7**	**93**
INDEPENDENT	40	57	40	44	54	44
IDEOLOGY						
◆ *LIBERAL*	**32**	**91**	**8**	**34**	**92**	**7**
MODERATE	46	59	38	45	59	40
CONSERVATIVE	21	28	70	21	23	76

	2008			2004		
	TOTAL	OBAMA	McCAIN	TOTAL	KERRY	BUSH
EDUCATION BY RACE						
WHITE, COLLEGE DEGREE	38	62	36	–	–	–
WHITE, NO COLLEGE DEGREE	41	57	42	–	–	–
NONWHITE, COLLEGE DEGREE	8	–	–	–	–	–
NONWHITE, NO COLLEGE DEGREE	12	–	–	–	–	–
BUSH JOB						
APPROVE	12	–	–	36	10	89
DISAPPROVE	88	60	37	62	95	4
WORRIED ABOUT THE NATIONAL ECONOMY						
WORRIED	89	55	42	–	–	–
NOT WORRIED	10	–	–	–	–	–

It is one of the most liberal states; one in three voters, 32%, called themselves liberal. And Massachusetts has one of the smallest proportions of Republicans in the country: only 17% Republican.

THE OBAMA BEFORE THERE WAS AN OBAMA

When the history of Barack Obama's ascension to the presidency is written, there will have to be some time spent on the successful 2006 gubernatorial campaign of African-American Democrat Deval Patrick. While Massachusetts is as blue as the Northern Atlantic Ocean, it's not always been seen as the most racially tolerant state (just ask former Boston Red Sox great Jim Rice). But Patrick's win erased a lot of doubt with Obama and his chief adviser, David Axelrod, whom Patrick counted on as a media consultant in his 2006 race. In fact, Patrick and Obama became so close that there was a brief controversy over some of the shared language the two used in their speeches and TV ads. Patrick hasn't had the easiest time in the state, but the Republican Party is a mess there and it may take a while before they can get competitive again on the statewide level. We're going on more than a decade since a Republican has held any seat in Congress from the Commonwealth of Massachusetts.

MISSISSIPPI
Still a Base Republican State but . . . Stay Tuned?
6 ELECTORAL VOTES

Mississippi, like the rest of the South, voted almost exclusively with the Democratic Party until the Democratic-sponsored civil rights legislation of the 1960s. The Republican Party took advantage of the situation and turned the state red. Since 1968, the state has voted Republican every time, except for 1976. The polls always showed a significant McCain lead but underestimated the margin.

	2008		2004	
McCain	**724,597**	**56.2%**	Bush	59.4%
Obama	**554,662**	**43.0%**	Kerry	39.8%
Other candidates	**10,606**			
	1,289,865			

Note: 100% 1,887 of 1,887 precincts; 100% 82 of 82 counties. Chart based on final, official vote totals.

Turnout was up an impressive 5.6 percentage points, to 61.3% of the eligible population. Mississippi tied South Carolina, another state with little attention paid by the presidential campaigns during the general election, for sixth in terms of increased turnout.

In the primary of March 11, 2008, Obama received 61.2% of the vote and Clinton received 36.7%.

	2008			2004		
	TOTAL	OBAMA	McCAIN	TOTAL	KERRY	BUSH
GENDER						
MALE	44	38	62	47	40	59
FEMALE	56	47	53	53	40	59
AGE						
♦ *18–29*	19	56	43	20	63	37
30–44	31	46	54	29	42	58
45–64	38	40	59	38	34	65
65+	12	–	–	13	25	75
RACE						
WHITE	62	11	88	65	14	85
♦ *BLACK*	33	98	2	34	90	10
♦ *HISPANIC*	4	–	–	–	–	–
PARTY						
DEMOCRAT	40	89	11	38	85	14
REPUBLICAN	45	6	94	47	6	94
INDEPENDENT	15	35	63	15	32	67

	2008			2004		
	TOTAL	OBAMA	McCAIN	TOTAL	KERRY	BUSH
IDEOLOGY						
LIBERAL	16	77	22	17	76	23
MODERATE	35	55	44	36	48	51
CONSERVATIVE	49	22	78	46	19	81
EDUCATION BY RACE						
WHITE, COLLEGE DEGREE	24	12	87	–	–	–
WHITE, NO COLLEGE DEGREE	38	11	89	–	–	–
NONWHITE, COLLEGE DEGREE	10	94	6	–	–	–
NONWHITE, NO COLLEGE DEGREE	28	94	6	–	–	–
BUSH JOB						
APPROVE	38	9	90	60	7	92
DISAPPROVE	61	67	32	38	95	4
WORRIED ABOUT THE NATIONAL ECONOMY						
WORRIED	83	42	57	–	–	–
NOT WORRIED	17	56	43	–	–	–

The youth voted for Obama in big numbers, but their proportion of the vote was not up. They actually showed up for Kerry in more significant numbers in 2004. Hispanics were a now measurable four percent of the electorate. (Repeat that statistic to yourself and realize that the increase in the Hispanic population is touching all sorts of states, not just the predictable Border States.) Blacks were a third of the electorate and 98% voted for Obama.

OUTSIDE SHOT AT BEING COMPETITIVE?

While Mississippi may have been an afterthought to Obama in the general election, it was an important victory marker for him in the primary campaign against Hillary Clinton. Just one week after Obama suffered a setback in primaries in Ohio and Texas, Obama stormed back with a huge victory in the Mississippi primary. While not as significant as the South Carolina primary victory, it was a big one for Obama and came at a time when he needed to appease his supporters. As for the general election, some Democratic demographers have thought that if enough care was given to registering more African-Americans in the state, the party could become competitive in presidential elections. Obama didn't work this state as hard as he worked others, but don't be surprised if Mississippi becomes a special project for the next four years by his political team as they search for a way to expand the map slightly. If nothing else, any work done increasing the Democratic vote for Obama in 2012 in this state will help the party down the ballot.

NEW JERSEY
The GOP's White Whale
15 ELECTORAL VOTES

New Jersey is a state that is always talked about as a swing state, but has gone Democratic in the last five elections. Before that, New Jersey voted Republican in eight out of the prior ten elections. The polls always showed an Obama lead in New Jersey and correctly predicted the margin.

	2008		2004	
Obama	2,215,422	57.3%	Kerry	52.9%
McCain	1,613,207	41.7%	Bush	46.2%
Other candidates	39,608			
	3,868,237			

Note: 100% 6,296 of 6,296 precincts; 100% 21 of 21 counties. Chart based on final, official vote totals.

Obama kept the Democratic streak alive easily in the Garden State, winning by more than 600,000 votes. Seven of the counties voted Republican in 2008, and the other 14 were in the Democratic column. Turnout edged up just a bit over two percentage points, to 65.9% of the voting eligible population. In the primary of February 5, 2008, Clinton received 53.8% of the vote and Obama received 43.9%.

	2008			2004		
	TOTAL	OBAMA	McCAIN	TOTAL	KERRY	BUSH
GENDER						
MALE	46	56	44	46	49	50
FEMALE	54	58	41	54	56	43
AGE						
18–29	17	67	31	17	64	35
30–44	30	59	40	31	49	50
45–64	38	55	45	37	51	48
♦ 65+	15	47	53	15	54	46
RACE						
WHITE	73	49	50	70	46	54
BLACK	12	92	8	14	82	17
♦ HISPANIC	9	78	21	10	56	43
PARTY						
♦ DEMOCRAT	44	89	11	39	90	10
REPUBLICAN	28	14	85	31	8	92
INDEPENDENT	28	51	47	30	54	44

(continued)

	2008			**2004**		
	TOTAL	OBAMA	McCAIN	TOTAL	KERRY	BUSH
IDEOLOGY						
LIBERAL	25	87	11	25	85	14
MODERATE	50	58	41	52	52	46
CONSERVATIVE	25	21	79	23	19	80
EDUCATION BY RACE						
WHITE, COLLEGE DEGREE	39	51	49	–	–	–
WHITE, NO COLLEGE DEGREE	34	47	51	–	–	–
NONWHITE, COLLEGE DEGREE	12	80	18	–	–	–
NONWHITE, NO COLLEGE DEGREE	15	81	19	–	–	–
BUSH JOB						
APPROVE	25	12	88	47	8	91
DISAPPROVE	74	68	31	52	94	5
WORRIED ABOUT THE NATIONAL ECONOMY						
WORRIED	86	56	43	–	–	–
NOT WORRIED	14	44	56	–	–	–

The Democratic portion of the electorate was up an astounding five points—to 44%. This is a tough number for Republicans to digest; if nearly half of the state's voters consider themselves to be Democrats, it means Republicans have to win all of their own voters plus some 75% plus of Independents to win statewide. Hispanics in New Jersey had a huge swing toward Obama. In 2004, they favored Bush 56% to Kerry 43%. In 2008, 78% voted for Obama, a 44 point swing in the margin. Obama narrowed his margins among Republicans by 13 points compared to Kerry. Forty percent were white Catholics, and more than half, 57%, voted for McCain. But this was five points less than Bush got in 2004. Seniors swung back 14 points to the Republicans.

THE GOP'S SUBURBAN COLLAPSE BEGAN HERE

New Jersey is the great white whale of Republican politics. Early polling in the state, whether for president or governor or the U.S. Senate, always shows Republicans looking competitive, and then the election happens. The problem, of course, is that there are just too many Democrats in the state. Republicans have to win over too many swing voters in order to stay competitive. It's been a generation since any Republican has received more than 50% of the vote in a statewide race in New Jersey. Republican Governor Christie Whitman never got over 50% in her two successful elections for governor in the 1990s. Republicans have a simple numbers problem in the state. And this problem is now showing up in congressional races. The GOP lost another seat and now has a three seat deficit in the delegation. When the book is written about the end of the Republican era of electoral dominance, the first place the book will start will be in New Jersey. It was the party's slippage in this all-suburban state that foreshadowed the GOP's slow loss of support in suburbs all over the country.

NEW YORK
Will the Last Republican Elected Official Get the Lights?
31 ELECTORAL VOTES

New York had the most electoral votes of any state until 1972 when California captured that distinction. Like many other northeastern states, New York has been primarily a Democratic state ever since the Great Depression. Polls showed a significant Obama lead throughout the campaign and correctly predicted the margin.

	2008		2004	
Obama	4,769,700	62.1%	Kerry	58.4%
McCain	2,742,298	35.7%	Bush	40.0%
Other candidates	162,786			
	7,674,784			

Note: 100% 16,300 of 16,300 precincts; 100% 62 of 62 counties. Chart based on final, official vote totals.

New York had given a 1 million vote margin to the Democratic presidential candidate in each of the past four elections, but it upped the ante in 2008 by giving Obama more than a 2 million vote edge in the Empire State. Turnout was flat, but the swing was all to the Democrats.

Republicans won 28 out of 62 counties, continuing to do well in upstate New York, while the Democrats dominated the far more populous New York City. Thirteen counties did move into the Democratic column from 2004. The two giant suburban counties on Long Island, Nassau and Suffolk, have long been discussed as Republican strongholds, but the last time either one voted Republican at the presidential level was 1992. But they are still not firmly in either camp: Obama won Suffolk by only four percentage points and Nassau a wider eight points.

In the primary of February 5, 2008, Clinton received 57.4% of the vote and Obama received 40.3%.

	2008			2004		
	TOTAL	OBAMA	McCAIN	TOTAL	KERRY	BUSH
GENDER						
MALE	46	59	40	45	56	42
FEMALE	54	67	32	55	60	40
AGE						
♦ *18–29*	22	76	21	17	72	25
30–44	29	61	39	29	61	38

	2008			**2004**		
	TOTAL	OBAMA	McCAIN	TOTAL	KERRY	BUSH
45–64	38	59	40	41	55	45
♦ *65+*	11	55	43	13	45	55
RACE						
WHITE	71	52	46	72	49	50
BLACK	17	100	0	13	90	9
HISPANIC	6	–	–	9	75	24
PARTY						
DEMOCRAT	50	91	8	45	89	10
REPUBLICAN	26	15	85	29	12	88
INDEPENDENT	25	56	41	26	57	40
IDEOLOGY						
♦ *LIBERAL*	31	92	7	27	88	11
MODERATE	43	68	31	48	59	39
CONSERVATIVE	25	18	82	25	24	75
EDUCATION BY RACE						
WHITE, COLLEGE DEGREE	42	58	41	40	57	42
WHITE, NO COLLEGE DEGREE	29	44	54	34	40	59
NONWHITE, COLLEGE DEGREE	13	86	12	12	82	17
NONWHITE, NO COLLEGE DEGREE	16	93	6	14	81	18
BUSH JOB						
APPROVE	17	–	–	42	12	87
DISAPPROVE	82	69	30	56	93	5
WORRIED ABOUT THE NATIONAL ECONOMY						
WORRIED	92	60	39	–	–	–
NOT WORRIED	8	–	–	–	–	–

Obama was favored across the generations in New York. The youth vote was up five points, and three-quarters voted for Obama. More than half of seniors, 55%, voted for Obama, a 22 point swing away from their 2004 Bush vote. With 31%, New York was one of the most liberal states since only 22% of voters identified as liberals nationally.

WHERE DID ALL THE REPUBLICANS GO?

Republicans took a beating up and down the Empire State ballot. In short, it was a bloodbath. The party lost three more seats in Congress and now holds just three of the state's 29 congressional districts. This is the smallest number of congressional seats the GOP has ever held from the state of New York. And the Democrats secured their biggest prize in the state legislature, winning narrow control of the state senate and therefore giving the Democrats total control of the state government for the first time since the New Deal. It's going to be a very busy political year in 2010, as Democrats will have to defend an incumbent senator and governor who were appointed to or ascended into their positions. This is just the type of opening the Republicans need in order to get some of their mojo back, if it is at all possible to do so.

NORTH DAKOTA
Not Quite There Yet for the Blue Team
3 ELECTORAL VOTES

North Dakota has only voted Democratic five times since it joined the Union in 1889. And North Dakota today is still a very safe state for the Republicans in presidential elections. The polls showed this state as a virtual tie, but they missed the mark significantly and underestimated the McCain margin.

	2008		2004	
McCain	168,601	53.3%	Bush	62.9%
Obama	141,278	44.6%	Kerry	35.5%
Other candidates	6,742			
	316,621			

Note: 100% 528 of 528 precincts; 100% 53 of 53 counties. Chart based on final, official vote totals.

Turnout was flat at just under 65%. But there has been change in North Dakota. Democrats did win 13 of the 53 counties, up from winning just four in 2004 and only two in 2000. And they did switch two of the biggest for the first time since 1968: Cass County, including Fargo, and Grand Forks County, with its namesake city.

In the caucus of February 5, 2008, Obama received 61.1% of the vote and Clinton received 36.5%.

	2008			2004		
	TOTAL	OBAMA	McCAIN	TOTAL	KERRY	BUSH
GENDER						
MALE	47	40	57	49	31	67
FEMALE	53	47	51	51	39	59
AGE						
◆ 18–29	22	51	47	20	32	68
30–44	29	41	57	26	27	70
45–64	37	42	55	39	39	50
65+	12	–	–	15	44	53
RACE						
◆ WHITE	92	42	55	98	35	63
BLACK	1	–	–	0	–	–
HISPANIC	2	–	–	1	–	–
PARTY						
DEMOCRAT	28	90	9	27	79	19
REPUBLICAN	38	7	92	41	2	97
INDEPENDENT	33	47	49	32	40	56

(continued)

	2008			**2004**		
	TOTAL	OBAMA	McCAIN	TOTAL	KERRY	BUSH
IDEOLOGY						
LIBERAL	16	81	19	13	72	27
MODERATE	48	52	45	54	42	55
CONSERVATIVE	36	15	83	33	10	89
EDUCATION BY RACE						
WHITE, COLLEGE DEGREE	42	46	52	–	–	–
WHITE, NO COLLEGE DEGREE	51	40	58	–	–	–
NONWHITE, COLLEGE DEGREE	3	–	–	–	–	–
NONWHITE, NO COLLEGE DEGREE	5	–	–	–	–	–
BUSH JOB						
APPROVE	39	10	90	60	7	92
DISAPPROVE	60	67	30	34	86	11
WORRIED ABOUT THE NATIONAL ECONOMY						
WORRIED	89	48	50	–	–	–
NOT WORRIED	10	–	–	–	–	–

Nine in ten, 92%, of North Dakota voters were white, and 55% voted for McCain. However, this is a 15 point narrowing in their vote over 2004. Of the 31% who were white Evangelicals, McCain won 72%. Among the 69% who are not white Evangelicals, Obama won 52%. And with 51%, Obama narrowly won the youth vote, a 40 point swing over Kerry's 2004 performance.

WILL DOWN BALLOT DEM SUCCESS EVER TRICKLE UP?

When Obama first played the "expand the battleground map" game, one of the first states mentioned was North Dakota. There were two reasons for this: 1) one of the state's largest media markets (Fargo) shares its viewers with another battleground state, Minnesota; 2) the state allows voters to register on Election Day, and the Obama camp was convinced they could simply change the math much easier than in other states. The Obama campaign wasn't completely wrong; they did swing the state 19 points, their third best swing behind Hawaii (36 points) and Indiana (22 points), but the Democrat still came up a whopping eight points short. In raw vote, eight points isn't a lot to make up in this small population state, but it isn't easy. The state sure is in the habit of electing Democrats to the Senate and U.S. House, as all three members of the state's Washington delegation share Obama's party ID. But that habit has yet to move up the ballot. Republicans are still in a strong position inside the state, controlling the governor's mansion and the entire state legislature.

OKLAHOMA
The Reddest State in the Union
7 ELECTORAL VOTES

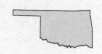

Oklahoma historically voted Democratic in all but two elections through 1948. The outcome in Oklahoma was never in doubt as the polls showed a significant McCain lead and correctly predicted the margin.

	2008			2004	
McCain	**960,165**	**65.6%**	Bush	65.6%
Obama	**502,496**	**34.4%**	Kerry	34.4%
	1,462,661			

Note: 100% 2,231 of 2,231 precincts; 100% 77 of 77 counties. Chart based on final, official vote totals.

Every one of the 77 counties backed McCain in the 2008 election. The last time any counties voted for the Democratic presidential candidate was in 2000, when nine managed to back Gore by small margins. In fact, Oklahoma is the only state in the Union where Obama failed to carry even one county. Along with a lack of attention from either campaign, turnout apparently slipped a bit in Oklahoma in 2008, hitting 56.7%, down from 58.3% in 2004. In the primary of February 5, 2008, Clinton received 54.8% of the vote and Obama received 31.2%.

	2008			2004		
	TOTAL	OBAMA	McCAIN	TOTAL	KERRY	BUSH
GENDER						
MALE	45	34	66	48	33	67
FEMALE	55	36	64	52	36	64
AGE						
18–29	19	40	60	19	38	62
30–44	30	38	61	27	31	69
♦ *45–64*	37	29	71	37	34	65
65+	14	–	–	17	35	65
RACE						
WHITE	82	29	71	77	29	71
BLACK	7	–	–	9	72	28
HISPANIC	3	–	–	4	–	–
PARTY						
DEMOCRAT	41	67	33	40	68	32
REPUBLICAN	44	5	95	43	4	96
INDEPENDENT	14	36	64	16	34	66

	2008			**2004**		
	TOTAL	OBAMA	McCAIN	TOTAL	KERRY	BUSH
IDEOLOGY						
LIBERAL	16	81	19	13	75	25
MODERATE	45	43	57	44	44	56
CONSERVATIVE	39	9	91	43	12	88
EDUCATION BY RACE						
WHITE, COLLEGE DEGREE	32	26	74	–	–	–
WHITE, NO COLLEGE DEGREE	50	31	69	–	–	–
NONWHITE, COLLEGE DEGREE	4	–	–	–	–	–
NONWHITE, NO COLLEGE DEGREE	14	61	39	–	–	–
BUSH JOB						
APPROVE	44	7	93	65	6	94
DISAPPROVE	55	56	43	34	90	10
WORRIED ABOUT THE NATIONAL ECONOMY						
WORRIED	88	35	65	–	–	–
NOT WORRIED	12	–	–	–	–	–

McCain was able to increase his share of the boomer vote 11 points beyond Bush's margin in 2004; just one example of how McCain improved on Bush's 2004 performance.

THE MOST ANTI-OBAMA STATE IN THE UNION?

Oklahoma was one of just four states where McCain bested Bush's 2004 margin; Arkansas, Louisiana, and Tennessee were the other three. Interestingly, they all border on one another (with Arkansas bordering the other three). For lack of a more politically correct term, some might describe these four states as the South's "white" belt, as it is hard to come up with another explanation for Obama's poor showing in these four specific states. The Democratic brand has been dying in the Sooner State for years. In fact, the final stronghold for the party fell in 2008 when Republicans took control of the entire state legislature after having split control for the last few years. Democrats usually only win statewide races when the Republicans have some nasty intraparty fighting. Look for that pattern to continue in the years ahead.

OREGON
Republicans Ought to Call It Ore-Gone?
7 ELECTORAL VOTES

Oregon broke its long string of support for GOP presidential candidates in 1988, as the state grew and became a technological center. But it retained a reputation for independence, giving Ross Perot hefty support in both 1992 and 1996. And without a third-party candidate to turn to, the battle between the Republican and Democratic candidates has been close in the twenty-first century. But not in 2008. Oregonians vote exclusively by mail. The polls showed a significant Obama lead throughout the campaign and correctly predicted the margin.

	2008			**2004**	
Obama	**1,037,291**	**56.7%**	Kerry	51.4%
McCain	**738,475**	**40.4%**	Bush	47.2%
Other candidates	**52,098**			
	1,827,864			

Note: 100% 1,000 of 1,000 precincts; 100% 36 of 36 counties. Chart based on final, official vote totals.

Obama won an easy victory in Oregon, brushing aside early McCain hopes that his image as a maverick would help him in the state. And the Democrats did it by winning just 12 of the state's 36 counties. With only a few exceptions, he won every county in the populous northwest quarter of the state, sweeping reliably Democratic Multnomah (Portland), Marion (Salem), and Lane (Eugene), as well as the Portland suburbs in Washington and Clackamas counties. It was the first time that Marion and Clackamas counties voted Democratic since 2000. Turnout slumped in Oregon, dropping by more than four percentage points to 67.4% of the voting eligible population.

In the primary of May 20, 2008, Obama received 58.8% of the vote and Clinton received 41.2%.

	2008			**2004**		
	TOTAL	OBAMA	McCAIN	TOTAL	KERRY	BUSH
GENDER						
♦ *MALE*	50	56	40	45	43	56
♦ *FEMALE*	50	59	39	55	59	41
AGE						
18–29	12	–	–	13	62	37
30–44	27	61	35	26	46	53

	2008			2004		
	TOTAL	OBAMA	McCAIN	TOTAL	KERRY	BUSH
45–64	42	55	41	41	54	45
♦ 65+	18	56	43	20	47	53
RACE						
♦ WHITE	89	57	40	93	50	50
BLACK	2	–	–	1	–	–
HISPANIC	5	–	–	3	83	17
PARTY						
DEMOCRAT	36	92	7	32	91	8
REPUBLICAN	27	9	89	34	7	93
INDEPENDENT	37	59	36	34	58	40
IDEOLOGY						
LIBERAL	24	94	4	27	95	5
MODERATE	43	67	29	39	57	43
CONSERVATIVE	33	15	82	34	10	89
EDUCATION BY RACE						
WHITE, COLLEGE DEGREE	41	61	35	36	59	40
♦ WHITE, NO COLLEGE DEGREE	47	54	45	57	44	54
NONWHITE, COLLEGE DEGREE	4	–	–	1	–	–
NONWHITE, NO COLLEGE DEGREE	7	–	–	6	–	–
BUSH JOB						
APPROVE	27	5	94	46	5	95
DISAPPROVE	72	76	20	54	93	6
WORRIED ABOUT THE NATIONAL ECONOMY						
WORRIED	84	61	37	–	–	–
NOT WORRIED	14	38	59	–	–	–

The gender gap in Oregon faded away as men and women voted in equal numbers, and both for Obama. Seniors switched partisan camps, with a 19 point swing to Obama. The white vote, which had split 50–50 in 2004, swung to Obama, largely driven by big shifts among those with less than a college degree, 19 points.

ANOTHER MODERATE GOPer GOES DOWN

When McCain was marketing himself to Republicans as the most electable potential nominee, one of the talking points he'd bring up is his ability to put more states in play, states like Oregon and Washington. Well, how wrong he was. Oregon and Washington are starting to look and vote a lot more like California than ever before. All three states were once battlegrounds but now provide a solid blue Left Coast anchor of nearly 75 electoral votes for any Democratic nominee. The Republican brand has been badly damaged in the Northwest thanks mostly to intraparty squabbling over ideology. And how Republicans in Oregon handle the loss of their moderate, now former Senator Gordon Smith will be interesting. Will state Republicans say Smith wasn't conservative enough, or simply that he was swamped in a bad year to be a Republican, thanks to Bush? How these ideological fights get settled in states like Oregon and elsewhere will largely dictate the near-term future prospects of the GOP's ability to thrive again in a state like Oregon.

RHODE ISLAND
No Longer New England's Lone Blue Island
4 ELECTORAL VOTES

Rhode Island has been Democratic since 1928, only voting Republican four times in that span: 1952, 1956, 1972, and 1984. Part of solid blue New England, Rhode Island is reliably Democratic. Polls here always showed a significant lead for Obama but underestimated his margin.

	2008		2004	
Obama	296,571	63.1%	Kerry	59.4%
McCain	165,391	35.2%	Bush	38.7%
Other candidates	7,805			
	469,767			

Note: 100% 541 of 541 precincts; 100% 39 of 39 towns, townships, and cities. Chart based on final, official vote totals.

Obama swept the state easily in 2008, losing only one town, Scituate, by 262 votes. In the primary of March 4, 2008, Clinton received 58.4% of the vote and Obama received 40.4%.

	2008			**2004**		
	TOTAL	OBAMA	McCAIN	TOTAL	KERRY	BUSH
GENDER						
MALE	46	52	42	47	57	41
FEMALE	54	70	29	53	62	37
AGE						
18–29	19	68	25	17	68	30
30–44	25	65	33	29	59	39
45–64	40	60	37	39	54	44
65+	16	–	–	15	69	31
RACE						
WHITE	83	58	39	88	57	41
BLACK	6	–	–	4	–	–
HISPANIC	7	–	–	5	–	–
PARTY						
DEMOCRAT	42	91	8	39	86	13
REPUBLICAN	16	11	87	16	8	92
INDEPENDENT	42	54	41	45	55	42
IDEOLOGY						
LIBERAL	28	89	10	27	81	17
MODERATE	47	66	31	52	63	35
CONSERVATIVE	25	23	73	21	25	74

(continued)

	2008			2004		
	TOTAL	OBAMA	McCAIN	TOTAL	KERRY	BUSH
EDUCATION BY RACE						
WHITE, COLLEGE DEGREE	42	59	37	–	–	–
WHITE, NO COLLEGE DEGREE	41	57	41	–	–	–
NONWHITE, COLLEGE DEGREE	6	–	–	–	–	–
NONWHITE, NO COLLEGE DEGREE	11	–	–	–	–	–
BUSH JOB						
APPROVE	16	12	86	42	13	86
DISAPPROVE	82	71	26	57	94	4
WORRIED ABOUT THE NATIONAL ECONOMY						
♦ *WORRIED*	92	63	34	–	–	–
NOT WORRIED	8	–	–	–	–	–

An overwhelming 92% are worried about the economy and 63% of them voted for Obama. Rhode Island has one of the largest white Catholic populations in the country, representing 49% of the vote, and they favored Obama just as they favored Kerry 57% to 41%.

DEMOCRATIC DOMINANCE CONTINUES

If there ever was a state in the Northeast that some analysts thought could show some signs of being race sensitive, it was Rhode Island. In the Democratic primary, the state's exit poll was off and some speculated it had to do with race. Clinton won the state handily, but the state's Democratic roots were just too deep for McCain to make any inroads. In fact, the Democratic coattails were so long that the party snatched a whopping eight state house seats, leaving the GOP with just six members in the 75 seat chamber.

SOUTH CAROLINA
It's South of the Border
and It's Red
8 ELECTORAL VOTES

South Carolina, like the rest of the South, voted almost exclusively Democratic until the Democratic civil rights legislation of the early 1960s. After that, it became a reliably Republican state. The only exception was 1976 when it supported Jimmy Carter. McCain always held a significant lead in this state, and the polls correctly predicted the margin that was significantly less than Bush's margin in 2004.

	2008		2004	
McCain	1,034,896	53.9%	Bush	58.0%
Obama	862,449	44.9%	Kerry	40.9%
Other candidates	23,624			
	1,920,969			

Note: 100% 2,291 of 2,291 precincts; 100% 46 of 46 counties. Chart based on final, official vote totals.

Turnout was up a surprising 5.6 percentage points to 58.6%, tying the Palmetto State with Mississippi for the sixth-biggest gain in turnout, and matching Mississippi in the low level of presidential general election attention to the state.

The state has been a bittersweet locale for McCain, killing his presidential hopes in 2000 and giving them new life in 2008. But Obama organized the state extensively for the Democratic primary and had some hope that his ground organization and the state's substantial African-American community might pull off an upset.

McCain drew more than enough support from 26 of the 46 counties to win easily, winning big majorities in the northwestern third of the state in places like Greenville and Spartanburg. Obama did manage to win a majority in Charleston, one of the five counties to move into the Democratic column in 2008. The last time Charleston County had voted Democratic was in 1980. In the primary of January 26, 2008, Obama received 55.4% of the vote and Clinton received 26.5%.

	2008			**2004**		
	TOTAL	OBAMA	McCAIN	TOTAL	KERRY	BUSH
GENDER						
MALE	46	41	58	43	36	63
FEMALE	54	48	51	57	45	55
AGE						
♦ *18–29*	18	55	44	18	48	51
♦ *30–44*	29	54	46	29	41	58
45–64	39	39	61	42	39	59
♦ *65+*	13	33	66	11	37	63
RACE						
WHITE	71	26	73	67	22	78
♦ *BLACK*	25	96	4	30	85	15
HISPANIC	3	–	–	1	–	–
PARTY						
DEMOCRAT	38	92	8	33	92	8
REPUBLICAN	41	4	96	44	3	96
INDEPENDENT	20	40	57	23	42	56
IDEOLOGY						
LIBERAL	17	84	15	15	76	24
MODERATE	43	58	42	46	50	49
CONSERVATIVE	40	14	86	39	16	83
EDUCATION BY RACE						
WHITE, COLLEGE DEGREE	34	32	68	–	–	–
WHITE, NO COLLEGE DEGREE	37	21	78	–	–	–
NONWHITE, COLLEGE DEGREE	8	–	–	–	–	–
NONWHITE, NO COLLEGE DEGREE	21	93	7	–	–	–
BUSH JOB						
APPROVE	36	8	92	59	8	92
DISAPPROVE	64	60	39	40	89	9
WORRIED ABOUT THE NATIONAL ECONOMY						
WORRIED	9	–	–	–	–	–
NOT WORRIED	90	44	55	–	–	–

There is a clear generational divide in South Carolina: those over 45 voted by a 25 point margin for McCain, while those under 45 voted for Obama 54% to 45%. This is partly due to the generation differences between black and white voters. On average the black vote is younger than the white vote, and the black margin for Obama was greater than the white margin for McCain.

WILL OBAMA SHAKE UP THIS STATE'S POLITICS?

When watching the virtual blue paint drip its way down the Atlantic seaboard from Maine through North Carolina, there had been some chatter that the large African-American population in South Carolina could be enough to paint even this red state blue. Obama never quite targeted the state in the general. However, if there are a couple Southern states he didn't win that his political team may decide to target for 2012, this is one of them. It appears his leftover primary operation allowed the Democrats to cut the GOP margin in half. What would have happened if the state had been receiving unlimited resources during the fall campaign? Obama probably would have still come up short, but the margin might have been closer to the Georgia victory for McCain (five points) than what he attained here. The state still has fairly strong Republican roots as the party controls the entire state legislature, the congressional delegation, and most of the major statewide offices.

SOUTH DAKOTA
Even a Daschle of Home State Love Wasn't Enough
3 ELECTORAL VOTES

South Dakota is a reliably Republican state, voting Democratic only four times, including 1964. But in 2008, the Republican margin was greatly reduced. The polls showed that this would be a closer race than normal in South Dakota and correctly predicted the final margin.

	2008		2004	
McCain	203,054	53.2%	Bush	59.9%
Obama	170,924	44.7%	Kerry	38.4%
Other candidates	7,997			
	381,975			

Note: 100% 799 of 799 precincts; 100% 66 of 66 counties. Chart based on final, official vote totals.

McCain swept 50 of 66 counties, but Obama managed to switch seven counties into the Democratic column in 2008, adding Sioux Falls and surrounding Minnehaha County by a narrow 587 vote margin. And turnout slipped substantially from 2004, when there was a fiercely contested U.S. Senate race in the state. Turnout was 63.7%, down more than four points from 2004. In the primary of June 3, 2008, Clinton received 55.3% of the vote and Obama received 44.7%.

	2008			2004		
	TOTAL	OBAMA	McCAIN	TOTAL	KERRY	BUSH
GENDER						
MALE	48	40	56	50	38	60
FEMALE	52	47	51	50	39	60
AGE						
♦ *18–29*	19	50	48	19	43	55
30–44	28	41	55	28	29	69
45–64	38	43	54	36	42	57
65+	15	45	55	17	40	57
RACE						
WHITE	90	41	56	95	37	61
BLACK	1	–	–	1	–	–
HISPANIC	3	–	–	0	–	–
PARTY						
DEMOCRAT	36	82	16	32	81	18
REPUBLICAN	42	12	87	47	6	93
INDEPENDENT	22	42	48	21	42	54

	2008			2004		
	TOTAL	OBAMA	McCAIN	TOTAL	KERRY	BUSH
IDEOLOGY						
LIBERAL	15	80	18	16	73	25
MODERATE	50	53	43	45	47	52
CONSERVATIVE	35	17	82	39	11	86
EDUCATION BY RACE						
WHITE, COLLEGE DEGREE	37	41	55	36	39	59
WHITE, NO COLLEGE DEGREE	53	42	56	57	34	63
NONWHITE, COLLEGE DEGREE	3	–	–	3	–	–
NONWHITE, NO COLLEGE DEGREE	7	–	–	4	–	–
BUSH JOB						
APPROVE	37	13	85	62	8	91
DISAPPROVE	63	64	33	37	89	8
WORRIED ABOUT THE NATIONAL ECONOMY						
WORRIED	86	47	50	–	–	–
NOT WORRIED	12	28	70	–	–	–

White Evangelicals were 38% of the electorate and 67% voted for McCain. Many folks probably don't realize how large the Evangelical vote is in the Plains and Midwest states. Evangelicals are not just a Southern phenomenon. There was no change in the proportion of the vote that was under 30; however, the margin did swing 14 points since 2004, narrowly giving Obama the youth vote.

PRO-GOVERNMENT CONSERVATIVES MOVING DEM?

Both Dakotas showed signs of being competitive. In the end, both broke for the Republicans, but the margins were drastically reduced. The question, of course, is whether this is a onetime thing or part of the slow matriculation of support in the Northern Plains and Midwest away from the Republican Party. It's possible McCain was simply uniquely bad in his attempts to appeal to these smaller, more government-dependent conservative states. While many in the GOP base like McCain's anti-pork rhetoric, some of the pork McCain railed against was stuff that even conservatives in South Dakota support because it's good for the local economy. It's going to take another cycle or two to see if this is a trend or a onetime thing.

TENNESSEE
A Swing State No Longer
11 ELECTORAL VOTES

Tennessee voted almost exclusively Democratic from Reconstruction until after World War II. Since then it has most often been Republican with a few exceptions such as the two Democratic victories in 1992 and 1996, when favorite son Al Gore was a candidate for vice president. However, Gore lost the state in 2000. The polls showed a significant McCain lead throughout the campaign.

	2008			2004	
McCain	1,477,405	56.9%	Bush	56.8%
Obama	1,085,720	41.8%	Kerry	42.5%
Other candidates	33,438			
	2,596,563			

Note: 100% 2,258 of 2,258 precincts; 100% 95 of 95 counties. Chart based on final, official vote totals.

McCain won 89 of the state's 95 counties, including 12 that switched into the Republican column in 2008, more than a quarter of the 44 counties nationwide that went in that direction. Only Arkansas had as many counties move in the GOP direction.

McCain did better in the big cities in Tennessee than he did in other states. He split the four largest metro areas with Obama, winning Hamilton County (Chattanooga) and Knox County (Knoxville), while losing Shelby County (Memphis) and Davidson County (Nashville). Turnout edged up just over one percentage point to 57.7%. In the primary of February 5, 2008, Clinton received 53.8% of the vote and Obama received 40.5%.

	2008			2004		
	TOTAL	OBAMA	McCAIN	TOTAL	KERRY	BUSH
GENDER						
MALE	47	36	60	45	41	57
FEMALE	53	47	52	55	43	56
AGE						
♦ 18–29	14	55	43	16	46	53
30–44	28	36	61	28	37	61
45–64	40	43	55	40	40	59
♦ 65+	18	36	59	16	50	48
RACE						
WHITE	84	34	63	84	34	65
BLACK	12	94	6	13	91	9
HISPANIC	2	–	–	1	–	–

	2008			2004		
	TOTAL	OBAMA	McCAIN	TOTAL	KERRY	BUSH
PARTY						
DEMOCRAT	32	86	13	32	90	9
REPUBLICAN	33	5	94	40	4	95
INDEPENDENT	35	37	58	28	40	57
IDEOLOGY						
LIBERAL	18	84	13	15	74	25
♦ *MODERATE*	38	48	47	39	59	40
CONSERVATIVE	44	17	82	46	17	82
EDUCATION BY RACE						
WHITE, COLLEGE DEGREE	35	37	61	–	–	–
WHITE, NO COLLEGE DEGREE	49	32	65	–	–	–
NONWHITE, COLLEGE DEGREE	7	–	–	–	–	–
NONWHITE, NO COLLEGE DEGREE	9	79	20	–	–	–
BUSH JOB						
APPROVE	35	6	93	57	6	92
DISAPPROVE	63	60	36	42	94	5
WORRIED ABOUT THE NATIONAL ECONOMY						
WORRIED	84	41	56	–	–	–
NOT WORRIED	15	34	64	–	–	–

While the youth vote swung into the Democratic column in 2008 by 19 points, the proportion of the electorate that were seniors was higher and they swung for McCain by a wider margin. Moderates swung 18 points more Republican, splitting their votes evenly between Obama and McCain. About the lone bright spot for Obama: 10% were new voters in 2008; they voted 56% for Obama, 44% for McCain.

A BELLWETHER NO LONGER

The last time a Democrat won the White House without winning Tennessee was in 1960. In fact, before 2008, that was the last time Tennessee had been wrong when it comes to picking a president. Tennessee had proven to be a pretty reliable bellwether in the past 100 years, choosing the eventual winner of all but two elections since 1912. But Tennessee is even more important to the Republican ticket. No Republican has won the White House without Tennessee since 1924. McCain improved upon Bush's 2004 performance in just four states and Tennessee was one of them (Arkansas, Louisiana, and Oklahoma were the other three). The Tennessee performance by Obama was somewhat surprising given that in 2006, the state's racial stereotypes appeared to be successfully challenged by Democrat Harold Ford Jr., who lost a surprisingly narrow contest for the U.S. Senate. It was Ford's performance, in fact, that convinced many analysts that if there had been such a thing as a "Bradley effect" in polling, it was no longer true. Obama's poor performance in Tennessee can't be explained away by race alone; there's clearly a problem with the Democratic Party's brand in the state. How else do you explain the GOP nabbing full control of the state's legislature in a year when, nationally, the GOP's governing brand was kicked to the curb?

UTAH
Vying with Oklahoma for Reddest State
5 ELECTORAL VOTES

Utah is a very Republican state and seems to stick out (along with Idaho) in its lack of two-party competitiveness. Other than voting Democratic from 1932 to 1948, Utah has voted Democratic only twice and never since the landslide of 1964. Polls always showed a significant McCain lead but underestimated the McCain margin.

	2008		2004	
McCain	596,030	62.6%	Bush	71.5%
Obama	327,670	34.4%	Kerry	26.0%
Other candidates	28,670			
	952,370			

Note: 100% 2,245 of 2,245 precincts; 100% 29 of 29 counties. Chart based on final, official vote totals.

McCain swept the state easily, winning all but two counties. The only glimmer of hope a Democrat might see is that Salt Lake County actually went for Obama by a margin of 296 votes, down quite a bit from the 79,779 Bush margin in 2004. Turnout plunged in Utah, dropping four percentage points to under 54%, putting the state in the company of Oregon, South Dakota, and West Virginia for biggest declines. In the primary of February 5, 2008, Obama received 56.7% of the vote and Clinton received 39.1%.

	2008			2004		
	TOTAL	OBAMA	McCAIN	TOTAL	KERRY	BUSH
GENDER						
MALE	47	34	63	46	25	72
FEMALE	53	34	63	54	28	71
AGE						
♦ 18–29	26	33	62	25	18	77
30–44	30	44	52	28	23	75
♦ 45–64	34	27	70	36	33	65
65+	10	–	–	11	32	67
RACE						
WHITE	90	31	66	91	24	73
BLACK	1	–	–	1	–	–
HISPANIC	5	–	–	5	–	–
PARTY						
DEMOCRAT	21	89	10	19	85	14
REPUBLICAN	50	6	93	58	4	95
INDEPENDENT	29	44	48	24	33	58

(continued)

235

	2008			**2004**		
	TOTAL	OBAMA	McCAIN	TOTAL	KERRY	BUSH
IDEOLOGY						
LIBERAL	14	–	–	11	74	19
MODERATE	39	52	45	44	37	60
CONSERVATIVE	48	9	88	45	4	95
EDUCATION BY RACE						
WHITE, COLLEGE DEGREE	39	28	69	–	–	–
WHITE, NO COLLEGE DEGREE	52	34	63	–	–	–
NONWHITE, COLLEGE DEGREE	4	–	–	–	–	–
NONWHITE, NO COLLEGE DEGREE	5	–	–	–	–	–
BUSH JOB						
APPROVE	47	6	92	69	3	96
DISAPPROVE	52	54	41	30	84	11
WORRIED ABOUT THE NATIONAL ECONOMY						
♦ *WORRIED*	96	30	67	–	–	–
NOT WORRIED	4	–	–	–	–	–

John McCain won across all categories of voters except self-identified Democrats and moderates. While there was some narrowing toward the Democrats among the younger voters, there was a marked 11 point swing further toward the GOP among boomers. The economy was the dominant issue for 72% and seven in ten voted for McCain.

MORMONS MORE PROMINENT IN NATIONAL POLITICS

It is very hard to call Utah a two-party state. If it wasn't for the fact that Democrats do hold one of the state's three U.S. House seats, it might be fair to say Utah was the most Republican state in the Union. And, you know, it really probably is. Democrats only find success in Utah when the GOP has messy primary fights. As the Mormon Church gets a little more proactive politically (including via Mitt Romney's once and future presidential campaigns and the Church's active support for the gay marriage ban in California), the state will find itself more and more in the political limelight.

VERMONT
The Bluest State in the Union?
3 ELECTORAL VOTES

Vermont is reliably Democratic in national elections, but it voted for Republicans from 1854 until 1988 with the exception of the landslide of 1964. It has voted Democratic starting in 1992. Polls showed a significant lead for Obama but underestimated the size of his margin.

	2008		2004	
Obama	**219,262**	**67.8%**	Kerry	58.9%
McCain	**98,974**	**30.6%**	Bush	38.8%
Other candidates	**5,346**			
	323,582			

Note:100% 260 of 260 precincts; 100% 246 of 246 towns, townships, and cities. Chart based on final, official vote totals.

Obama swept every county and town with only three exceptions. One town that McCain won was Lemington, where the Republican "swept" it, 30 to 29. That's right, by one vote. Turnout was down to slightly just over 66%. In the primary of March 4, 2008, Obama received 59.4% of the vote and Clinton received 38.7%.

	2008			2004		
	TOTAL	OBAMA	McCAIN	TOTAL	KERRY	BUSH
GENDER						
MALE	47	63	33	45	58	41
FEMALE	53	71	28	55	60	37
AGE						
18–29	14	81	18	15	71	27
30–44	26	60	37	31	58	39
45–64	45	68	31	42	58	39
♦ *65+*	16	69	31	12	47	52
RACE						
WHITE	95	68	31	97	58	40
BLACK	1	–	–	1	–	–
HISPANIC	1	–	–	1	–	–
PARTY						
♦ *DEMOCRAT*	37	97	3	31	94	6
REPUBLICAN	23	13	85	27	10	90
INDEPENDENT	39	73	24	41	67	27
IDEOLOGY						
♦ *LIBERAL*	32	94	5	32	93	4
MODERATE	44	69	29	44	60	37
CONSERVATIVE	24	33	65	25	17	80

(continued)

	2008			2004		
	TOTAL	OBAMA	McCAIN	TOTAL	KERRY	BUSH
EDUCATION BY RACE						
WHITE, COLLEGE DEGREE	50	73	24	–	–	–
WHITE, NO COLLEGE DEGREE	45	61	38	–	–	–
NONWHITE, COLLEGE DEGREE	2	–	–	–	–	–
NONWHITE, NO COLLEGE DEGREE	3	–	–	–	–	–
BUSH JOB						
APPROVE	16	13	87	40	7	92
DISAPPROVE	84	79	18	59	93	4
WORRIED ABOUT THE NATIONAL ECONOMY						
WORRIED	94	70	28	–	–	–
NOT WORRIED	6	–	–	–	–	–

Thirty-two percent of Vermont voters chose liberal rather than moderate or conservative to describe themselves, which makes the state the most liberal state in the country, exceeded only by the District of Columbia. Is it any wonder a onetime Socialist, Bernie Sanders, is able to be a U.S. senator from here? The Democratic share of the electorate was up six points over 2004. All voting groups went more heavily Democratic in 2008. But seniors had the most remarkable shift, voting for Obama 69% to 31%, a 43 point swing.

THE BLUE VERMONSTER

After Washington, D.C., and Hawaii, Vermont provided Obama with his widest margin of victory and therefore can claim to be the most pro-Obama state in the continental United States. The Democratic sweep wasn't so dramatic that it swept out the state's very moderate Republican Governor Jim Douglas. In a mirror image of how Democrats find success in places like Kansas and Utah, Republicans usually find success in Vermont when the Democratic coalition is split. There's a very active liberal party called the Progressive Party, which has more than once paved the way for a Republican to win an occasional race or two.

WASHINGTON

How Could the Home of
Starbucks Vote Any Other Way?

11 ELECTORAL VOTES

There was a time when Washington was a swing state. Not anymore. The state has voted for Democrats in the last five elections. A large majority of the state votes by mail. Polls showed a significant Obama lead throughout the campaign and slightly underestimated the margin.

	2008		2004	
Obama	**1,750,848**	**57.7%**	Kerry	52.8%
McCain	**1,229,216**	**40.5%**	Bush	45.6%
Other candidates	**56,814**			
	3,036,878			

Note: 6,719 of 6,719 precincts; 100% 39 of 39 counties. Chart based on final, official vote totals.

Obama and McCain divided the state in terms of counties, with Obama winning 20 counties and McCain 19. But Obama's success followed the pattern in other states: he won the bigger cities and counties. In Washington, Obama won the Democratic heartland of King County (Seattle) by nearly 400,000 votes, as well as Snohomish County (northern suburbs of Seattle) and Pierce County (Tacoma). McCain managed to win only Spokane, and that was by only 2,528 votes.

Turnout was essentially unchanged, at just under 67% of the voting eligible population. In the caucus of February 9, 2008, Obama received 50.0% of the vote and Clinton received 46.9%.

	2008			2004		
	TOTAL	OBAMA	McCAIN	TOTAL	KERRY	BUSH
GENDER						
♦ *MALE*	48	57	40	45	48	50
♦ *FEMALE*	52	58	40	55	57	43
AGE						
18–29	10	–	–	12	50	47
30–44	29	56	41	27	54	44
45–64	42	58	39	42	56	43
65+	19	51	47	19	45	54
RACE						
WHITE	83	55	42	88	52	46
BLACK	4	–	–	2	73	25
HISPANIC	7	–	–	5	52	48

(continued)

239

	2008			2004		
	TOTAL	OBAMA	McCAIN	TOTAL	KERRY	BUSH
PARTY						
♦ DEMOCRAT	36	95	5	36	93	6
♦ REPUBLICAN	26	9	91	32	5	94
♦ INDEPENDENT	39	55	39	33	55	41
IDEOLOGY						
LIBERAL	27	93	6	27	91	8
MODERATE	41	65	30	40	62	37
CONSERVATIVE	32	16	82	33	10	88
EDUCATION BY RACE						
WHITE, COLLEGE DEGREE	40	60	38	41	57	42
WHITE, NO COLLEGE DEGREE	43	51	47	47	47	51
NONWHITE, COLLEGE DEGREE	8	–	–	5	66	33
NONWHITE, NO COLLEGE DEGREE	9	–	–	6	47	52
BUSH JOB						
APPROVE	27	7	93	46	6	93
DISAPPROVE	72	77	20	53	93	5
WORRIED ABOUT THE NATIONAL ECONOMY						
WORRIED	85	62	36	–	–	–
NOT WORRIED	15	33	65	–	–	–

Democrats remained a stable 36% of the electorate, while Republicans were down five points to 26% and Independents up six points to a 39% share. Independent voters broke for Obama 55% to 39%. In 2004, there was a gender gap in Washington, with Bush winning 50% of men to Kerry's 48%. Kerry won 57% of the women's vote. In 2008, men swung 19 points toward Obama, thus voting for him in equal numbers as women. Working-class whites with less than a college education also switched parties; in 2008, they voted for Obama 51% to 47%. Only 5% of voters said 2008 was their first time voting in this very high turnout state.

THE GOP'S DIVIDED HOUSE SOLIDIFIES STATE'S BLUE STATUS

As with Oregon, there was some happy talk from the GOP that they could put Washington in play. It's a state George W. Bush tried to get into play in both 2000 and 2004. But this is now the third straight presidential election in which the Democratic share of the vote has grown. There's clearly a trend away from the GOP. As the Seattle population swells, it's getting harder and harder for non-Seattle politicians to win, and while some Republicans have held up in the Seattle area (see Republican Congressman Dave Reichert, who has survived two straight close calls now), the trend line is not good. As with Oregon, the Washington GOP's intraparty feuding has probably cost the party more support in the state than any branding issues nationally.

WEST VIRGINIA
Not Since 1912 . . .
5 ELECTORAL VOTES

West Virginia was a reliably Democratic state until 2000. Democrats carried the state in every election from 1968 until 2000 with the exception of 1972 and 1984. Obama is the first Democrat since Woodrow Wilson in 1912 to win the White House without carrying West Virginia. Polls showed a McCain lead but much less than the final margin. Some polls in October even showed an Obama lead. The polls underestimated the final margin by quite a bit.

	2008		2004	
McCain	398,061	55.7%	Bush	56.1%
Obama	304,127	42.6%	Kerry	43.2%
Other candidates	12,058			
	714,246			

Note: 100% 1,887 of 1,887 precincts; 100% 55 of 55 counties. Chart based on final, official vote totals.

McCain won 48 of the 55 counties, including four that went from the Democratic column in 2004 to the GOP in 2008. Two counties shifted narrowly to the Democratic side of the ledger. Turnout was down more than three percentage points to 50.6% of the voting eligible population, based on preliminary estimates. In the primary of May 13, 2008, Clinton received 67.0% of the vote and Obama received 25.7%.

	2008			2004		
	TOTAL	OBAMA	McCAIN	TOTAL	KERRY	BUSH
GENDER						
MALE	47	42	56	47	43	55
FEMALE	53	44	55	53	43	56
AGE						
♦ *18–29*	18	47	52	16	52	48
30–44	23	37	61	26	41	58
45–64	45	44	55	42	40	59
♦ *65+*	14	43	54	16	51	48
RACE						
WHITE	94	41	57	95	42	57
BLACK	2	–	–	3	83	15
HISPANIC	3	–	–	0	–	–
PARTY						
♦ *DEMOCRAT*	48	69	28	50	69	30
♦ *REPUBLICAN*	34	7	92	32	6	94
INDEPENDENT	19	39	58	18	42	56

	2008			**2004**		
	TOTAL	OBAMA	McCAIN	TOTAL	KERRY	BUSH
IDEOLOGY						
LIBERAL	18	71	28	17	73	25
MODERATE	48	51	46	49	53	46
CONSERVATIVE	34	15	84	33	15	85
EDUCATION BY RACE						
WHITE, COLLEGE DEGREE	32	42	56	33	43	56
WHITE, NO COLLEGE DEGREE	62	41	57	62	42	57
NONWHITE, COLLEGE DEGREE	2	–	–	1	–	–
NONWHITE, NO COLLEGE DEGREE	4	–	–	2	–	–
BUSH JOB						
APPROVE	35	8	92	57	8	92
DISAPPROVE	63	63	34	42	93	6
WORRIED ABOUT THE NATIONAL ECONOMY						
WORRIED	90	44	54	–	–	–
NOT WORRIED	10	–	–	–	–	–

The state showed improvement for Republicans. A third were Republican, with 92% voting for McCain, and the 19% who were Independent also favored McCain 58% to 38%. Even though West Virginia still has one of the highest percentages of self-described Democratic voters (at 48%, it's down two points since 2004), at the same time the partisans have not been voting Democratic at the same rate as in other states; Obama tied Kerry's percentage among Democrats here, giving Obama one of his lowest margins, 69% to 28%, of any state in the Union. The youth vote and seniors, who had marginally supported Kerry in 2004, swung to McCain in 2008. White Evangelicals were 52% of the electorate and 66% voted for McCain.

DID RACE HURT OBAMA'S CHANCES?

After Hillary Clinton trounced Obama in the Democratic primary in this state (in a primary that was held after it was generally accepted that Obama had the nomination in the bag), the Obama campaign pretty much wrote off the state. But as the economy began spiraling downward, Democrats thought they were sensing an uptick in this economically sensitive state. But clearly the economy wasn't a big enough issue to move many voters, as Obama lost the state by the same margin as Kerry. The state is still Democratic in statewide elections, but the Republican Party is slowly (*very* slowly) starting to move the needle down the ballot. But until the state GOP somehow distances itself from the national party's anti-union rhetoric, it may have a hard time gaining hold in some of the local offices in this state.

WYOMING
Dick Cheney Would Be Proud
3 ELECTORAL VOTES

Wyoming joins Utah and Idaho as one of the most reliable Republican states in the Rocky Mountain region. The only time Wyoming has voted Democratic since 1952 was the 1964 Democratic landslide. The polls showed a significant McCain lead throughout the campaign and correctly predicted the margin of victory.

	2008		2004	
McCain	**164,958**	**65.2%**	Bush	68.9%
Obama	**82,868**	**32.7%**	Kerry	29.1%
Other candidates	**5,311**			
	253,137			

Note: 100% 490 of 490 precincts; 100% 23 of 23 counties. Chart based on final, official vote totals.

Wyoming, Oklahoma, and Utah might vie for the title of most consistently Republican state in the nation, but Wyoming's claim is a good one. Not only has it voted for a Democrat in the presidential race only twice since World War II, Democrats have struggled to top 30% of the vote in the past two elections.

McCain won here easily, with Obama notching only the sixth best percentage since 1964. McCain won 21 of 23 counties. Obama did win in Teton County, which contains the Grand Teton National Park, much of Yellowstone National Park, and the affluent community of Jackson Hole, Wyoming. Thanks to Jackson Hole, Teton County has one of the highest per capita incomes in the country. Turnout slid slightly to about 65% of the voting eligible population. In the caucus of March 8, 2008, Obama received 61.4% of the vote and Clinton received 37.8%.

	2008			2004		
	TOTAL	OBAMA	McCAIN	TOTAL	KERRY	BUSH
GENDER						
MALE	47	30	67	51	26	71
FEMALE	53	35	63	49	32	67
AGE						
18–29	20	35	61	20	25	72
30–44	24	25	74	29	30	68
45–64	42	37	62	39	28	70
65+	14	–	–	12	35	64

(continued)

| | **2008** | | | **2004** | | |
	TOTAL	OBAMA	McCAIN	TOTAL	KERRY	BUSH
RACE						
WHITE	91	32	66	92	28	70
BLACK	0	–	–	1	–	–
HISPANIC	5	–	–	6	–	–
PARTY						
♦ *DEMOCRAT*	26	80	19	25	73	27
REPUBLICAN	52	6	93	53	4	95
INDEPENDENT	22	42	51	22	42	54
IDEOLOGY						
LIBERAL	14	77	22	14	60	38
MODERATE	47	40	57	48	38	60
CONSERVATIVE	39	8	90	38	7	92
EDUCATION BY RACE						
WHITE, COLLEGE DEGREE	36	44	54	–	–	–
WHITE, NO COLLEGE DEGREE	55	24	74	–	–	–
NONWHITE, COLLEGE DEGREE	2	–	–	–	–	–
NONWHITE, NO COLLEGE DEGREE	6	–	–	–	–	–
BUSH JOB						
APPROVE	43	3	96	71	5	94
DISAPPROVE	57	55	42	28	90	6
WORRIED ABOUT THE NATIONAL ECONOMY						
WORRIED	92	34	64	–	–	–
NOT WORRIED	8	–	–	–	–	–

While there were not big partisan shifts in the Wyoming electorate, those who call themselves Democrats did vote seven points more Democratic this time. White Evangelicals were 29% of the electorate and 83% voted for McCain.

DEMS HAVE JACKSON HOLE, REPUBS HAVE EVERYTHING ELSE

There was a time when some Democrats in the state thought Obama could somehow sneak over the 40% mark because of the massive TV advertising he was doing in two media markets that bleed into the state (Billings, Montana, and Denver, Colorado). But Wyoming's true Republican self showed itself big-time, helping the GOP secure the one post the party was nervous about losing: the state's lone seat in the U.S. House.

INTERESTING SHARES OF THE ELECTORATE

Note: This does not necessarily mean "youngest" or "oldest," etc., state population as that would be calculated based on census information and might not be an accurate assessment of voters. As an example, note that the census lists Pennsylvania as one of the states with an older population. But that doesn't translate to their share of seniors voting being greater relative to others. States that Obama won are indicated in bold.

WHITE VOTERS

	2008			2004		
	TOTAL WHITE %	OBAMA	McCAIN	TOTAL WHITE %	KERRY	BUSH
ALASKA	78	33	64	83	33	64
ALABAMA	65	10	88	73	19	80
ARKANSAS	82	30	68	83	36	63
ARIZONA	76	39	58	79	41	58
CALIFORNIA	**63**	**52**	**46**	**65**	**47**	**51**
COLORADO	**81**	**50**	**48**	**86**	**42**	**57**
CONNECTICUT	**78**	**51**	**46**	**86**	**51**	**48**
DISTRICT OF COLUMBIA	**35**	**86**	**12**	**38**	**80**	**19**
DELAWARE	**77**	**53**	**45**	**76**	**45**	**55**
FLORIDA	**70**	**42**	**56**	**70**	**42**	**57**
GEORGIA	66	23	76	69	23	76
HAWAII	**41**	**70**	**27**	**42**	**58**	**42**
IOWA	**91**	**51**	**47**	**96**	**49**	**50**

(continued)

WHITE VOTERS

	2008			2004		
	TOTAL WHITE %	OBAMA	McCAIN	TOTAL WHITE %	KERRY	BUSH
IDAHO	90	33	65	93	29	69
ILLINOIS	73	51	48	78	48	51
INDIANA	88	45	54	89	34	65
KANSAS	90	40	59	90	34	64
KENTUCKY	85	35	63	90	35	64
LOUISIANA	65	14	84	70	24	75
MASSACHUSETTS	79	59	39	87	58	39
MARYLAND	64	47	49	71	44	55
MAINE	96	58	40	97	53	45
MICHIGAN	82	50	47	82	44	54
MINNESOTA	90	53	46	93	50	49
MISSOURI	82	41	57	89	42	57
MISSISSIPPI	62	11	88	64	14	85
MONTANA	90	45	52	95	39	58
NORTH CAROLINA	72	35	64	71	27	73
NORTH DAKOTA	92	42	55	98	35	63
NEBRASKA	92	39	59	95	33	66
NEW HAMPSHIRE	94	54	44	95	50	49
NEW JERSEY	73	49	50	70	46	54
NEW MEXICO	50	42	56	57	43	56
NEVADA	69	45	53	77	43	55
NEW YORK	71	52	46	73	49	50
OHIO	83	46	52	86	44	55
OKLAHOMA	82	29	71	77	29	71
OREGON	89	57	40	93	49	49
PENNSYLVANIA	81	47	51	82	45	54
RHODE ISLAND	82	58	39	88	57	41
SOUTH CAROLINA	71	26	73	67	22	78
SOUTH DAKOTA	90	41	56	95	37	61
TENNESSEE	85	34	63	84	34	65
TEXAS	64	25	72	66	25	74
UTAH	90	31	66	91	24	72
VIRGINIA	70	39	60	72	32	68
VERMONT	95	67	31	97	58	39
WASHINGTON	83	55	42	88	52	46
WISCONSIN	89	54	45	90	47	52
WEST VIRGINIA	94	41	57	95	42	57
WYOMING	92	32	66	92	28	70

States with the Highest Proportion of Whites

STATE	WHITE
MAINE	**96%**
VERMONT	**95%**
WEST VIRGINIA	94%
NEW HAMPSHIRE	**94%**
NORTH DAKOTA	92%
NEBRASKA	92%
WYOMING	91%
IOWA	**91%**
IDAHO	90%
UTAH	90%
MONTANA	90%
KANSAS	90%
SOUTH DAKOTA	90%
MINNESOTA	**90%**

States with the Lowest Proportion of Whites

STATE	WHITE
DISTRICT OF COLUMBIA	**35%**
HAWAII	**41%**
NEW MEXICO	**50%**
MISSISSIPPI	62%
TEXAS	63%
CALIFORNIA	**63%**
MARYLAND	**64%**
ALABAMA	65%
LOUISIANA	65%
GEORGIA	65%

States with the Highest Proportion of African-Americans

STATE	BLACK
DISTRICT OF COLUMBIA	**56%**
MISSISSIPPI	33%
GEORGIA	30%
ALABAMA	29%
LOUISIANA	29%
SOUTH CAROLINA	25%
MARYLAND	**25%**
NORTH CAROLINA	**23%**
VIRGINIA	**20%**
DELAWARE	**17%**
ILLINOIS	**17%**
NEW YORK	**17%**

States with the Lowest Proportion of African-Americans

STATE	BLACK
MONTANA	0%
WYOMING	0%
VERMONT	**1%**
NEW MEXICO	**1%**
SOUTH DAKOTA	1%
MAINE	**1%**
HAWAII	**1%**
NEW HAMPSHIRE	**1%**
NORTH DAKOTA	1%
IDAHO	1%
UTAH	1%

States with the Highest Proportion of Hispanics

STATE	HISPANIC
NEW MEXICO	**41%**
TEXAS	20%
CALIFORNIA	**18%**
ARIZONA	16%
NEVADA	**15%**
FLORIDA	**14%**
COLORADO	**13%**
NEW JERSEY	**9%**
HAWAII	**8%**
CONNECTICUT	**8%**

States with the Lowest Proportion of Hispanics

STATE	HISPANIC
VERMONT	**1%**
MAINE	**1%**
NEW HAMPSHIRE	**2%**
NORTH DAKOTA	2%
NEBRASKA	2%
KENTUCKY	2%
TENNESSEE	2%
MISSOURI	2%

STATE	HISPANIC
SOUTH DAKOTA	3%
WEST VIRGINIA	3%
IOWA	**3%**
MINNESOTA	**3%**
WISCONSIN	**3%**
OKLAHOMA	3%
ARKANSAS	3%
MICHIGAN	**3%**
DELAWARE	**3%**
NORTH CAROLINA	**3%**
SOUTH CAROLINA	3%
GEORGIA	3%

States with the Highest Proportion of Voters Under 30

STATE	18–29
UTAH	26%
IDAHO	26%
DISTRICT OF COLUMBIA	**25%**
LOUISIANA	23%
NORTH DAKOTA	22%
MONTANA	22%
ALABAMA	22%
WISCONSIN	**22%**
MINNESOTA	**22%**
NEW YORK	**22%**

States with the Lowest Proportion of Voters Under 30

STATE	18–29
WASHINGTON	**10%**
OREGON	**12%**
COLORADO	**14%**
TENNESSEE	14%
VERMONT	**14%**
GEORGIA	14%
FLORIDA	**15%**
TEXAS	16%
MAINE	**16%**
HAWAII	**16%**

States with the Highest Proportion of Seniors

STATE	65+
FLORIDA	**22%**
WASHINGTON	**19%**
OREGON	**19%**
ARKANSAS	19%
TENNESSEE	18%
NEBRASKA	18%
ARIZONA	18%
IOWA	**18%**
MONTANA	18%
OHIO	**17%**

States with the Highest Proportion of Catholics

STATE	CATHOLIC
RHODE ISLAND	**55%**
MASSACHUSETTS	**53%**
NEW JERSEY	**48%**
CONNECTICUT	**45%**
NEW HAMPSHIRE	**38%**
NEW YORK	**37%**
NEW MEXICO	**35%**
WISCONSIN	**33%**
PENNSYLVANIA	**32%**
LOUISIANA	31%
ILLINOIS	**31%**

States with the Highest Proportion of White Evangelicals

STATE	WHITE EVANGELICAL
ARKANSAS	56%
OKLAHOMA	53%
WEST VIRGINIA	52%
TENNESSEE	52%
ALABAMA	47%
MISSISSIPPI	46%
KENTUCKY	45%
NORTH CAROLINA	**44%**
INDIANA	**43%**
KANSAS	41%
SOUTH CAROLINA	40%

States with the Highest Proportion of College-Educated

STATE	COLLEGE
COLORADO	58%
DISTRICT OF COLUMBIA	58%
CONNECTICUT	55%
NEW YORK	55%
NEW HAMPSHIRE	53%
VERMONT	52%
VIRGINIA	52%
MARYLAND	52%
NEW JERSEY	51%
MASSACHUSETTS	51%

States with the Lowest Proportion of College-Educated

STATE	NON-COLLEGE
WEST VIRGINIA	66%
MISSISSIPPI	66%
IDAHO	66%
INDIANA	65%
MICHIGAN	65%
OKLAHOMA	64%
KENTUCKY	64%
MISSOURI	64%
ARKANSAS	63%
LOUISIANA	63%

States with the Highest Proportion of Liberals

STATE	LIBERAL
DISTRICT OF COLUMBIA	46%
VERMONT	32%
NEW YORK	31%
MASSACHUSETTS	31%
CONNECTICUT	29%
HAWAII	28%
RHODE ISLAND	28%
WASHINGTON	27%
MAINE	27%
MARYLAND	26%
MINNESOTA	26%
NEW HAMPSHIRE	26%

States with the Highest Proportion of Moderates

STATE	MODERATE
MARYLAND	52%
NEW JERSEY	50%
DELAWARE	50%
PENNSYLVANIA	50%
SOUTH DAKOTA	50%
MASSACHUSETTS	49%
HAWAII	48%
ILLINOIS	48%
WEST VIRGINIA	48%
NEBRASKA	48%
NORTH DAKOTA	48%
GEORGIA	48%

States with the Highest Proportion of Conservatives

STATE	CONSERVATIVE
MISSISSIPPI	49%
UTAH	48%
ALABAMA	47%
TEXAS	46%
ARKANSAS	45%
TENNESSEE	44%
IDAHO	43%
LOUISIANA	42%
SOUTH CAROLINA	40%
GEORGIA	39%
WYOMING	39%
ALASKA	39%
KENTUCKY	39%
OKLAHOMA	39%

States with the Highest Proportion of Democrats

STATE	DEMOCRATS
DISTRICT OF COLUMBIA	78%
MARYLAND	51%
NEW YORK	50%
WEST VIRGINIA	48%
DELAWARE	48%
KENTUCKY	47%
ILLINOIS	47%
HAWAII	45%
NEW MEXICO	44%
PENNSYLVANIA	44%
NEW JERSEY	44%

States with the Highest Proportion of Independents

STATE	INDEPENDENT
NEW HAMPSHIRE	45%
MASSACHUSETTS	43%
RHODE ISLAND	42%
ALASKA	41%
VERMONT	39%
WASHINGTON	39%
MAINE	39%
COLORADO	39%
OREGON	37%
MONTANA	35%

States with the Highest Proportion of Republicans

STATE	GOP
WYOMING	52%
KANSAS	49%
IDAHO	48%
NEBRASKA	48%
ALABAMA	45%
MISSISSIPPI	45%
OKLAHOMA	44%
SOUTH DAKOTA	42%
INDIANA	41%
SOUTH CAROLINA	41%
UTAH	40%

EXIT POLL METHODS STATEMENT

National Exit Poll

Most of the exit polling in this book was conducted by Edison Media Research and Mitofsky International for the National Election Pool (ABC, AP, CBS, CNN, FOX, and NBC). Exit polls prior to 2004 were conducted by VNS for the same networks and the AP. Earlier exit polls were conducted by various organizations such as NBC News and CBS News.

The National Exit Poll was conducted at a sample of 300 polling places among 17,836 Election Day voters representative of the United States.

In addition, 2,378 absentee and/or early voters in all 50 states were interviewed in a preelection telephone poll. Absentee or early voters were asked the same questions asked at the polling place on Election Day. The absentee results were combined in approximately the correct proportion with voters interviewed at the polling places. The interviews were conducted among respondents who said that they were definitely voting in the general election. The interviews were conducted between October 24 and November 2 using a Random-Digit-Dialing (RDD) telephone sample.

The polling places were selected as a stratified probability sample of each state. A subsample of the state samples was selected at the proper proportions for the National Exit Poll. Within each polling place an interviewer approached every nth voter as he or she exited the polling place. Approximately 50 voters completed a questionnaire at each polling place. The exact number depends on voter turnout and their cooperation.

For the national tabulations used to analyze an election, respondents are weighted based on two factors. They are: 1) the probability of selection of the precinct and the respondent within the precinct; 2) by the size and distribution of the best estimate of the vote within geographic subregions of the nation. The second step produces consistent estimates *at the time of the tabulation*, whether from the tabulations or an estimating model used to make an estimate of the national popular vote. At other times the estimated national popular vote may differ somewhat from the national tabulations.

All samples are approximations. A measure of the approximation is called the sampling error. Sampling error is affected by the design of the sample, the characteristic being measured, and the number of people who have the characteristic. If a characteristic is found in roughly the same proportions in all precincts the sampling error will be lower. If the characteristic is concentrated in a few precincts the sampling error will be larger. Gender would be a good example of a characteristic with a lower sampling error. Characteristics for minority racial groups will have larger sampling errors.

The table below lists typical sampling errors for given size subgroups for a 95% confidence interval. The values in the table should be added and subtracted from the characteristic's percentage in order to construct an interval. Ninety-five percent of the intervals created this way will contain the value that would be obtained if all voters were interviewed using the same procedures. Other non-sampling factors, including nonresponse, are likely to increase the total error.

% Error Due to Sampling (+/–) for 95% Confidence Interval

% VOTERS WITH CHARACTERISTIC	100	101–200	201–500	501–950	951–2,350	2,351–5,250	5,251–8,000	8,001–15,000
5% or 95%	6	5	3	2	2	1	1	1
15% or 85%	11	7	5	4	3	2	1	1
25% or 75%	13	9	6	5	3	2	2	1
50%	15	10	7	5	4	3	2	1

NUMBER OF VOTERS IN BASE OF PERCENTAGE

The exit poll in specific states was conducted using the same methods. A full methods statement for each state poll is available from Edison Media Research.